城市治理的
理论与实践

（2019~2020）

THEORY AND PRACTICE IN RELATION TO
URBAN GOVERNANCE (2019-2020)

陆　丹　包雅钧　主编

社会科学文献出版社
SOCIAL SCIENCES ACADEMIC PRESS (CHINA)

目录
CONTENTS

工业4.0时代网络化城市空间构建与治理模式创新

吕　斌*

【摘　要】20世纪90年代以后，全球化、信息化和区域一体化成为世界发展的主旋律，城市已经不可能孤立地发展。随着每天海量人、物、信息交换的发生，城市和城市之间的关系变得比以往更加重要。伴随着2013年德国提出"工业4.0"战略以后出现的"第四次产业革命"浪潮，在中国，互联网经济、轨道交通等的迅速发展促进了虚拟联系和实体联系的网络化，城市网络化发展态势正不断强化，网络化城市空间结构成为城市新的空间组织形态。网络化城市空间结构是大都市区空间演化的高级阶段，是国家和区域中心城市必然的外在形态，而构建网络化城市空间结构就是着力解决大城市病问题、推动以人民为中心的城市高质量发展、优化城市治理体系和提升治理能力的重要路径。本文在论述了构建网络化城市空间结构的目标和意义并揭示了网络化城市空间结构基本特征的基础上，以成都市为例，阐述了网络化城市空间治理模式的创新路径。

【关键词】工业4.0；社会5.0；网络化城市空间结构；城市空间治理

---

* 吕斌，北京大学城市与环境学院教授，北京大学城市治理研究院学术委员会主任，中国城市规划学会副理事长。

一　工业 4.0 时代城市空间形态的演变与适应

近 10 多年来，大数据分析、人工智能、物联网等数字技术、网络技术、智能技术的研究开发成果正在急速地浸透到我们普通人的日常生活中，比如由于智能手机的普及，包括购物方式、工作方式在内的生活方式与 10 年前相比，已经发生了很大的变化，这是我们 50 年前，甚至 30 年前所不能想象的进步。

2013 年 4 月，德国提出了"工业 4.0"战略，被世界认为这是制造业生产方式全面物联网化（IoT 化）的开始，是利用信息化技术促进产业变革的时代，又被称为"第四次产业革命"。伴随这个浪潮，2015 年 5 月，国务院印发了《中国制造 2025》，部署全面推进实施制造强国战略，这是中国版的"工业 4.0"。打造具有国际竞争力的制造业，一个很重要的背景，就是物联网化、智慧化，通过充分利用信息通信技术与网络空间虚拟系统相结合的手段，将制造业向智能化转型。近几年智能技术在我国及一些发达国家发展非常快，比如机器人、无人驾驶汽车等，对全社会影响很大。工业一定是有产品的，产品会渗透到我们的生活中，从而改变我们的生活方式和城市形态，虚拟技术应用的最终目标还是要为人类社会本身服务，要提高人们的生活质量和幸福感。然而"工业 4.0"构想并没有明确谈及如何将"第四次产业革命"的进步成果惠及市民或一般社会，日本在推行"工业 4.0"时，就提出了一个现实问题：如何把"工业 4.0"的成果惠及人类社会本身？于是，2016 年 1 月，日本在《第 5 次科学技术基本规划》中提出了构建以新的科学技术引领即将到来的"5.0 版社会"，即"社会 5.0"的构想。"社会 5.0"构想是指最大限度地活用 ICT（信息和通信技术），通过实现网络空间与现实空间的高度融合，构建能为人们带来丰富感的、以人为中心的"超智慧社会"。

与"工业 4.0"明显不同的是"社会 5.0"特别强调要构建以人为中心的宜居宜业社会，技术开发的成果一定要惠及市民社会，同时还强调要照顾到个人的嗜好或多样性的诉求，构建具有包容性的社会。我们国家目前没有提"社会 5.0"这个概念，但提出了以人民为中心的高质量发展理念，这也是基于这个大背景。一切以人民为中心，顺应人民群众对美好环境和幸福生活的新期待，全力推动城乡人居环境的高质量发展，不断提升人民群众的幸福感、获得感和安全感。在技术上，"社会 5.0"则特别强调把网络空间与现实空间相融合，用物联网、机器人（Bot）、人工智能（AI）、大数据等技术，从衣、食、住、行各方面提升生活的便捷性。"工业 4.0"强调全面物联网化，"社会 5.0"是要把物联网、互联网与人类社会的实体空间相结合，在以人为中心的基础上构建超智慧化的社会，这对我们的人居环境空间将产生深远的影响。

人的生活、生产等行为模式的变化，必然会对城市空间形态产生新的要求和影响。在"社会 5.0"时代，城市空间形态将形成"大分散小集中"的格局。所谓"大分散"，是指在网络社会、虚拟技术很发达的时代，一部分业态、工种不需要大规模聚集在一个高密度空间之内，特别是那些生产性服务业，不一定要集中到所谓的 CBD，工作方式可以从 face to face 转向 table to table。比如，近年一些双创型企业就已经显示了小规模分散发展的态势，甚至一个人居家也能完成创新创业。这种变化对于我们选择工作地址、居住地址会有很大的影响，进而对城市空间形态产生影响。另外，这种分散又不能是无序的发散或蔓延，必须是自律型的分散或紧凑型的分散，即须在城市区域某些适当的节点位置形成具有复合土地利用的紧凑型城市（Compact City）功能空间，其中最重要的是商业、文化、义务教育等服务功能与居住空间的近接、紧凑，以及职住空间的相对接近，这样就会在城市区域范围内形成多中心分散型网络化空间结构，这就是所谓"大分散小集中"的概念。国际上典型的呈多中心分散型网络化空间结构的城市区域之一就是东京都市圈。在东京都市圈，国内国际大型企业总部并非都集聚在东京都中心城区，很多都是分散集聚在周边位于 30 公里半径圈的新城中，如神奈川县的横滨未来港湾 21 世纪新城（MM21）、埼玉县的大宫新城、千叶县的幕张新都市等。这些分散在东京都外圈、作为东京副中心的新都市既集聚了很多国内外大企业研发总部，又拥有适合创新性产业人士的高质量居住环境及滨海休闲空间，成为东京都市圈的重要成长极。

二 网络化城市空间结构的特征与构建

1. 网络化城市空间构建的意义

20 世纪 90 年代以后，全球化、信息化和区域一体化成为世界发展的主旋律，城市已经不可能孤立地发展。随着每天海量人、物、信息交换的发生，城市和城市之间的关系变得比以往更加重要。"工业4.0"时代互联网经济、轨道交通等的发展促进了虚拟联系和实体联系的网络化，城市网络化发展态势正不断强化，网络化城市空间结构成为城市新的空间组织形态。国外主要城市如伦敦、巴黎、东京等，均经历了由单中心圈层式扩张向轴带带动再向多中心网络化发展的演化过程。20世纪90年代，网络城市理念引入中国，成为城市区域空间发展的新战略，国内主要城市如上海、北京、广州、成都等在总体规划中均提出了构建网络化发展格局。网络化城市空间结构是大都市区空间演化的高级阶段，是国家和区域中心城市必然的外在形态，研究大都市区网络化空间结构的形成路径和发展演变尤为重要。2015年中央城市工作会议明确提出"转变城市发展方式，完善城市治理体系，提高城市治理能力，着力解决城市病等突出问题"，而构建网络化城市空间结构就是着力解决大城市病问题、推动城市转型发展、优化城市治理体系和提升治理能力的重要路径。

2. 网络化城市空间结构的特征与构建

网络化城市空间结构研究的基本视角不同于传统的以二维土地利用为基础的城市空间规划研究，而是将城镇视作城市区域中的一个点，规划研究聚焦于这个点与城市区域中其他点之间的结构关系，进而研究城市群体构成体系的整体演化规律，我们常见的都市圈及城市群等规划研究都属于此种视角下的城镇体系研究范畴。网络城市是以交通等实体网络和信息网络等虚拟网络为支撑，构成的多中心、网络化、集约型的新型城市区域。网络化城市空间结构建构具有两个关键要素：一是节点，这是网络城市构建的基础；二是联系，包括交通等实体网络联系与网络信息等虚拟网络联系。网络化城市空间结构不同于传统的等级结构城市发展模式，各网络节点之间存在密切的横向和纵向联系，功能互补，互相协作，推动网络的整体发展。通常，构建网络化城市空间结构应具备以下基本特征。

（1）多节点、扁平化、均衡性的空间结构。在传统城镇体系中，城镇规模越大、行政等级越高，则城市地位越高、作用越大、所获得的发展资源也会越多。而在网络化城市空间结构中，网络节点的地位不再取决于规模和行政等级，而是由节点的特色功能和在网络中对外交通、信息等资源的控制作用所决定，通过多个网络节点的联系和相互作用，形成多节点、扁平化、均衡性的网络化空间结构。比如，国外许多著名高校、世界500

强企业等，并非都集中在大城市，而是分布在中小城市甚至小城镇。例如，沃尔玛公司、微软公司、通用电气、强生、摩托罗拉、麦当劳等世界500 强企业的总部大都位于小镇上，这些小镇规模很小，只有几万到几十万人口，却在全球生产销售、研发网络中占据重要地位，是全球城市网络的重要节点。

（2）面向全球和区域网络的对外联系的开放系统。网络化城市空间结构并非自成体系，而是通过嵌入全球网络体系，形成内外联通的开放系统。网络化城市空间结构往往拥有高水平的对外交通枢纽，如国际航空港、航运港、铁路港等，连通着世界网络，并承担更大区域和国际化的功能，网络化城市空间结构更强调通过在外部网络中的节点作用来体现价值和地位。

（3）内部具有完善的实体和虚拟网络支撑。网络化设施是网络化城市空间结构的骨架和基础，包括交通线网、供水、供电管线等实体网络和金融汇兑、信息交换等虚拟网络设施。网络化城市空间结构中的各节点通过完善的网络化设施联系，尤以发达的轨道交通网络为主要支撑。东京都市圈、巴黎大都市区均依托发达、便捷的轨道交通网络将都市圈内部各城市紧密联系在一起，形成典型的网络城市。

（4）城乡一体的联动关系。网络化城市空间结构中农村地区不仅承担农业生产和生态功能，同时还承担科技研发、总部办公、文化创意、休闲旅游、养老服务等功能，与城市功能互补，相辅相成，共同融入区域和全球网络。以东京筑波新城为例，新城周边乡村聚集着 300 多家民间研究机构，同时保留原有自然和乡村环境，既发展乡村农业，又承担着休闲旅游、乡村文化、科学研究、康养等功能，乡村居民享有和都市居民一样的优质教育、医疗及其他公共服务。

（5）人与自然协同共生的生态环境。网络化城市空间结构将改变传统城市蔓延的单一模式，网络节点与绿色基础设施协同发展，拥有人与自然共生的生态环境。以荷兰兰斯塔德地区为例，阿姆斯特丹、鹿特丹、海牙、乌特勒支四个功能互补的核心城市良性互动，分布在该区域的巨大绿心周围。在城市发展过程中，既很好地保护了绿心，也避免了单个城市的无序蔓延，形成了自律的分散式紧凑型城市群。

三　网络化城市空间治理模式的创新

中央城市工作会议上提出"完善城市治理体系，提高城市治理能力"。[①] 党的十九届四中全会于 2019 年 11 月 5 日公布的《中共中央关于坚持和完善中国特色社会主义制度 推进国家治理体系和治理能力现代化若干重大问题的决定》中也指出坚持和完善"中国特色社会主义制度、推进国家治理体系和治理能力现代化"[②]，是全党的一项重大战略任务。我国正在经历世界历史上规模最大、速度最快的城镇化进程，并逐步实现由城市管理向城市治理的跨越。

城市治理能力是衡量新型城镇化高质量发展水平的重要标志之一，从治理效率和实际效果看，既有的城市治理模式显然难以适应新型城镇化发展要求，治理模式转型势在必行。近年来，数字城市、感知城市、无线城市、智慧城市等新概念层出不穷，"互联网+"正在付诸实践，这为解决城市治理的难点问题提供了机遇和条件。然而，"城市治理+互联网"仅是单纯技术层面的工具性应用，是城市治理的加法，从本质上看还是一种物理变化。要真正为城市治理增质提效，应催生基于网络化城市空间结构的城市治理体系，引领城镇化向更高阶段发展。具体地说，就是要打破垂直型的城市治理体系架构，减少管理层级。通过对话，协调正式与非正式的多方合作平台，构建更为扁平化的治理格局。不以城镇行政级别和规模为标准分配资源，而把资源向具有发展条件和潜力的网络节点投放。比如，杭州市就将网络化大都市建设领导小组会议转变为常设机构——"网络化大都市董事会"，组建了一级半官方的联盟，同时充实了其区域协调功能。此外，还把部分镇转变为市管镇，减少管理层级，推动扁平化管理，激发了小城镇的发展活力。

成都市近年来也改变了传统依据城镇行政等级和规模分配资源的模式，把资源向具有发展条件和潜力的网络节点投放，促进了土地、财政等要素向承担国际化和区域功能的镇投放，并推动了市级优质公共服务资源（如医疗、教育等）有效延伸到这些镇。同时，成都市实施了"强镇扩权"

[①] 陈政高：《完善城市治理体系　提高城市治理能力》，《人民周刊》2007 年第 11 期。
[②] 《习近平谈治国理政》第 2 卷，外文出版社，2017，第 289 页。

和"合村并镇"两大行动计划，首先赋予重点镇县级管理权限，扩大事权，改变了"车大马小"的现状。此外，基于调查研究适当地调整行政区划，将一般乡镇就近并入重点镇，扩大了重点镇的腹地范围。成都市现在乡镇平均面积约 40 平方公里，乡镇点位多、密度大，城镇规模偏小，导致城镇化带动能力弱，网络节点发育滞后。通过合村并镇有助于进一步扩大重点镇的辐射范围，改变点多分散的乡镇发展格局，能够推动市域网络化空间结构的形成和发育。

实现城市治理现代化是一个系统工程，既涉及城市治理多元参与主体素质的提升，又需要推进治理体制机制的变革和治理工具的现代化，而网络化城市空间结构的构建则会有效地助力城市治理体制机制的变革与治理工具的创新。

The Construction of Networked City Area and Its Governance Model Innovation in the Age of Industry 4. 0

Lv Bin

Abstract：Since the 1990s, globalization, informatization and regional integration have become the main theme of world development, and cities have become impossible to develop in isolation. With the daily mass exchange of people, logistics and information, the relationship among cities becomes more important than ever. With the "Fourth Industrial Revolution" wave that emerged after Germany proposed the "Industry 4. 0" strategy in 2013, the rapid development of the Internet economy and rail transit in China has promoted the networking of virtual and physical connections, and the trend of urban network development is constantly being strengthened, and the networked city area structure has become a new form of urban spatial organization. The networked city area structure is an advanced stage of the spatial evolution of metropolitan areas, and the inevitable external form of national and regional central cities. The construction of a networked city area structure is an important approach to solving the problems of large cities, promoting the people-centered high-quality urban development and improving the urban governance system and governance capabilities. This article discusses the goal and significance of constructing a networked city area structure and reveals the basic characteristics of the networked city area structure. Taking Chengdu city as an example, it expounds an innovative approach to the governance model of the networked city area.

Keywords: Industry 4.0, Society 5.0, Networked City Area Structure, Urban Spatial Governance

政府治理现代化是城市现代化的关键

罗一民[*]

【摘 要】城市现代化的实现，不仅需要专业性技术性手段，更需要带有综合性、根本性、统领性的现代化治理途径。政府治理现代化主要涉及两个方面：一是政府职能的现代化，二是政府治理体系的现代化。城市的现代化离不开政府治理的现代化。在推进城市现代化的进程中，既要注重现代化专业技术手段的运用，更要注重现代化治理体系建设，以政府治理现代化引领城市现代化。

【关键词】城市；政府治理；现代化

2013 年 11 月，党的十八届三中全会指出："全面深化改革的总目标是完善和发展中国特色社会主义制度，推进国家治理体系和治理能力现代化。"① 党的十九届四中全会专题研究坚持和完善中国特色社会主义制度、推进国家治理体系和治理能力现代化若干问题，并作出重要决定。党中央这一重大战略决策，对于全面深化改革，通过国家治理现代化推进社会主义现代化总目标的实现，具有极为重要的现实意义。毫无疑问，这对于通过地方政府治理现代化推进城市现代化，也具有极为重要的现实意义。

城市现代化，是工业、农业、科技、国防四个现代化的基础和动力源，只有实现了城市现代化，才能全面实现"四化"。而要想实现城市现代化，首先要实现城市治理现代化。城市治理现代化，也可看作城市政府

---

* 罗一民，南京大学政府管理学院兼职教授，北京大学政府管理学院兼职研究生导师。曾任南通市市长、市委书记，江苏省政协副主席。现为江苏国际文化交流中心理事长。

① 《十八大以来重要文献选编》上，中央文献出版社，2014，第 512 页。

治理的现代化。因此，城市的现代化离不开政府治理的现代化。这是笔者在江苏南通担任 10 多年市长、市委书记的切身感受。

我们知道，城市的现代化内涵十分丰富，包括城市建设的现代化、功能的现代化、产业的现代化、居住环境的现代化、社会秩序的现代化，甚至包括居住在城市中的人的现代化。这些现代化的实现，不仅仅需要城市建设和管理的专业性、技术性手段，更需要带有综合性、根本性、统领性的现代化治理途径。这涉及政府治理体制机制和能力的现代化，也是现代政治文明建设的重要方面。现代政治文明建设所要着重解决的，就是现代治理体系和能力的问题。或者说，也就是政治现代化的问题。从某种意义上说，政治现代化，也就是政府治理现代化。有了政府治理的现代化，就会有城市各个方面的现代化；没有政府治理的现代化，城市的现代化就无从谈起。这就犹如光有"大楼"，而没有"大师"，还不能称作"大学"。

2019 年 11 月 2 日，习近平总书记在考察上海时强调：深入学习贯彻党的十九届四中全会精神，提高社会主义现代化国际大都市治理能力和水平。① 这再一次为我们指明了城市治理现代化的方向。笔者认为，政府城市治理的现代化，主要包括两个方面：一是政府城市工作职能的现代化，二是政府治理体系的现代化。这两方面的水平都应切实提高。政府城市工作职能的现代化，就是按照现代化的要求，确定和完善城市工作职能，主要体现在"画""建""管""用"四个方面。

所谓"画"，就是对城市各方面，包括城市的形态布局和经济社会发展蓝图进行勾画、描绘，是一种广义的城市规划。在这里，主要是依托城市原有的资源，包括自然资源（自然条件、地形地貌、环境空间等）和人文资源（历史文脉、文化积淀、既有产业布局、传统建筑风格等），以新发展理念和现代城市规划理论为指导，对城市进行整体性、统筹性、引领性的规划和设计。这是城市建设和治理的"龙头"，其水平的高低，直接决定着城市现代化的程度和方向。现代化的"画"法至关重要。"画"不出现代化的水平，现代化的治理就无从谈起。

---

① 《习近平在上海考察时强调 深入学习贯彻党的十九届四中全会精神　提高社会主义现代化国际大都市治理能力和水平》，新华网，http://www.xinhuanet.com/politics/leaders/2019-11/03/c_1125187413.htm，最后访问日期：2020 年 7 月 23 日。

所谓"建"，就是对城市进行全方位的建设，把描绘的蓝图变为现实模样。其中包括交通系统、绿地系统、湿地系统、景观系统建设，创业创新所必备的基础条件，便民工程及公共服务设施等城市功能建设。这是地方政府日常工作中着力较多的方面，也是城市现代化状况的直观表现。人们从表面上观察一个城市的现代化程度，即通常所说的现代感如何，往往着眼于这些方面。以现代化的标准建设好城市，是城市治理现代化的基础，也是政府现代化治理职能所在。广义的"建设"，应包括物质文明和精神文明建设两大方面。精神文明建设的现代化，主要是提高市民的思想素养和科学文化素质，培育以社会主义核心价值观为内核、市民广泛认同的城市精神，这也是城市现代化的题中应有之义。

所谓"管"，就是对城市的各种有形物体和社会秩序进行全面管理。这是政府治理现代化的重要职责。城市的各种建设设施和公用物品应该管理，各个领域的工作和生活秩序及社会治安更应该管理。地方政府对城市的管理职能，更接近"治理"内涵，也更能反映治理的现代化水平。一座现代化的城市，首先管理水平必须是一流的。目前，随着城市规模越来越大，"城市病"越来越多，城市中的矛盾和冲突越来越突出，地方政府"管"的任务越来越重，所遇到的挑战和难题也越来越多。在克服重建轻管倾向的同时，必须有新思路、新举措，积极推动由单一的行政化管理向行政化与社会化并举的综合治理转变，由单纯的强制性管理向人性化治理转变，由简单的管理型向管理与服务相融合型转变。这是现代城市管理者的重要任务，大学里政府管理学院的教学科研内容，也应更偏重于此。

所谓"用"，就是在"画""建""管"的基础上，对城市进行合理而有效的综合利用。实际上也就是要使城市为人服务的功能最大化。比如，要发挥城市为居民的生产和生活提供最优服务的功能，为经济社会健康发展发挥最佳的集聚辐射功能，为工业化、城镇化发挥最强驱动引领功能，等等。"用"好城市的过程，既是发挥城市作用的过程，也是使城市不断保值、增值的过程，更是使城市居民享受现代化成果的过程，从而使城与人和谐共生、融合发展。正如习总书记在考察上海时所指出的那样：城市是人民的城市，人民城市为人民。要努力创造宜业、宜居、宜乐、宜游的良好环境，让群众有更多获得感，为人民创造更加幸福的美好生活。① 这是城市治理的出发点和落脚点，但当地方政府被表面的急功近利的"政绩"所牵引时，人民利益往往容易被忽视。一些地方一方面大兴土木、盲目建设，另一方面"城市病"频发，各方面的使用效能不佳，盖源于此。当下，地方政府应特别重视在"用"字上下功夫。城市"用"得好，才能最终体现城市治理现代化的水平。

总之，城市的"画""建""管""用"，是城市工作的基本职能。运用现代化的理念、标准、方法，完善和履行这些基本职能，是城市治理现代化的基本要求，也是实现城市现代化目标的基本条件。但是，城市的政府治理体系更为重要。因为，城市工作职能现代化，乃至整个城市的现代化，最终还要依赖于地方政府治理体系的现代化。城市工作职能的现代化，与地方政府治理体系的现代化，共同构成了城市治理的现代化。地方政府治理体系的现代化，使作为城市治理的主体——政府，按照现代民主政治的要求，建立一整套科学合理的运作制度和机制，从而确保城市治理沿着现代化的轨道运行，取得现代化的成效。所谓地方政府治理体系的现代化，主要表现为以下"四个化"。

第一，决策的民主化。众所周知，现代治理和现代民主政治的重要标志，就是决策的民主化。在城市治理的过程中，政府决策的正确性和正当性，取决于广泛而充分的民主。决策的正确合理和决策行为的正当合法，依赖于扎实的民主基础。缺乏民主，不仅会使决策错误或违规，而且即使是正确的决策，也往往难以贯彻落实。因为缺少民主的决策，缺少正当性，不正当的决策则缺少公信力和执行力。由此可见，决策民主化既是现代政府的基本标志，也是城市治理现代化的必由之路。政府作为城市现代化建设的决策者、推进者，应尊重城市历史、立足城市现状、把握时代要求、回应人民期盼、端正城市发展指导思想，作出顺应城市发展规律的科学决策。首先，要在决策程序合规合法的前提下，与城市中的广大居民一道，深化对城市历史和未来的认识。城市是历史的记录者，作为决策者来讲，在自己任期内所做的一切，只是城市发展长河中的一朵浪花、一个瞬间。因而必须首先学会用历史的、系统的眼光去认识和看待城市，在敬畏历史、保护历史中传承好历史，特别是要搞明白在不同的历史时期应该做

---

① 《习近平：城市是人民的城市，人民城市为人民》，搜狐网，https://www.sohu.com/a/351500549_114731，最后访问日期：2020 年 7 月 23 日。

什么，不应该做什么，从而作出符合城市实际、体现群众意愿的决策。

21世纪之初，随着苏通长江大桥、大型海港相继开工建设，南通进入桥港发展新时代。如何不失时机地推动城市走向"大而美""富而强"，我们发动各方面进行了深入研讨，甚至可以说是全民大讨论。在研究和讨论中，大家对南通历史上的重要人和事逐步形成了共识。比如，认识到著名爱国政治家、实业家、教育家、近代城市建设的先驱张謇，在家乡南通规划经营"一城三镇"，勾勒了近代城市现代化的雏形。他经营、规划和建设城市的先进理念，早于英国城市规划大师埃比尼泽·霍华德"田园城市"的建城思想，南通因此成为当时全国的"模范县"。对此，我们组织各方面专家学者"大胆假设、小心求证"。规划设计大师、两院院士吴良镛经过研究后，认为南通堪称"中国近代第一城"。这一判断，显著提升了城市的独特历史地位和影响力，极大激发了全市上下的自豪感和自信心，以及建设美好城市的愿望。我们因势利导开展"城市精神"和"弘扬先贤伟业、续写时代辉煌"的大讨论，不仅把张謇先生建城思想的研究推向了前所未有的高度，而且凝聚起了推进"近代第一城"大放异彩的智慧和力量。在此基础上，形成"依托江海、崛起苏中、融入苏南、接轨上海、走向世界、全面小康"的城市发展大战略，并及时决策实施通州撤市建区和启动新城区建设，中心城市发展迅速拉开了大框架。另外，我们在规划、建设、管理和经营城市的时候，每一项决策、每一个工程，都贯彻以人民为中心的发展思想，真正体现以人为本、城人合一的理念。民主政治的原则，应贯穿于城市工作的指导思想、决策及实施的各个方面。实践证明，没有城市公众的有序参与、民主监督、协商共治、权力制衡，地方政府对城市治理的决策及实施将陷入难以避免的偏颇和无力。毋庸讳言，当前许多地方出现的城市治理乱象，包括乱拆乱建、乱管乱治，大多与决策不当有关，而决策不当的背后，是因为决策不民主。如果事先发扬民主，听取意见，许多恶果是完全可以避免的。决策不能按程序集思广益，仅凭少数领导人不切实际、背离群众"拍脑袋"，肯定会出现决策不当，甚至严重失误。当然，若深究起来，决策不民主的背后，是民众对政府及其官员的选择和监督等民主权利尚未真正落实。无所顾忌、为所欲为的不当决策，源于缺乏民主制约的无所约束、无所规范的决策机制。在民主选举和民主监督机制健全的国度和城市里，决策者是不敢、不愿、不能乱决策的。

第二，管理的法治化。依法治理是现代文明国家的规范性要求，法治是国家治理现代化的基本原则和重要标志。离开法治，所谓的治理体系和治理能力的现代化，就是一句空话。同理，政府治理的法治化是政府治理现代化，乃至城市现代化的根本所在。善于用法治理念、法治思维和法治方式去治理城市，实现从"统治"向"治理"、从"人治"向"法治"、从"管制"向"善治"的转变，这是城市现代化发展的必然趋势，是政府治理现代化和城市现代化的核心体现。靠一套完善的法治体系管理城市，可以一通百通、事半功倍。摒弃法治、推崇"人治"，则会疲于奔命、一事无成。对此，笔者深有体会。2001年，笔者在南通担任市长，发现城市面貌"脏、乱、差"的背后，是因为城市管理执法工作存在职责边界不清、管理方式简单、执法行为粗放等问题。说到底，是法治的缺失。解决这些问题的根本手段是完善法治。于是，我们在江苏最早争取到国家综合执法城市管理改革试点，成立了城市综合执法管理部门，集中执法、统一执法、规范执法，从法制、体制、机制、编制等方面解决城市管理问题，并明确市、区、街道职责分工和运行机制，形成"两级政府、三级管理、四级网络"的管理格局，从而一举改变了"七八个大盖帽管不住一个破草帽"的现象，也改变了脏、乱、差的城市面貌。市长再也不用像以前那样具体管小商小贩乱摆摊点、行人车辆乱闯红灯之类的事了。曾被当时的总理朱镕基严厉要求"要把城市从垃圾堆中解放出来"的南通，几年后得到了他的高度认可。他高兴地称赞南通是江苏发展变化最大的城市，南通的濠河是"东方的威尼斯"。

与此同时，针对当时社会转型期出现的诸多矛盾，我们依法探索标本兼治、重在治本的新路子，在全国首创社会矛盾纠纷大调解机制，那些法院管不着、村委会管不了、乡镇管不好、治安处罚根治不了的疑难杂症，通过这个机制给解决了，并且在全国推广开来。南通连续十二年被评为全国社会治安综合治理先进城市。这实际上就是法治的力量。实际上，法治比人治更省力，也更有效。习近平总书记在2017年两会期间参加上海代表团审议时，特别强调"要强化依法治理，善于运用法治思维和法治方式解决城市治理顽症难题，努力形成城市综合管理法治化新格局"。① 这说到了要害，说到了根本。今天的南通，已从早期的城管体制改革试点拓展到创新政府治理的全方位改革，综合执法体制改革一直走在全国前列，并且在城乡建设与管

---

① 《走出一条超大城市社会治理新路》，人民网，http://m.people.cn/n4/2017/0309/c1405-8534214.html，最后访问日期：2020年7月23日。

理、环境保护、历史文化保护方面有权制定地方性法规，城市治理规范了，城市发展也更具活力了。特别令人高兴的是，南通行政审批制度改革全国领先，非许可审批事项全面取消，"一枚印章管到底"被国务院第三次督查确定为典型经验通报表扬。

第三，运作的高效化。政府运作的高效化，意味着运作程序最简练、方式最快捷、成本最低廉、成效最显著。现代城市治理事务繁多、变化多端，政府必须以高效的运作跟上城市变化发展的节奏，没有政府的高效运作，就没有现代化的治理。政府运作的高效化应主要从三个方面着手。

一是强攻改革快干事。推进城市现代治理，每时每刻都会遇到新情况、新问题，政府必须快速应对、有效处置，特别是遇到突发事件更应如此。目前，随着城市化进程的加快，城市管理面临诸多问题，突发事件（生产交通安全事故、公共自然灾害、社会矛盾引发的群体性事件）不断发生，"黑天鹅"和"灰犀牛"频频而来。通常所谓的公共应急管理，成了政府治理城市的重要职责和严峻考验。这必须以管理方法的创新、治理体系的改革、政府效能的提高来解决。当前，要着重解决政府功能紊乱、职能缺失、效能低下这"三能"问题。另外，要通过改革提升效率，政府必须有所为、有所不为，而不能充当无所不包、无所不揽的管家婆。从2000年开始，我们在全省率先对406家国有企业、108家市属事业单位实施改革，并重新界定政府部门职能，一场"静悄悄的革命"，使市场主体和社会主体活力得以充分释放，也使政府摆脱了纷繁复杂的事务，从"全能"走向"有限"，从"封闭"走向"透明"，从"分神"走向"专心"，实现了职能归位、效能提升。

二是统筹协调干好事。政府运作的高效，最终应体现在经济、政治、社会、文化、生态"五位一体"的协调发展上。这是衡量政府高效运作的主要标准，也是城市现代化进程与治理成效的具体反映。这就要求政府管理者打好"组合拳"，努力推动遵循经济规律、社会规律、自然规律的科学发展。多年来，南通政府与南通人民共同探索实践，走出来一条在科学发展观和习近平新时代中国特色社会主义思想指导下的跨越发展道路，形成了全面协调可持续发展的"南通现象"，取得了良好的发展绩效。目前，江苏省委对南通的定位要求是争当全省的"三个先锋"（解放思想超越发展的先锋、高质量发展的先锋、新时代干事创业的先锋）。

三是降低成本干成事。"高效"和"低耗"相辅相成，"低耗"主要表现为：开支低、机构少、人员精；领导班子内部及政府各部门之间内耗摩擦少，运转有序；按市场化原则利用资源，提高经济和社会效益。政府应通过深化行政体制改革等措施，降低行政成本和制度交易成本，包括减少内部摩擦损耗，节省人财物支出，提高行政管理效能。同时，发挥市场在资源配置中的决定性作用，引导非公市场主体参与城市公共设施建设。当年我们在南通，就是利用民营企业的资本建起了大型公共体育场馆，利用外资企业资本建起了大型海洋港口。至今，这还是全国首例。

第四，自身建设的科学化。"打铁还需自身硬"，政府治理的现代化有赖于政府自身的现代化。作为城市治理主体，政府决策的民主化、管理的法治化、运作的高效化，最终还要靠自身建设的科学化来实现。所谓政府自身建设的科学化，实际上也就是遵循现代政府的运作规律，按照政治现代化的要求，科学地建立政府、建设政府、运行政府，包括从政府设立到政府运作全过程。科学化应着重突出四点。①政府建立和施政的合法化——人民授权、人民选举、人民监督。政府依法成立、依法行政，最终体现了人民的意志和权利。这是确保政府科学化的前提和基础。②政府机构设置和日常运作的合理化——精干、高效、规范、有序。这是政府科学化的主要表现和基本要求，也是政府充分发挥职能作用、提高工作效能的基础性条件。③政府工作人员的高素质化——专业、敬业、勤政、廉政。这是政府科学化的人力保障和必备条件。④政府效能建设的制度化——权力制衡、问责激励、绩效评估、奖优罚劣。这是政府科学化的制度建设和目标追求。我们南通在 2001 年就围绕"高效、规范、创新、廉洁"政府自身建设总目标，切实推行政府绩效管理考评制度，推进政府效能"自我革命"，促使政府自身运作效率大大提高，政府服务质量一度数年连续位居全国 50 个最具竞争力城市排名之首，成为全省行政审批事项最少、审批时限最短、审批速度最快的城市。同时，我们发扬光大"包容会通、敢为人先"的城市精神，促进官与民互动共治，助推人与城共同成长。总之，做到了以上四点的政府，必定是科学合理的政府、人民信任的政府、治理有方的政府，必将能把城市引向现代化。

总而言之，只有通过治理体系的现代化，才能实现整个城市的现代化。政府只有通过自身建设的科学化，才能做到政府决策的民主化、管理的法治化、运作的高效化，从而实现整个治理体系的现代化。从根本上说，城市的现代化离不开政府治理的现代化。我们城市现代化水平不高，并不仅仅是因为缺乏专业技术手段和专业技术人才，还因为缺乏健全的现代化治理体系。我们有时"画"不好城市，是因为缺乏民主决策和民主监督；我们有时"建"不好城市，是因为缺乏高效有力的政府运作；我们有时"管"不好城市，是因为缺乏科学完备的法治手段；我们有时"用"不好城市，是因为缺乏有远见卓识、敢于担当的政府官员。因此，我们与其头痛医头、脚痛医脚地"治理"城市，不如从根本上建立起一整套现代化的治理体系，从而使城市的现代化成为必然和触手可及的现实目标。这方面的任务，特别重要而又异常艰巨。我们必须义无反顾地全力以赴。这是克服目前城市治理中所存在的各种弊端和障碍，又好又快地推进城市现代化的根本之道。我们在推进城市"画""建""管""用"等方面现代化的过程中，既要注重现代化专业技术手段的运用，更需要按照党的十九届四中全会要求，注重现代化治理体系和能力建设，以政府治理现代化引领城市现代化。

Modernization of Government Governance Is the Key to Urban Modernization

Luo Yimin

Abstract: The realization of urban modernization requires not only specialized and technical means, but also a comprehensive and fundamental management approach. Modernization of government governance mainly involves two aspects: first, the modernization of government functions; second, the modernization of the government governance system. The modernization of cities cannot be separated from the modernization of government governance. In pushing forward the process of urban modernization, we should pay attention to the application of modern professional and technical means, but also to the construction of modern governance system and urban modernization led by modernizing government governance.

Keywords: Urban, Government Governance, Modernization

文化规划与城市建设及城市治理的关系研究

陈国欢[*]

【摘　要】当前，全国城市发展与治理进程进入了关键期，一边是可以量化的具体成绩，另一边是不可量化的文化缺憾。在新时代背景下，城市发展与治理过程中如何规避普遍存在的问题，城市如何在稳步发展中保持自己独特的个性，文化规划显得尤其重要，不可或缺，迫在眉睫。

【关键词】文化规划；城市建设；城市治理

文化是一个城市的灵魂。此观点现已被普遍认可。但在具体实践过程中如何去解读，如何去体现，这需要深思，也值得去深思。在当下，中国的城市建设和治理，有着两个重要的时代背景。

其一，在我国快速的城市化进程中，存在文化战略思考和规划的严重缺失问题，文化策划和规划尚没有形成常态和有效机制，以至于忽略了城市建设中的"软规划"，也就是设计规划之外的文化规划。其结果便是全国各地大小城市"千城一面"或"一城千面"，而不再是"一城一面"，同时也造成了传统优秀文化的流失和西方文化的严重侵蚀，各城市地域个性湮灭和消解，大众审美水平庸俗化和退化，甚至出现了严重失误导致城市规划严重失调的案例，使得城市建设陷入特色危机之中，城市文化生态亟须挖掘和修复。

---

*　陈国欢，国家一级美术师，研究员级高级工艺美术师，现任江苏省文联副主席，东南大学文化战略规划研究中心主任。

其二，党的十七届六中全会提出了"文化自信""文化自觉"理念，到了党的十八大，则正式将其提升为国家战略内容。而要真正将"文化"从理念转化为具体实践，真正将"文"化入建设、发展和生活的方方面面，具体的"规划"与"应用"，显得尤为重要。具体到城市建设与管理，文化规划与建设规划、设计规划要并驾齐驱，多轨并行，决不可弱化和缺席。在当前局面下，文化规划参与城市建设与治理，迫在眉睫，刻不容缓。

一 城市的区域共性与文化个性

城市是人类文明发展的必然结果。每一个城市，都有自己独特的个性与独特风格，并有其独特的文化肌理和"主色调"。比如，京杭大运河沿线城市，其中江苏段就有多种文化表征，同样的一条河，各地域的文化个性并不相同，如徐州的楚汉文化，南京的金陵文化，苏州的吴越文化……这应该跟沿线与运河交汇的黄河、长江、太湖融汇所成不同"水质"的底色有关。

当然，作为"城市"，它们也是有共性的，至少有着相似的区域共性。因此，大到一个区域，小到一个城市、一个街区，都应有其自己的文化定位，都应确立自己的文化战略与规划。比如我国的京津冀、长三角、大湾区等核心区域，最终要实现的，不仅仅是经济的一体化、交通的一体化，更应是文化规划的一体化。

又比如长三角，"江南文化""江海文化"就是苏、浙、沪、皖四地所共认的文脉，它们在风俗、习惯、生活方式、审美取向等方面是相通的。具体说到上述四地的城市规划，需要立足于大区域的城市规划意识，既要考虑到共性，也要考虑到个性，做到共性中有个性，个性中有共性，各自发掘最典型的文化底蕴，呈现自己的文化肌理和城市风貌，既能各美其美，又能美美与共。

考虑到城市共性与个性因素，城市的群体记忆、情感认同、生活观念和生命体验等文化资源，如能通过系统的文化规划得以真正地传承和延续，势必会成为一种特殊的美学符号，会让城市更加像它自己，更加别具一格。

具体来说，城市文化个性，与各自的自然环境、人文历史、风俗习惯等均有内在关联，正是长期的积累和叠加才逐步形成了各个城市各自的"底色"。比如广东的树叶绿中带黑，土地是红得发黑；江南一带却是浅绿中带蓝；黄土高坡又是另一种感觉。地域音乐曲艺方面亦是如此，江南的丝竹、昆曲和吴语，陕北的信天游、秦腔，内蒙古的长调，西藏的天籁，等等，无不个性鲜明，具有极强的文化识别性。

以"我们的节日"为案例来说，中国传统节庆在不同城市既有共性，也有个性。我们在为南京春节、元宵节提出策划建议时，提出紧扣南京年味特色，以多层面、多角度、多样性体现全民年节为基础，提炼核心爆点，关键以"灯""联"为核心载体承载南京城市文化精髓。其中，"灯"，以秦淮灯彩为亮点，空间延展，形式拓展，有手扎彩灯，有现代灯光秀，有焰火；将做灯、挂灯、赏灯、观灯、约灯、戏灯细分出来，并结合灯谜，将"灯"与"联"结合起来，跨界拓展为灯与彩，灯与音，灯与诗，灯与画，灯与树，灯与楼，灯与河，灯与桥，灯与影，灯与车，灯与舞……描绘出一幅"金陵夜景图卷"，实现"人在灯中，灯在人中"的节日胜景。其中"联"，老城门挂春联，已成为南京春节新亮点，正好结合"世界文学之都"的城市定位，将春联活动放大，空间上扩展至车站、地铁、店铺；将征联、撰联、写联、贴联、赏联整个流程贯穿。在"我们的节日"的文化规划中，古都南京抓住"灯""联"二字做足文章，"家家挂灯、户户贴联"，"万灯点亮金陵夜，千联写就新南京"，打造"灯·联金陵年"。

城市正如美人，城市文化不存在高低之分，唯特色与个性各有差异。城市的软实力，从根子上来说，集中在文化综合力上，我们可以通过文化要素提炼，系统把握其内涵本质，将其外化和强化在城市建设和治理的形象和行为上，使之能够体现出从内而外一致的鲜明的城市格调，让城市在共性基础上个性鲜活，让人哪怕仅是一面之缘，也能够永生不忘。

二 城市建设与治理存在诸多问题

目前，在城市发展与治理中存在诸多实际问题。比如，不管城市大小，规模上一味求大；不管历史长短，风格上一味求新，所谓"不破不立"，"旧的不去，新的不来"。

我们的古城老街，总喜欢出新，在"创卫"建设中，常常整条街粉刷一新，不知不觉中遮盖掉了城市千百年的历史痕迹。比如笔者现在所居住的老城南，某日突然心血来潮，外墙出新时涂成了五颜六色的幼儿园风格，据说这是领导去新加坡学回来的"阳光灿烂"。相反，在意大利威尼斯水城老街上，可以随处看到各世纪各时期建筑在外墙、门窗上的不同记录。其实，这才是一座活态的博物馆，记住历史，才能感知未来。

又如笔者居住的南京核心城区秦淮区，提出了"文化立区"，即便重视如此，近期听说位于夫子庙地区的杨公井老牌书店"古籍书店"要歇业转型了。这是一家老南京都知道的老书店，因维持不下去只能歇业。南京被评为"世界文学之都"之后不久，一家老字号古籍书店就要从这个文气氤氲的城市消失，这实在让人惋惜。作为一个在南京居住了几十年的老市民，笔者不得不说，现在的南京夫子庙与明清时期相比就是缺少了书卷气，多了烟火气，夫子庙没有了夫子样，周边的实体书店，实在太少了。这是不是与文化规划介入城市建设和治理的程度不够深入有关？

另外，一些城区以统一的风格和视觉效果，将沿街商铺的招牌设计成同一尺寸、同一材质、同一色彩，其结果是失去了商业文化和广告标识的品牌识别特色，毫无个性可言。

再如，许多地产楼盘名称不顾自身特点，喜好模仿外国名字，甚至于编造貌似洋气的名字，像什么"玛斯兰德""拉德芳斯"等，既不好记又不好读。

更如城市绿植设计跟风随潮，有的到处将香樟作为行道树，而放弃垂柳、芦苇、蒲草等代表水乡地域生态的植物。更有甚者，地处山城环境的高楼将远处的高山压成了盆景，视线上，住宅小区远高于自然山体的高度，山城的风貌全然被破坏；湖边的建筑将湖围成一个密不透风的"水桶"，将原本辽阔的城市水景变成了住宅小区的私家池塘。

其实，对每个城市的文化认识与挖掘，都是需要下功夫的，当然，这远不如猎奇、抄袭来得快。正是因为如此，文化规划参与城市建设与治理势在必行。

三 文化规划是城市发展与治理的根与魂

文化具有内涵和外表两个层面，外表形式可以多样，但内核是统一的，样式在不断变化，而内涵相对稳定。文化虽然是多元的、交互的，但其地域性不会根本消解。

当今社会，已经进入审美经济时代，空间与景观，视觉的体验，都会融入地域历史人文的根脉和底色中。所以，文化既是"根"，也是"魂"，其深度地将时空交融形成了一个特有的生态系统。

文化与地域的关联，也常常会随着当地的政治、经济地位的起伏而变化。比如江苏，有着楚汉文化、淮扬文化、金陵文化和吴地文化，这些文化因时代变化而多层叠加形成了复式结构。

又如南京，被命名为世界"文学之都"，这与从六朝、南唐、大明、清代、民国千年积累而来的文化密不可分。而如何从江南的诗性文化和文学审美中进一步彰显南京独特的美学精神，是否需要补充一座"南京文学艺术馆"，并延展至民众的生活美学之中，这都值得文化规划者思考。同时，城市文化自信也体现在开放性和交流上，与其他文化的交流对话，可以极大丰富自己的文化。这些都需要文化规划的深度介入。

最近，南京的红花机场正在建设文化客厅，该机场是20世纪30年代初的空军大校机场，是中国历史上最大的航空基地之一。机场现已搬迁，对于老机场留下来的机场跑道材料，正在考虑如何再利用，变废为宝。随着文化规划的逐步介入，机场跑道石将被设计制作成各种城市家具、导视系统、景墙、汀步、铺装、建设外墙、艺术装置、文创产品等，以用废料再生方式体现区域特色，承载历史记录，留住城市文化与历史的根与魂。这是文化规划参与城市建设与治理的一个很好的案例。

怎么将文化规划植入城市发展中是一个综合性的大课题。比如在形象应用方面，最基本的途径是，先提炼出城市的文化调性，找准文化底色和肌理，明确文化图谱，然后再规划总结出总体的框架结构，细分至城市空间中去。

比如文化空间的布局，要专门规划，大到自然山水景观、建筑群落，小到街巷店铺、景区、社区、商区，直至街口巷角的微空间，关注城市的文化界面和空间对话，形成包括雕塑、装置、景观、绿植、灯光、各类标识、店招、广告、公共场所的座椅、垃圾箱、路灯、建筑外立面、空调室外挂机、道路铺装等在内的综合体系，结合民俗民风、传统现代，将老城与新区进行差异化布局，真正做好文化统领下的亮化、美化、绿化，形成一个特色鲜明的文化生态系统。

文化规划，要精细化：内容包括朝代、名人、典故、民俗等。

文化规划，要整体化：要从景区扩大至街区，从街区扩大至社区。

文化规划，要统领化：要通过总定位，去影响业态规划、产业规划、建设风格、色彩调性、景观设计、文化空间等。

文化规划，要研究各区域的文化肌理，梳理各区域的文化资源，分析各区域的文化之感，确定各区域的文化气质。

当下，文化竞争力在城市发展中已从边缘走向了中心。城市的精神追求是历史底蕴和时代气息的总和，代表了一个城市的总体"气象"和"格调"。城市文化可以培育市民品格，可以塑造城市风貌，可以凝练城市精神。更多地关注和研究城市文化形态的独特性与多样性，城市文化发展的继承性与延展性，城市文化建设的地域性与国际性，可以让我们的城市更有品位，更有气质，更有风骨，更有魅力。

四 小结：文化规划参与城市建设与治理迫在眉睫

可以说，在中国目前的城市建设与治理过程中，文化规划，势在必行，文化规划，迫在眉睫。

城市的高质量发展，急需顶层设计的提升，综合规划的创新。

东南大学文化发展战略规划研究中心是一个应时应运而生的文化规划机构案例。中心于2019年6月下旬落地南京，以研究、传承中华优秀文化艺术，并将其融入当代区域经济与城市发展为目标，发挥高校优势，跨界融合艺术学、社会学、历史学、建筑学、美学、传播学、设计学等诸多学科；整合校内外资源，着力于艺术学的社会应用方向，为各相关政府的文化发展战略与规划提供智力支撑，以项目为龙头，集中攻关，跨单位、跨学科、跨领域研究与应用。

文化规划在城市建设与治理中的作用十分重要，通过"硬规划"和"软规划"的结合，能够使城市发展在硬实力基础上增加软实力。而文化软实力又是引领性、统筹性的核心。只有在文化规划先行的导向之下，去细化其他各项功能规划，才是城市建设高质量发展的正确之路。以城市建设与治理为文化规划的导向，可以彰显个性、特点，可以提升审美效果，可以凝聚城市精神内涵价值，可以节约集约建设，可以实现城市持续良性发展。

A Looming Trend of the Cultural Planning Participating in Urban Construction and Governance

Chen Guohuan

Abstract: In current situation, the process of urban development and governance in China has entered a critical period. On one hand, there are concrete achievements that can be quantified, and on the other hand, there are cultural defects that cannot be quantified. Under the background of the new era, how to avoid the common problems in the process of urban development and governance, how to maintain its own unique personality in the steady development of the city, cultural planning is particularly important, indispensable and imminent.

Keywords: Cultural Planning, Urban Construction, Urban Governance

城市基层公共文化服务自主供给的生发逻辑研究[*]

李少惠　吴嘉欣[**]

【摘　要】基层公共文化服务自主供给是由基层群众自发组织、自主提供的，具有娱乐自我、服务大众的双重效应，与当前群众旺盛的文化需求相吻合，已经成为城市公共文化服务体系建设的必然趋势之一。本文运用 Nvivo11 质性研究工具，对城市基层公共文化服务自主供给的生发逻辑进行探索。研究发现，公共文化服务自主供给遵循着包含内生需求与外在支持的逻辑起点、载体构建与空间整合的逻辑进路以及心理默契与情感价值回归的逻辑终端在内的整体逻辑走向。生发逻辑隐含着城市基层公共文化服务自主供给从无到有、步步走向成熟的发展路径，对于构建以群众为主体的公共文化服务供给模式大有裨益。

【关键词】基层；公共文化服务；自主供给；生发逻辑

一　问题的提出

公共文化服务体系作为国家文化建设战略的重要组成部分，关系着广

---

* 基金项目：国家社科基金项目"乡村振兴战略实施中完善西部农村公共文化服务体系研究"（18BZZ102）；中央高校基本科研业务费专项资金项目"西部民族地区公共文化服务整体性治理研究"（2019jbkyxz005）。

** 李少惠，兰州大学管理学院教授，博士生导师，研究方向为文化治理、行政发展；吴嘉欣，兰州大学管理学院硕士研究生，研究方向为民族地区文化治理。

大群众基本文化权益的实现。随着"政府主导、市场运作、社会参与"的复合供给模式逐渐嵌入公共文化服务供给的运作中，以群众为供给主体的"自主供给"模式登上了基层公共文化服务体系的舞台，旨在以多重力量增加公共文化服务的有效供给，满足人民群众追求美好生活的文化需求。城市基层公共文化服务自主供给是由基层群众自发组织、自主供给的，具有娱乐自我、服务大众的双重效应。民众自发聚合在街头广场、公园等公共场所，以舞蹈、合唱、戏曲、乐器演奏为主要内容开展形式多样的文化活动。由是，公共文化服务自主供给范围越来越广、群体越来越大、形式愈加多样，与目前国家大力提倡构建现代公共文化服务体系的目标要求高度契合。在此背景下，确有必要回溯发掘基层公共文化服务自主供给的生成逻辑与发展理路，以此开拓公共文化供给新思路，创新供给模式，继续巩固适宜群众生活的文化活动和形式，对于完善基层公共文化服务体系将大有裨益。

现阶段中国的市民社会尚未发育成熟，民间提供和管理文化服务的能力不足。公共文化服务主要依靠政府提供①，还可以根据各地经济发展状况，通过中央政府主导或促成地方政府合作的方式供给。② 例如在市场和第三部门的合作下建立公共文化服务体系③，形成以政府为主导，非政府组织、企业以及社区等社会各方协同参与的"交互理性"的制度框架。④其中，自主供给模式是公共文化服务多元化供给的一个崭新模式，它是通过自愿的方式主动提供公共物品或公共服务以满足民众需求。相比于政府权威型供给、市场商业型供给以及社会化供给模式，自主供给更加符合供给主体的实际需要，且供给成本更低，效率更高。戴维·奥斯本和特德·盖布勒认为让顾客挑选资源，是公益服务提供者快速响应顾客需求的最佳方式；⑤ 埃莉诺·奥斯特罗姆也证明人类社会中存在大量的公共池塘资源

---

① 丁煌：《当代政府管理新范式》，《行政论坛》2000 年第 3 期。
② 高喜月：《我国公共文化服务供给的主体、特征和路径选择——基于政府间关系》，《学理论》2014 年第 16 期。
③ 周晓丽、毛寿龙：《论我国公共文化服务及其模式选择》，《江苏社会科学》2008 年第 1 期。
④ 李少惠：《公共文化服务体系建设的主体构成及其功能分析》，《社科纵横》2007 年第 2 期。
⑤ 〔美〕戴维·奥斯本、特德·盖布勒：《改革政府——企业精神如何改革着公营部门》，周敦仁译，上海译文出版社，1996，第 163 页。

问题，不是依赖国家或市场来解决的，而是资源使用者通过自愿合作的集体行动为公共事物管理提供更有效的制度安排。① 可见，无论是私有化还是权力下放，"自主运作"的建立都是近年来公共治理改革的主导趋势。②

纵观公共文化供给模式领域的研究，基层公共文化服务自主供给是多元供给模式的纵向裂变与拓展，是基于广大人民群众日益增长的文化需求及民众文化权利意识的广泛提升所产生的新型供给模式，自主供给更能紧密契合基层群众的文化需求，凸显了基层群众的文化主体性。然而，现有研究成果多侧重对公民参与公共文化服务多重因素的解释，而疏于具体分析各因素之间的内在关系，且针对基层公共文化服务自主供给的生发逻辑的研究较少。现有研究不足为本研究的开展留下了充足的余地。

二　基于 Nvivo11 质性研究工具的研究过程

（一）研究设计

本文旨在回答的核心研究问题是"城市基层公共文化服务的自主供给是如何产生与发展的"，目的是挖掘城市基层公共文化服务自主供给的一般性规律，为公共文化服务自主供给实践提供参考依据。研究过程中以 L 市基层公共文化服务的实践样态为研究场景，通过实地调研获取一手资料，借助 Nvivo11 质性研究工具，深入分析城市基层公共文化服务自主供给的诱致性因素，明确其逻辑走向。

（二）案例选择

L 市是一个包含回族、东乡族、藏族、维吾尔族等多民族的省会城市，各少数民族聚集形成了别具特色的民族文化。在预调研的基础上，本文最终选取 L 市楼兰之韵新疆舞蹈队（XJ）、夕阳红老年合唱团（XY）、和谐秦腔自乐班（QQ）和锅庄舞蹈队（GZ）四个文化自组织作为本调研对象。案例选取遵循以下原则：一是案例可接触；二是案例具有较长的公共文化

---

① 〔美〕埃莉诺·奥斯特罗姆：《公共事物的治理之道——集体行动制度的演进》，余逊达译，上海人民出版社，2000，第 122 页。

② Klenk T., Lieberherr E., "Autonomy in Public Service Provision and the Challenge of Accountability," *ETH-Zürich* 38（2014）.

服务自主供给的发展过程；三是所选案例要避免同质性和单一性。

（三）半结构式访谈与资料收集

在半结构式访谈过程中，综合运用深度访谈法、参与式观察法和焦点团体，共访谈 18 人，访谈对象既包括参与公共文化服务的个人（组织者或参与者），也包括团体，同时也将旁观者（PG）纳入其中。在实地调研中，访谈提纲仅作为参考，实际访谈内容会根据受访者的回答适时调整，最终共获取 6 万余字的原始资料，整理出 3000 余字的备忘录。

（四）编码与资料整理

本文运用 Nvivo11 质性研究工具进行编码工作，在编码过程中遵循扎根理论的三级编码要领，通过不断比较，逐步使研究资料"概念化""范畴化"，并最终归纳出"城市基层公共文化服务自主供给的生发逻辑"。

三　城市基层公共文化服务自主供给的生发逻辑透视

"生发逻辑"意在表明事物的生成和发展过程所遵循的基本规律，是指事物从无到有、从低级到高级、从青涩走向成熟的内在机理。

（一）文化需求衍生——自主供给的逻辑起点

主观爱好与健康意识的彰显。"需求"源于集体内部不满足、不平衡的一种心理或生理状态，这种状态刺激机体产生去寻求满足、弥补缺失的某种行为。文化需求作为人的精神需要，是基于生理需求、安全需求等更高阶段的需求，彰显着个体的精神内涵、价值观念、意识形态等面向的欲望，也正是这种与经济发展水平相伴相生的内生需求，成为城市基层公共文化服务自主供给产生的最原始动机。社会发展进入转型期，人们的思想逐渐开化，更加注重精神层次的文化享受和主体价值的彰显。然而高额的生活成本，激烈的竞争压力，让不少人长期处于身心俱疲的生活状态中，消耗健康已经成为很多人奋斗的代价。老年人在享受晚年生活的过程中，将物质需求看得更为寡淡，相反则更加注重身体状况是否良好，而中青年人则有意识地提前规避生活压力带来的健康损耗，越来越多地走出家门参与文化活动。在这样一种心理状态下，免费的自发性文化活动也就成为不同群体锻炼身体、增强体质的完美选择。

观念认知的转变与心理情愫的唤起。时代的快速流动带来的不仅仅是物质外表的更新换代，也促进民众内心的观念转变。在愈发宽松的社会环境中，人的主观能动性得到了持续性增长，突破了物质压力，人们更多地向往轻松愉悦的精神享受，不再像过去那般封闭保守，而是渴望得到展示自我的机会。中老年群体普遍怀有对过去生活的记忆，加上某种心理情愫的催化，他们将这种记忆和情愫寄托于生动的文化活动而得以重现。因此，无论是感官上单向度的享受，还是积极投身其中的主体性参与，都无不彰显着群众多元向度的文化需求。"文化需求衍生"的编码举例见表1。

表1　"文化需求衍生"的编码举例

范畴	原始语句（初始概念）
主观爱好	PG39 我喜欢太极拳，打了二十多年了，看这有人打太极拳，我都会跟着一起打（主观兴趣） GZ61 我对藏族的锅庄舞是情有独钟，我以前跟藏民打过交道，藏民的生活习惯各个方面我都了解（生活经历）
健康意识	XY53 关键还是以锻炼身体为主，人的观念在变化（健康意识）（观念转变） QQ292 就是为了领着大家一起开心、快乐地锻炼身体，为了健康着想，没有别的目的（健康意识）（活动目的）
观念认知转变	XJ73 过去人的思想太封闭了，现在慢慢就开放了（思想逐渐开放） XY51 年轻人可以随便唱歌，我们有什么不可以呢？社会这么好，应该多出来活动活动（认知转变）
心理情愫唤起	QQ31 因为一般老年人怀旧，秦腔他听得亲切、听得懂（怀旧情结） XY217 我们都是岁数大一点的中老年人，我们是唱的红歌多一点，我们年轻的时候唱的是这些歌曲，就是觉得比其他歌曲都好听（心理情愫）（历史记忆）

（二）社会条件进步——自主供给的外在支持

社会形态更迭。社会环境的变化展现着日新月异的变换节奏，城镇、农村人口的潮流涌动加速了城乡融合的社会形态。人口的地域转移既有赖于经济的地域转移，也带动着文化的地域转移。笔者在调查研究过程中发现，例如秦腔自乐班、腰鼓队、花儿演唱等很多文化团体的主要组成人员是近年来从 L 市周边的农村转移而来，或是进城务工，或是随儿女进城养老，他们的到来在一定程度上改变了 L 市的人口结构、经济结构以及文化形态，因此成为一种社会形态的微观变换，这种变换具体表现为三方面：第一，主要供给者——以城市居民为主要参与者变为城市居民和农村居民结合的供给结构；第二，文化资源形态——在城市原本单一的文化资源的基础上增添了农村地区的文化元素，如秦腔、花儿、腰鼓等；第三，基层公共文化服务的客体——由于文化资源日益多样，提高了其他居民参与活动的可能性，基层公共文化服务的群众基础更为广泛。"社会条件进步"范畴的编码例举见表 2。

表 2 "社会条件进步"范畴的编码例举

范畴	原始语句（初始概念）
社会形态更迭	PG29 我原先在农村，过去的人逢年过节都唱一唱（秦腔），来这（城市）之后呢，反而还看到有人唱呢（从农村到城市） QQ55 我们都是一起来打工的，周末闲了就聚到一起唱上几个小时（进城务工）
文化政策支持	XJ89 现在社会进步了，政府也更加重视文化的发展了（政府重视） GZ258 我们团队参加过市里的广场舞比赛，还得到了奖金（比赛奖励）
生活质量改善	PG284 现在的人生活条件好了，闲暇时间也多了，需要精神享受（条件好转） QQ98 过去老是为了生活奔波，现在不用再为钱的事情操心了（生活富裕）
参与成本低廉	XY155 我们一个月只交十块钱电费，谁都能交得起（费用成本） PG198 现在网络这么发达，不会跳了可以从网上学，很方便（学习成本）

文化政策支持。基于社会形态的不断变换，国家层面大力提倡的普惠共赢的文化政策更让基层公共文化服务发展如沐春风。L 市政府采用以奖代补、项目补贴、演出资助和招标采购等办法，对文化惠民及各类公益性演出予以补贴，扶持基层群众业余文艺团队发展，并逐步形成了"文化活动月""文化艺术节"等群众文化活动品牌，为广大群众的文化活动提供良好的展示机会。无论是兴修街道、社区综合文化服务中心等基础设施的硬件支持方面，还是政府提供演出机会和经费奖励的软件支持方面，这些实践的落实无疑填补了以往空有说辞的"政策鸿沟"，给予城市基层公共文化服务自主供给实践莫大的鼓励和支持。

生活质量改善与参与成本低廉。不断提高的生活水平，在很大程度上助推了基层公共文化服务的向好态势。一方面，当人民的生活水平达到某一基点时，便会出现追求文化品质和精神享受，同时又能够实现自身价值的深层次诉求；另一方面，社会的进步不仅体现于人均消费水平的提高，也体现在生活成本的降低，尤其是在以移动互联网为主的科技时代，群众可以借助便捷的网络渠道进行学习，提升了群众主动学习的兴趣。可以说，不断提升的生活水平提升了群众树立自身价值的精神欲望，低廉的参与成本又助推了群众自组织的良态发展，二者反向行之构成了城市基层公共文化服务自主供给得以发展的客观条件。

（三）文化团队组建——自主供给的载体构建

文化精英：文化精英的引领示范。城市基层公共文化服务的自主供给以各类文化团队为主要载体。在团队组建过程中，少不了文化精英的引领示范作用。"精英"是指精明强干、具有显著影响力和号召力的群体。在文化领域内，如果拥有较多的文化资源，并能有效地利用资源服务于大众群体，获得他人认可的人，则被称为"文化精英"。这些文化精英主要由"文化爱好者"和"专业人员"两种类型组成。文化爱好者一般基于长久以来保持的浓厚兴趣，加之在生活中历练积累的文化才能，从而产生组建文化团队的意向。专业人员一般以艺术老师、退休教师、民间艺人和少数民族群众等为主要代表组成，他们通常具有高尚的艺术审美和纯熟的经验技术，能够对普通群众产生指导作用，引领集体性文化活动沿着培养高尚情趣、培养艺术气息的轨道前行，避免了活动的单调和低俗。

身临其境：陌生成员的浸入体验。当文化团队的雏形搭建起来后，便是新成员不断进入的阶段。团队开展文体活动时，往往会吸引感兴趣的来往行人驻足观看，此时文化团队成了"表演者"，过往行人成了"旁观者"，他们常常表现出跃跃欲试的心理状态，甚至会在旁观者人群中不由自主地跟唱或跟舞，进入了一种"身临其境"的表演场域。文化团队因其自发性的组建方式，必然具备了"开放而非封闭"的特征，也即文化团队并无明确的"准入界限"和"准入规则"。在这种情境下，团队为了扩大规模，往往以热情的姿态接纳"旁观者"进入组织尝试，于是陌生成员能在备受鼓舞的氛围下形成一种"浸入式体验"。"文化团队组建"范畴的编码例举见表3。

表3 "文化团队组建"范畴的编码例举

范畴	原始语句（初始概念）
文化精英	QQ188 团队成员在退休之前大多是从事专业的戏曲工作的（成员专业性） XJ18 她本身就是维吾尔族人，年轻时候就在舞蹈团待过（个人资源）
身临其境	GZ247 如果有观众想学的话就直接进来体验（体验环节） XJ258 看多了也想进去和他们一起跳（跃跃欲试）
关系嵌入	QQ247 有人想学习这个，我们就一起教着唱（成员互助） XJ125 时间长了，我们就熟悉了，把他看作是我们的成员了（互相熟络）
情感共鸣	XY201 既能自娱自乐，大家互相帮助，演唱技巧也提高了（相互促进） QQ291 有些事情要和大家一起商量，才能把这个队伍壮大起来（人际和谐）
形象价值	XY228 叫作"夕阳红老年合唱团"，慢慢我们要把队伍组织起来呢（团队目标） QQ184 因为我们都是从农村来打工的，好不容易能聚到一起唱秦腔，所以叫"和谐秦腔自乐班"，希望我们的队员一直都和谐（团队名称）

关系嵌入：文化团队的认同吸纳。当陌生成员经过"浸入式体验"环节后，往往有很多人愿意加入其中。此时，文化团队以非正式方式接纳新成员，经过不断地磨合和交流拉近成员关系。当新旧成员互相熟悉之后就逐渐形成了文化团队的"身份认同""关系认同""价值认同"。此时，以新成员为嵌入的主体，以现有文化团队为嵌入客体，以个人资源、关系、价值观等为嵌入的主要内容的"吸纳-嵌入"机制就成为促进自发性文化团队提升扩容度的第三步骤。

情感共鸣：团队成员的凝聚共融。当个人与个人、个人与群体处于同一情境下，他人的情感变化能够引起个体主观相同或相似的反应倾向时，就产生了"情感共鸣"。对一个群体或团队来说，情感共鸣展现的是内部成员共同的"心理振幅"。新成员加入团队，客观上将个人文化偏好、价值观念、行为意识等要素嵌入组织中，在时间的不断积累中，成员消除了彼此的陌生感和隔阂感，更具有一种零距离、直面化的交流互动。正是源于团队成员长期以来通过磨合、沟通、交流的方式而达成的心照不宣的心理机制，一个团队从而产生文化认同，这种文化认同在某一程度上又形成了成员的"心理参照"，让团队成员的行为方式、思想观念都逐渐接近，趋于同一，进而以"共同参与—心理参照—情感共鸣—团队凝聚"的逻辑走向牢牢粘合的团队关系。

形象价值：团队品牌的内涵塑造。团队发展趋于成熟后，必然少不了"形象价值"的彰显。因为形象本身具有价值，所以由此带来的效益便往往是一种品牌的外显性展示。如"楼兰之韵新疆舞蹈队"，其名取自"西域楼兰之风韵"的美意，以穿戴维吾尔族特色服装为标志，清晰地展示了团队风情浓郁的新疆特色，在文化活动场所极为引人注目，成功地打造了一个独一无二的品牌形象。与此相同，很多自发性文化团队在发展过程中都为自己取名，一些较为成熟的团队还身穿统一服装，策划团队口号，从而在形式上树立一种鲜明的团队品牌，使得团队更具有仪式感，达到了一定的宣传目的。文化团队构建的逻辑关系见图 1。

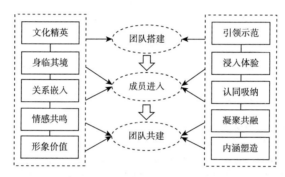

图 1　文化团队构建的逻辑关系

文化团队的构建使得群众文化活动有了一个特定组织，不仅有利于促进群众日常生活中的情感交流，也有利于构建生活空间，从而推动认同感、归属感、心理安全感的建立。

（四）文化空间整合——自主供给的情境叠加

硬件支持：物理场所的基础性供给。聚焦于社会学视域下的文化空间，是指具有文化意义的物理空间、地点、场所。① 无疑，文化空间首先是一个物理场所的客观存在。城市居民在进行自发性文化活动前，首先要选定一个合适的场所作为活动地点，通常以人民广场、文化广场、公园、社区活动中心，或是大面积空地为选择对象。这些场所通常都具有"开放

---

① 向云驹：《论"文化空间"》，《中央民族大学学报》（哲学社会科学版）2008 年第 3 期。

性""无门槛"的特点，不需要缴纳场地使用费，不被限制活动时间，且都设在居民生活圈中心，交通便利，因而是群众开展公共文化活动的最佳选择。文化团队的空间选择通常具有随意性和临时固定性，也即团队成员并不将活动位置长期固定在某一领域，场所的选择大多以人口流动性、活动密集程度、空间开放程度等作为定位标准，若场地产生了资源争夺的情况，那么成员能够在一致同意的前提下更换活动位置，因此组织场域也具有空间流动性。"文化空间整合"范畴的编码例举见表4。

表4 "文化空间整合"范畴的编码例举

范畴	原始语句（初始概念）
物理场所	PG78 公园人多，大家能跳起来（场合优势） PG84 这里环境好，主要是地方宽敞（环境优势）
文化资源	QQ203 秦腔是咱们甘肃这一带的传统文化（传统文化资源） XJ241 新疆舞是民族舞里面比较独特的，文化底蕴深厚，更有美感（民族特色）
娱乐氛围	GZ109 来这个公园遛弯就看见有人在跳锅庄舞，所以后来就加入进来了（氛围带动） XJ100 发现这些舞蹈很有感染力，音乐欢快，听着开心，人就喜欢（氛围感染）
文化与情感互融	QQ248 经常来唱一唱，心里的烦心事好像就消散了（舒缓心情） GZ301 跳舞时间长了，好像心里就产生了一种感情，觉得生活离不开它（文化依赖感）

软件支持：文化资源的补给性填充。在公共文化服务供给过程中，多样文化资源的注入使得文化活动精彩纷呈。以广场舞为例，因其大众化、平民化的特点曾经一度成为风靡群众的娱乐活动，但是广场舞也曾经被贴上"低俗化"的负面标签，究其根本，是源于其内容的"空虚化"、形式的"单一化"，可以说，文化资源的匮乏一度成为广场舞的发展瓶颈。然而随着人口迁移、社会形态变换、现代信息技术的覆盖，文化资源呈现重生态势。在活动内容上，特色民族文化、古老民俗文化、现代流行文化元素交相辉映。在人才资源上，不仅有少数民族朋友、民间艺人，也不乏具备专业才能的职业艺人。在信息资源上，群众常常会借助网络工具及时学习新的文化表演形式，以形成团队的绝对竞争力。因此，文化资源已经成为群众对基层公共文化服务自主供给内容的重要补给，是引导群众性文化

活动脱离媚俗化、平庸化的有力武器，深度彰显了文化资源的价值性，使群众自娱自乐的文化活动获得了长久发展的生命力。

环境机制：娱乐氛围的调剂性渲染。从公共文化空间建构的过程来看，物理场所奠定了空间基础，文化资源填充了活动内容，在二者建立的基础上，便形成一定的环境机制——娱乐氛围。城市基层公共文化服务的自主供给，表象是文化活动在公共场所的开展，实则是文化环境的无形营造。当团队整体开展活动时，悠扬的歌声、欢快的舞姿，其中所散发出来的娱乐气息交织在一起，围绕在城市上空，周围的旁观者则可以寻找他们的兴趣点驻足停留、默默欣赏。由于大多数文化团队有着常态化的表演机制，活动时间和地点相对固定，旁观爱好者就可以在固定的时间去观看一场免费的文化演出。久而久之，当旁观者与活动者产生情感共鸣时，便会尝试加入其中。由此，以娱乐氛围为主要内容的环境机制因其渲染性功能而对旁观者产生一种深刻的感染力，从而成为文化空间的拓展工具。

心理机制：文化与情感互融。当人们在一定的物理空间进行文化活动的生产和实践时，文化空间对群众有一种"引导性制约"作用，面对不同情景，群众往往由"被动式反射"行为转化成"耳濡目染式习惯"，最后走向一种"主动式参与"行为。因此文化空间在影响人们行为的同时，也形塑着思维和心理。群众开展自主性的文化活动时，无论是活动者还是旁观者都能感受到最为生动的文化生活和文化体验，产生文化与情感的交互效应。久而久之，人们逐渐会产生一种文化依赖——一旦生活中缺少文化活动，则会感到生活的寂寥和清冷，陷入一种无所适从的生活状态中。随着时间的绵延，文化环境不仅改变了群众的娱乐心态，随之而来可能是人们的行为习惯、意志情趣、生活理念、价值取向的转变，达到了文化内涵与情感的互融效果。因此，文化环境不仅是文化活动的存在方式，更是一种具有文化气息的意义空间，它体现着人们的价值追求和理想表达，是文化空间构建的核心内蕴。文化空间整合逻辑关系见图2。

（五）社会资本积累——自主供给的默契重组

联系机制：社群网络的模式化构建。在持续的社会交往中，联系机制无疑成为发展社会关系网络的第一步骤。一方面，在团队组建初期，通常成员的认识表现为尝试心理下的默默跟随。当团队趋于稳定后，成员之间会确定一种联系机制，一般以成立微信群的方式呈现，团队中的大事小情

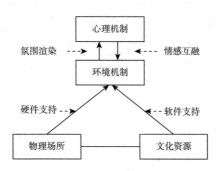

图2　文化空间整合逻辑关系

都可以借此工具进行通知，极大地方便了团队成员之间的交流。当这种联系机制成为常态，团队成员的沟通与交流转而可以拓展到生活中的琐事，延伸了成员的沟通渠道。另一方面，从团队外部来看，无论是何种类型的文化团队，都会不定时地参与一些文化展演、比赛等活动，这需要与其他团队成员、活动举办方、参赛对手进行联系和沟通，此时便形成团队内部—外部的联系机制。在社会关系网络中，成员不断交换着信息资源、技术资源、人脉资源，甚至是关系资源，而不同团队的成员们便存在于亲属关系、职业关系、组织关系、邻里关系等之中，这样的社群关系在时间的脉络里演化成一种模式化的建构，通过非制度化的人际关系和相对固定的行为而得到保障。"社会资本积累"范畴的编码例举见表5。

表5　"社会资本积累"范畴的编码例举

范畴	原始语句（初始概念）
联系机制	XY112 和其他团队联系比赛，我们就都相互熟悉了（建立联系） XY113 比如保险公司开业就会找到我们为他们演出（联系演出）
互惠机制	GZ176 大家在一起跳舞，就是一个相互学习的过程（相互学习） XJ375 社区联系到我们，让我们去表演，对双方都是一个机会（各取所需）
信任机制	QQ201 我们原先是一个地方出来打工的，所以才聚到一块唱秦腔（原始信任） XJ332 大家都是志同道合的人，也都能说到一起去，大家是彼此关照的（志同道合）
非正式制度	XY99 每人每月交十块钱的电费，都是自愿交的，队里不强制（自担费用） GZ156 每次跳舞的时候要把服装穿上，这样才显得整齐（心理契约）

互惠机制：社群成员的常态化帮扶。文化团队作为关系集合体，团队成员已经在潜移默化的团队关系中形成了彼此的关系认同和情感弥合，并且树立了一致性的团队发展目标，因此成员之间就会逐渐形成非正式的帮扶机制。对待新进成员，既有成员会义务性地给予指导，帮助他们尽快融入团队。新老成员之间以文化活动为纽带会形成"日常生活性"交往，主要体现在彼此的娱乐、聊天、生活互助等方面，该交往方式一般并不涉及利益或特定目的，有利于提升群众之间关系的紧密性。随着时间的推移，以群众性文化团体为基本单元的关系网络会逐步扩展到更大范围的合作体，他们或是联结其他文化团体、社会组织、市场、基层政府部门等，通过合作形式达成互惠互利模式。例如一些文化团队会义务性出演社区、企业等部门组织的活动。与此同时，这些部门也为团队提供了更为丰富的表演机会，双方在互惠合作中不断创造着新的资源集合体和社会关系网络，不仅建立了表达友好的沟通机制，形成了更为广泛的社会交往，也在实践过程中契合了彼此需求。因此，由团队内部向外围不断渗透的行动过程为社群成员的个人发展提供了常态化的帮扶，也为多元的社会关系网络建立了互惠机制，成为社会资本的主要观测点。

信任机制：社群网络的潜在性成长。信任是构成社会资本的核心要素，是个体对于他人行为是否会遵守规则或标准的一种积极的反馈行为。基于团队成员在交往过程中个体或群体之间形成的普遍信任关系，信任主要分为认知信任和情感信任。一方面，成员的相互交往形成了一定的交流空间和信息集合体，尤其以"零距离"的方式获取大量的信息来源，这为成员之间建立信任关系提供了重要基础。与此同时，当个体感知到自己与其他成员具备相同的文化符号、思想意识、价值观念时，个体间更容易在团队中产生信任感。另一方面，公共活动空间为团队成员提供了一个交往平台，在长期交往过程中成员产生了自然的情感联系和心理认同，随即形成了成员之间的情感信任。文化团队作为一个关系集合体，必然具有一定的团体意识，团体意识则为成员增强团队归属感提供了情感信任的"培育场"，成员在长期的交流互动中更能增加团队归属感与凝聚力，无形之中也就建立和强化了团队中的信任关系。

非正式制度：社群网络的共在性惯习。相比国家的法律、政策、规章等正式制度，非正式制度具有一种潜移默化的属性，一旦形成，就会对人们的观念意识、行为模式具有某种约束作用。即使在日常文化活动中团队成员也身着统一演出服装，演出服装作为一个团队最为鲜明的文化符号，彰显着团队品牌的内涵，也意味着团队发展已经步入正轨。另外，由于文化团队均由群众自发性组建，为了应对日常活动的电费缴纳、设备服装的购置、材料印发等开销，成员需要自行承担相应费用，但此项费用由个人自愿上交，并非强制。这种自愿承担活动费用的行为也成为一种非正式制度，体现着团队成员着眼集体利益的自愿行为。如果将一个文化团队看作一个"微单元"，那么这些非正式制度就是成员之间的心理契约和共识，也即当成员维持一定人际关系时，依靠共同的参照和微妙的心理机制，非正式制度往往以一种隐性规范的角色彰显团队发展过程中的"自我管理""自觉维护"的共在性惯习。相比硬性而冰冷的正式制度，非正式制度通常能更加有效地推动团队及社群发展。基层公共文化服务自主供给中社会资本形成过程见图3。

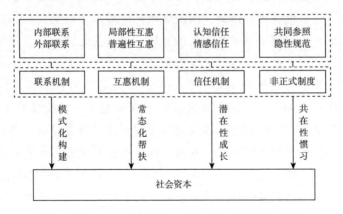

图3　基层公共文化服务自主供给中社会资本形成过程

（六）情感价值回归：自主供给的文化呈现

自我效能感的逐步渗透。"自我效能感"是指"人们对能否运用自己的技能完成某种工作行为的自信"[①]，也即对个体能力保有一种确切的信念。群众之所以热衷于自主性的公共文化活动，是因为多元的文化活动使

---

① Duane Brown, *Career Choice and Development*, M. A.：San Francisco Press, 2002, pp. 87-88.

得群众能够收获着实丰富的"自我效能感",主要体现在生活状态的改观和心理状态的调整两个方面。基层公共文化活动以中老年人为主要参与者,他们往往处于一种寂寥的生活状态中,而文化活动则可以充当生活调味品,不仅可以填充老年时光的空白,还可以有效拓宽人际交流,找回个人存在感。参与者常常能在文化活动中达到展示自我的目的,从而收获心理上的获得感与自豪感,这种获得感或来自团队成员的鼓励,或来自旁观者赞许,尤其对于队长、领唱(舞)者等"明星角色"来说,集体性活动更能增加他们的优越感和荣誉感,这种荣誉感也成为增强团队凝聚力的关键因素。无论是生活状态还是心理状态,文化活动参与者总能在其中找到自我存在的意义,从而增强了参与群体性文化活动的意愿。"情感价值回归"范畴的编码例举见表6。

表6 "情感价值回归"范畴的编码例举

范畴	原始语句(初始概念)
自我效能感	GZ20 跳舞不是给别人看的,是给自己享受的(自我享受) GZ202 把这个快乐带给自己也带给大家(传播快乐)
公共精神	XY98 音响是我自己家的,这是大家共同的爱好,没必要斤斤计较(志愿精神) QQ206 我们应该把自己的文化重新捡起来,发扬光大(社会责任感)

公共精神的不断延伸。基层公共文化服务最为显著的特征是"公共性",不仅存在于开放性的公共空间内,也体现在群众内化的公共精神上。群众自主供给的行为本身就是公民参与意识和主体意识的鲜明体现,基于社群网络的联结、规范、互惠与信任,成员之间很容易形成强韧的聚合力,同时也衍生出基于个人道德规范、奉献意识的公共精神。一方面,在群体性活动中,因权利和义务的无规定性,成员往往自主地承担团队事务,尤其以队长或团队负责人为主要带头人,以互惠关系为团队发展和自我发展的认同基础,成员逐渐树立了一种积极参与、平等合作、邻里友好的公共意识。另一方面,囿于传统文化流失危机日渐严重,一些老艺人以拾起传统文化为最质朴的初衷,努力唤醒人们对传统文化的历史记忆,展现了一种深厚的社会责任感。公共精神的存在不断突破人们自私冷漠的

"德性困境"①，呈现的则是"人人相善其群"的传统公德。公共精神的延伸给予了广大群众道德范式的指引，才使得群众对自发性的公共文化活动有了情感价值的体现，使得公共文化服务自主供给有了"精神—现象"的路径轨迹。基层公共文化服务中情感价值的回归路线见图4。

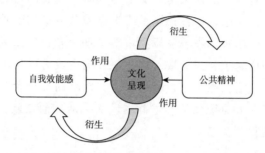

图4　基层公共文化服务中情感价值的回归路线

四　结论与启示

（一）内生需求与外在支持：自主供给的逻辑原点

群众公共文化服务自主供给的逻辑原点由"内生需求"和"外在支持"两大范畴构成。"需求"源于集体内部不满足、不平衡的一种心理或生理状态，这种状态刺激机体产生去寻求满足、弥补缺失的某种行为。文化需求作为人的精神需要，是基于生理需求、安全需求等更高阶段的需求，彰显着个体的精神内涵、价值观念、意识形态等面向的欲望，也正是这种与经济发展水平相伴相生的内生需求，成为城市基层公共文化服务自主供给产生的最原始动机。加之中老年群体普遍怀有对过去生活记忆和某种心理情愫的催化，他们将这种记忆和情愫寄托于生动的文化活动而得以重现。因此，无论是感官上单向度的享受，还是积极投身其中的主体性参与，无不彰显着群众多元向度的文化需求。

社会环境的变化展现着日新月异的节奏变换，城镇、农村人口的潮

---

① 王永益：《社区公共精神培育与社区和谐善治：基于社会资本的视角》，《学海》2013年第4期。

流涌动加速了城乡融合的社会形态，人口的地域转移既有赖于经济的地域转移，也带动着文化的地域转移。加之国家层面大力提倡的普惠共赢的文化政策让基层群众的文化需求如沐春风，不断提高的生活水平，在很大程度上推动着基层公共文化服务的向好态势，都为群众的公共文化生活增添了"一臂之力"，基层群众的公共文化需求有了内外兼具的逻辑开端。

（二）载体构建与空间整合：自主供给的逻辑进路

基于群众普遍的文化需求和社会条件的外在支持，城市基层公共文化服务自主供给的发展路径步入"载体构建"和"空间整合"范畴。首先，自发性文化团队往往最初由几位主要发起人组建起一个非正式团队，志趣相投的"旁观者"以"浸入式体验"的方式加入团队。在长期的共同活动中，团队成员的文化偏好、行为意识等趋于一致，于是出现了团队共同的"心理参照"，使成员逐步产生了情感共鸣。情感共鸣一旦产生，对团队整体发展有着强有力的粘合作用，是推动成员产生"共融心理"的催化剂。最后，当团队发展至成熟阶段，往往会以树立一定的品牌来提升形象价值，通常表现为"取名称""喊口号""统一服装"等具体方式，不仅使团队特征更加鲜明，也树立了一种积极的外在形象。

如果将文化团队看作一个"子系统"，那么文化空间则是多个"子系统"的集合体。其中，以物理场所为基本的硬件支持，以文化资源为必要的软件支持，构成了文化空间的客观存在。近年来，在国家政策的映照下，各级政府部门以保障群众文化权利为重点工作，尤其以建立健全文化服务设施为工作开展的首要任务，这为群众集体性文化活动提供了最基本的保障。与此同时，群众集体性的活动所散发的文化魅力无疑又为群众营造了一种具有"云氛围"的文化场域，形成一种具有晕染效果的娱乐氛围，构成了文化空间重要的支撑力，在这种氛围感染中，群众内心极易形成"文化依赖感"，从而引导群众走向"主动式参与"阶段。由是观之，在物理场所和文化资源的基础之上，娱乐性的环境氛围和文化情感的相互交织构成了文化的内生空间，打通了基层群众自主供给的逻辑进路。

（三）心理默契与价值回归：自主供给的逻辑终端

经过编码，自主供给的逻辑终端由"社会资本"与"情感价值"两大主范畴构成。城市基层公共文化服务自主供给行为的本质是群众自发组织的具有开放性的群体活动，从该行为伊始，联系机制无疑成为打破封闭环境的第一步。依托团队成员在长期相处过程中常态化的帮扶、资源的共享与交换，形成了互惠互信、情感联结、价值认同的动力要素，促进了社群网络的成长，而组织内部非正式制度的结构性嵌入，又使得社群单元有了共同参照，也成为成员的心理契约。综上，社会资本的形成既是构建和谐有序的社会关系网络的基础，也是形成互助互惠互信的关系格局的保障，使得群众自主供给公共文化服务有了更为深厚的心理默契。

"情感价值"范畴由"自我效能感"和"公共精神"两个副范畴构成。自我效能感体现着个人对于行为的预期心理和真实感受。群众在集体性的文化活动中获得丰富的自我效能感，这种情感丰富的心理机制往往扮演着内生需求的"催化剂"的角色——自我效能感越强烈，则参与公共文化服务自主供给的动机越强烈。随着社会不断向更高阶段发展，公民的"主体意识"和"个人价值"呈现出愈加明显的延展趋势，越来越多的人能够在公共事务上展现出一种积极参与、邻里友好的公德意识。这种以公共利益为基准点的精神逐步渗透到更广泛的群体活动中，使自主性参与更上一层楼，对于推动群众树立公共性规范、社会性道德有着最为生动的教育意义，也是基层公共文化服务自主供给最佳的文化呈现。城市基层公共文化服务自主供给的生发逻辑的理论模型见图5。

城市基层公共文化服务自主供给的生发逻辑遵循了"逻辑起点—逻辑进路—逻辑终端"三个阶段，在这一过程中，不仅体现了城市基层公共文化服务从无到有、从弱到强的发展路径，还折射出基层群众在不同场域内心理活动与社会环境的叠加效应。总体来说，城市基层公共文化服务自主供给的行为展现了文化供给者和文化受益者双重角色的统一，实现了基层公共文化服务的精准对接，这种极具群众主体意识的供给模式是国家大力发展公共文化服务体系的有益补充，展现着基层公共文化服务供给的新理念，也为完善未来的公共文化服务的供给机制提供了新思路，这是走向文化治理现代化的必然过程。

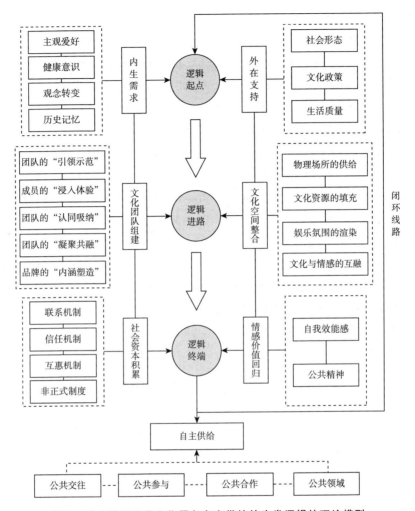

图5 城市基层公共文化服务自主供给的生发逻辑的理论模型

A Study on the Logic of Autonomous Supply of Public Cultural Services at the Grass-roots Level in Cities

Li Shaohui and Wu Jiaxin

Abstract：The autonomous supply of grass-roots public cultural services is spontaneously organized and provided by grass-roots people. It has double effects of entertainment and serving the public. It is consistent with the current strong cultural needs of the masses and has become one of the inevitable trends in the construction of urban public cultural service system. Using Nvivo 11 qualitative research tools, this paper explores the development logic of autonomous supply of urban grass-roots public cultural services. The study finds that the independent supply of public cultural services follows the overall logical trend including the logical starting point of endogenous demand and external support, the logical path of carrier construction and spatial integration, and the logical period of psychological tacit understanding and emotional value regression. The growth logic implies the development path of autonomous supply of urban grass-roots public cultural services from scratch to maturity step by step, which is of great benefit to the construction of the supply mode of public cultural services with the masses as the main body.

Keywords: Grass-Roots, Public Cultural Services, Independent Supply, Germinal Logic

城市治理的顽疾

——城中村问题研究的可视化分析

朱 立 封晓健*

【摘 要】城中村是中国城市化进程中产生的一种特殊社会现象。城中村产生有其复杂的历史和现实背景。城中村主要存在建筑物密集且有众多违章搭建房、环境脏乱差、人口结构复杂、治安管理难、多数居民文化素质较低、就业难等问题。这些问题严重影响城市经济社会的整体发展及社会的和谐稳定,成为城市治理的一大难题,也成为国内众多学者的关注点。本文以中国知网 (CNKI) 核心期刊文献为基础,借助 CiteSpace、Bicomb、Ucinet 三种可视化软件导出知识图谱,对城中村问题的发展脉络、特征、演化趋势做出梳理分析。以期为在全球经济下行、各种矛盾冲突激化、贫富两极分化加速的背景下,推进我国城中村改造、破解城市化进程难题提供有价值的建议。

【关键词】城市治理;城中村;可视化分析;改造模式

一 城中村问题的研究现状

改革开放 40 多年来,我国经济建设取得了辉煌成就。特别是城市化建设进入高速发展的阶段。随着城市化过程中经济持续增长,尤其是工业总

---

* 朱立,青岛大学政治与公共管理学院副教授;封晓健,青岛大学政治与公共管理学院研究生。

量的扩大，城市边缘开始向外持续扩张。一方面，受到城市规模发展的影响，另一方面，得益于户籍制度和人口流动政策的开放。大批劳动力的涌入产生了城市化过程中诸多问题中的一个——城中村问题。城中村是指伴随城郊区化、产业分散化以及乡村城市化的迅猛发展，为城建用地所包围或纳入城建用地范围的原有农村聚落，是乡村—城市转型不完全的具有明显城乡二元结构的地域实体。[①] 我国对于城中村的研究自 20 世纪末开始，受到不同时期内政策的变动，以及实际需要和理论支持存在断层线的影响。目前针对城中村的治理在实际操作中存在不同程度的差异，厘清城中村问题的研究脉络并分析未来发展趋向对于提高城中村人口居住质量、提升城市整体形象具有重要影响。

城中村问题的发生和发展一方面深受我国加速城市化进程的影响，另一方面又受到我国的土地政策和历史文化的影响。目前，国内学者对于城中村问题的研究分为以下几个方面。第一方面，以实地调研考察为主。吴智刚[②]、闫小培[③]、刘伟文[④]等学者以广州地区为调研考察对象，在经过深入分析后，对城中村的出现、其存在的合理性、存在的具体问题以及从政府角度改造城中村的思路等做出解释。朱婉莹[⑤]、赵晔琴[⑥]、汪明峰[⑦]等学者以上海地区的某城中村为调研对象，从流动人口的角度出发，说明强制性清理城中村对外来务工人员的影响，提出了政府的主观能动性作用。第二方面，从理论入手，解读政策，对城中村改造这一问题进行剖析。袁伟[⑧]、李志生[⑨]、

---

① 闫小培、魏立华、周锐波：《快速城市化地区城乡关系协调研究——以广州市"城中村"改造为例》，《城市规划》2004 年第 3 期。

② 吴智刚、周素红：《城中村改造：政府、城市与村民利益的统一——以广州市文冲城中村为例》，《城市发展研究》2005 年第 2 期。

③ 闫小培、魏立华、周锐波：《快速城市化地区城乡关系协调研究——以广州市"城中村"改造为例》，《城市规划》2004 年第 3 期。

④ 刘伟文：《"城中村"的城市化特征及其问题分析——以广州为例》，《南方人口》2003 年第 3 期。

⑤ 朱婉莹、赵伟宏、汪明峰：《城中村拆迁与外来人口居住选择的影响因素研究——以上海市联明村为例》，《人文地理》2018 年第 4 期。

⑥ 赵晔琴：《法外住房市场的生成逻辑与治理逻辑——以上海城中村拆违为例》，《华东师范大学学报》（哲学社会科学版）2018 年第 4 期。

⑦ 汪明峰、林小玲、宁越敏：《外来人口、临时居所与城中村改造——来自上海的调查报告》，《城市规划》2012 年第 7 期。

⑧ 袁伟：《我国城中村改造模式研究》，《华东经济管理》2010 年第 1 期。

⑨ 李志生：《关于城中村改造的问题》，《城市发展研究》2002 年第 5 期。

郭艳华[①]、周森[②]等学者认识到当前城市化进程中城中村改造的必要性和紧迫性，提出城中村改造虽然是一项纷繁复杂的工程，但是有章可循，需要从管理机制入手，并详细阐述了这一观点。第三方面，从经济学角度分析城中村的存在合理性及其存在的价值问题。李立勋[③]、吴英杰[④]、刘中一[⑤]等学者认为城中村作为传统农村和现代城市的混合体，经济生活方式存在差异，而城中村的未来需要与城市发展、经济利益进行协同。第四方面，从城中村改造的利益相关者出发，探讨利益群体对城中村发展的作用。邵鹏[⑥]等学者认为在城市化改造过程中，对于前期的拆迁及后期再分配问题，需要考量多方利益主体，同时界定好公共利益，对于当前城中村改造中尚存的问题，认为需要选择最优路径。

以上研究，学者们对城中村问题已经进行了比较深刻的剖析，涉及城中村的起因、治理、改造等多方面内容，内容全面详实。为深刻认识城市背后的城中村问题，整体把握关于城中村问题的研究脉络，梳理我国学者目前关于城中村研究的方向、关注点以及未来对城中村问题的研究方向，本文采用文献分析方法，借助中国知网期刊核心论文，通过 CiteSpace、Bicomb、Ucinet 三种可视化软件进行知识图谱推演，总结提炼改革开放 40 多年来的城市化问题研究主题脉络、演进特征和发展趋势，探讨城市化问题领域未来可能的研究方向，以期对我国城市治理进行科学化研究以及为解决城中村问题提供参考。

二 治理城中村问题的研究设计

（一）数据来源与数据处理

在城市化建设中，城中村问题越来越突出，城中村治理是城市治理不

---

① 郭艳华：《论改造城中村的现实途径》，《探求》2002 年第 4 期。
② 周森：《城中村改制和改造的思路与对策》，《南方经济》2002 年第 2 期。
③ 李立勋：《城中村的经济社会特征——以广州市典型城中村为例》，《北京规划建设》2005 年第 3 期。
④ 吴英杰、罗皓：《"城中村"改造：寻求城市发展与经济利益的协调》，《乡镇经济》2004 年第 7 期。
⑤ 刘中一、刘中炜：《城中村改造的经济学思考》，《经济论坛》2004 年第 2 期。
⑥ 邵鹏：《城中村改造中的权益维护研究——以公共利益为视角》，《法制与经济》2017 年第 12 期。

可欠缺的重要部分，越来越受到学者的关注。因此，本文以"城中村"为主题进行文献搜索。文献源于中国知网（CNKI）数据库，时间跨度为1996～2019年，关键词搜索相关主题文章12366篇，文章来源类别设定为CSSIC和核心期刊，获得相关主题文章1126篇。剔除新闻、述评、会议报告等不符合文章，最终获得973条核心文献。操作时间截止到2019年12月。

CiteSpace数据处理：通过知网refworks导出txt，进行CiteSpace分析，生成时区图和高频关键词图谱；Bicomb数据处理：对所选文献进行自定义导出，修改格式后进入Bicomb提取界面，成功提取后完成统计，并导出共现矩阵；Ucinet数据处理：将Bicomb导出的共现矩阵导入Ucinet进行格式文件转换，利用netdraw生成聚类网络图。

（二）研究过程与方法

本文采用CiteSpace、Bicomb、Ucinet软件作为数据分析工具，对本次的973条样本预案进行可视化分析，生成知识图谱。通过知识图谱可以分析出当前关于城中村问题的研究聚焦点。CiteSpace知识图谱不同的十字架大小，十字架之间连接线的粗细和数量，能够分析城中村问题中各种因素之间的相互联系和强弱关系。通过突变检测来研究未来城中村的研究趋势和研究热点。Bicomb的词篇矩阵可以直观总结关键词，并与CiteSpace进行对比，提升知识图谱可信值。Ucinet图谱中正方形越大、越居中则代表该关键词出现频率、所占地位越高。

（三）研究对象

以"城中村"为研究对象。"城中村是一个相对成熟的概念，一般是指在快速城镇化进程中，一些距离城市较近的村庄被纳入城市建设用地范围，但仍保留和实行农村集体所有制与经营体制的社区。"[①] 城中村的原住居民凭借便利的居住条件和低廉的租住成本招揽租客，吸引大批外来人员，在此基础上进行个体经营，使城中村成为城市人口流动的重要聚集地，反作用下原住居民为获得更可观的利益，随意搭建简易房等违规建

---

① 李润国、赵青、王伟伟：《新型城镇化背景下城中村改造的问题与对策研究》，《宏观经济研究》2015年第8期。

筑，屡禁不止，由此引发一系列的城市治理难题。

三 "城中村"研究时空分布分析

根据中国知网显示的数据进行分析，宏观上能够发掘各个时间段内关于城中村治理的重点和发展脉络，微观上厘清城中村是什么，城中村各阶段存在的问题及当前的主要问题、解决路径等内容。通过图谱进行数据分析，形成对城中村认识的逐渐深入。

（一）城中村问题发文数量分析

知网检索以"城中村"为关键词的中文核心期刊论文最早出现于1996年。在此后的研究中论文数量呈现小幅度波动上升趋势（见图1），研究热潮出现在2011~2015年，2004~2011年升幅加快。2015年以后呈现下降趋势，但总体仍保持较高的发文数量。进入21世纪以来，发文量持续保持在50篇核心论文以上。表明近年来，在城市化过程中，城中村问题持续受到学者的关注。

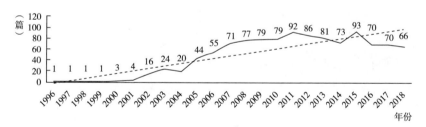

图1 1996~2018年CSSCI及核心期刊关于城中村发文数量

根据历年城中村发文数量，导出CiteSpace的时区图（见图2），结合文献资料进行发掘，可以将国内对城中村问题的研究分为三个时间段。

第一个时间段为1996~2001年。在本阶段内，存在两个社会现象。第一个现象是随着城市化建设开始逐渐加速，城市向周边郊区蔓延的速度也逐渐加快。在此时间段内，广州、北京等地区的城中村开始逐渐成型并引起关注。在城市化推进过程中拆迁难、安置难成为主要问题。为使农民妥协，减轻后期政府安置压力，往往采取保留宅基地等措施。"这些各式各样的妥协办法给城市换来了宝贵的发展空间，但却又给城市留下了日益严

重的问题。"① 第二个现象是中国共产党第十四次全国代表大会确立了建立
社会主义市场经济体制的改革目标以后，我国社会和经济进入转型期，农
民进城务工成为趋势。城中村凭借其区位优势，吸引大量外来人口聚集。
村民为获得更大利润，以自建或者与开发商协作的方式违规建房，"在原有
分得的百余平方米的宅基地上满负荷或超负荷的建设，以较低的成本建成
多层楼房"②，这样高密度和低质量成为城中村建筑的一大特色，由此引发
各种环境、生态、社会问题。这一阶段的学者首先关注到城中村问题的出
现、城中村问题在具体城市的特征，挖掘城中村问题初期出现的原因并开
始寻找解决城中村问题的路径。

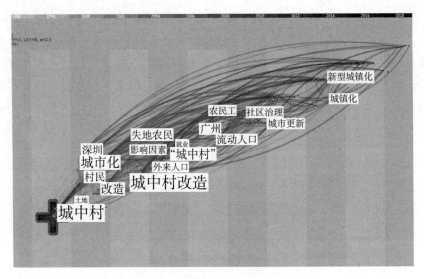

图 2　城中村研究时区图

　　第二个时间段为 2002～2015 年。在本阶段，城中村矛盾凸显，学者们
试图多角度挖掘城中村问题的根源并提出针对性的建议。在此过程中可以
将思路分为三点，第一点是学者们从城中村的本质上进行深入的分析，城
中村的实质是一种农村社区，实行的是农村典型的集体管理体制，与城市
管理方式存在差异成为这一时期城中村问题的重要原因。这一阶段比前一

---

① 房庆方、马向明、宋劲松：《城中村：从广东看我国城市化进程中遇到的政策问题》，《城
　　市规划》1999 年第 9 期。
② 罗赤：《透视城中村》，《读书》2001 年第 9 期。

阶段的研究更为精准。北京市、广州市等主要人口集聚城市的城中村初具雏形，可选取的城中村案例更为普遍。① 第二点是对城中村的特征进行分析，包括城中村的社会特征②、空间特征③、人口特征④等。各地区城中村存在的问题在当前阶段被逐渐放大且趋于统一，大中城市均出现城中村治理难、治理效果差的问题。部分学者在研究地区问题时提出要对城中村进行清理的意见。⑤ 第三点是城中村如何改造。这一点在 2010 年以后开始逐渐被提及。学者针对不同类型的城中村提出不同的建议。部分学者侧重于权衡政府、村民和外来人口等多方利益，杨爽等和张侠等学者运用动态博弈理论分析了各利益主体间的关系及其制约条件，得出博弈情境下多方协作的城中村改造策略。⑥ 也有部分学者从单主体角度进行探索解释，王建民等通过构建城中村改造前后的利益均衡模型来说明政府在城中村改造中的作用。⑦ 并且，随着对于廉租房确实能够帮助低收入家庭解决住房问题认识的逐渐深入，学者开始将廉租房政策和解决城中村住房拥挤私搭乱建相联系。⑧ 本阶段学者们的研究强调城中村动态的改造过程，强调在这一过程中对城中村进行合理合规的改造以适应城市化发展的趋势。

　　第三个是时间段为 2016~2019 年。这一阶段关于城中村改造的文献开始偏重于"移民"与城市的融合问题以及权益分配问题。上一阶段中的城中村完成或者即将完成改造，接下去的问题就是改造完成之后的城中村与

① 周锐波、闫小培：《集体经济：村落终结前的再组织纽带——以深圳"城中村"为例》，《经济地理》2009 年第 4 期。

② 刘伟文：《"城中村"的城市化特征及其问题分析——以广州为例》，《南方人口》2003 年第 3 期。

③ 李晴、常青：《城中村改造实验——以珠海吉大村为例》，《城市规划》2002 年第 11 期。

④ 谢志岿：《村落向城市社区的转型——制度、政策与中国城市化进程中城中村问题研究》，中国社会科学出版社，2005，第 30~39、282~291 页。

⑤ 黎云、陈洋、李郇：《封闭与开放：城中村空间解析——以广州市车陂村为例》，《城市问题》2007 年第 7 期；尹晓颖、薛德升、闫小培：《"城中村"非正规部门形成发展机制——以深圳市蔡屋围为例》，《经济地理》2006 年第 6 期；魏成、赖寿华：《珠江三角洲大都市地区高密集城中村的形成——一个分析框架》，《现代城市研究》2006 年第 7 期。

⑥ 张侠等：《城中村改造中的利益关系分析与应对》，《经济地理》2006 年第 3 期；杨爽、周晓唯：《"城中村"改造中制度安排的选择》，《重庆工商大学学报》（西部论坛）2006 年第 4 期。

⑦ 王建民、刘明达、刘碧寒：《城中村改造利益均衡模型构建与检验》，《地域研究与开发》2015 年第 6 期。

⑧ 郑文升、金玉霞、王晓芳、丁四保：《城市低收入住区治理与克服城市贫困——基于对深圳"城中村"和老工业基地城市"棚户区"的分析》，《城市规划》2007 年第 5 期。

城市的融合。有学者指出城中村改造的后续工作是社区融合。① 陈凯仁等②通过数据调研对当前城中村存在的四个利益群体进行了改造意愿的分析。同时，陈凯仁等通过调研分析认为外来流动人口对于城中村有一定的归属感，这种归属感可以理解为是否愿意融入城中村这一社区，但归属感受到多种因素的影响。③ 在这一阶段，居民和城中村，城中村和城市，城市和居民，三者之间的权益如何保障以及分配成为关注的重点，学者们强调平衡好各方利益的同时需要加大城中村的融合建设，以此推动城中村向城市靠拢。

（二）城中村问题研究机构分析

通过中国知网自带的文献分析对研究城中村问题的前15个研究机构进行统计（见图3），排序前三的分别是中山大学、北京大学和中国人民大学。分析排名前15的机构可以看出，目前对于城中村问题的研究阵地以高校为主，表明目前高校仍然是进行城市治理问题研究的主要阵地。

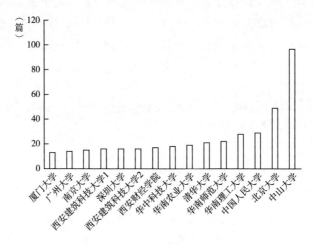

图3 中国知网自带机构分析发表城中村文献机构前15名

① 刘于琪、刘晔、李志刚：《居民归属感、邻里交往和社区参与的机制分析——以广州市城中村改造为例》，《城市规划》2017年第9期。
② 陈凯仁、龙茂乾、李贵才：《城中村利益相关者改造意愿影响因素——以深圳市上步村为例》，《城市问题》2017年第8期。
③ 陈凯仁、龙茂乾、李贵才：《超大城市城中村外来人口归属感研究——以深圳上步村为例》，《地域研究与开发》2017年第5期。

通过 CiteSpace 对导出的文献进行发文机构分析（见图4），能够更加细化地了解研究机构。图谱显示发文机构中，中山大学地理科学与规划学院占比最高，北京大学的四个相关学院中城市与环境学院占比最高。中山大学地处广州，北京大学位于北京，广州和北京是城中村现象最为明显的两个城市，中山大学和北京大学依托优秀的科研基础和区位优势，能够对城中村进行细致研究，为解决城中村问题提出了多种可行性方案。

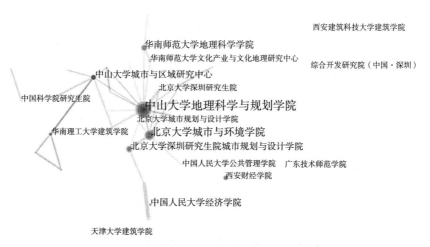

图4　发表城中村核心文献发文机构分析

为使图谱内容更为直观可读，将 CiteSpace 图谱的相关数据转化为条状图进行展示（见图5）。通过与中国知网自带的机构分析进行对比能够看出，中国知网的数据覆盖面更为广阔，CiteSpace 的分析更为精确，两者的数据相吻合。

（三）城中村问题研究资助基金分析

根据中国知网数据对所选文献进行涉及的基金分析（如表1），可知获得支持的文献数量为437篇，占总有效文献数据量的45%。其中排名前三的分别是国家自然科学基金（180篇）、国家社会科学基金（128篇）、广东省自然科学基金（18篇）。表明国家层面以及地方政府对于城中村问题的重视，都能够鼓励支持针对城中村问题的研究。

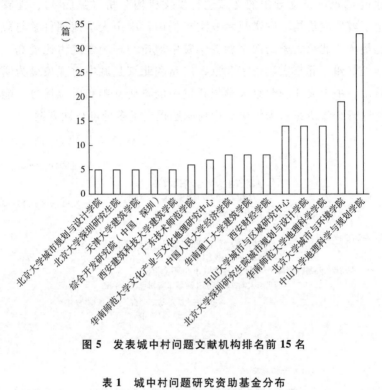

图 5 发表城中村问题文献机构排名前 15 名

表 1 城中村问题研究资助基金分布

基金名称	数量	基金名称	数量	基金名称	数量
国家自然科学基金	180	国家软科学研究计划	5	国家重点基础研究发展规划	3
国家社会科学基金	128	高等学校博士学科点专项科研基金	4	建设部科学技术计划项目	3
广东省自然科学基金	18	教育部留学回国人员科研启动基金	4	江苏省教育厅人文社会科学研究基金	3
中国博士后科学基金	16	河南省科技攻关计划	4	广州市科技计划项目	2
国家科技支撑计划	12	广东省软科学研究计划项目	3	山西省软科学研究计划	2
陕西省教育厅科研计划项目	7	美国福特基金会基金	3	上海市重点学科建设项目	2
教育部人文社会科学研究项目	6	教育部新世纪优秀人才支持计划	3	中国科学院知识创新工程项目	2
陕西省软科学研究计划	6	福建省自然科学基金	3	山东省软科学研究计划	2

续表

基金名称	数量	基金名称	数量	基金名称	数量
陕西省自然科学基础研究计划项目	2	青岛市社会科学规划项目	1	浙江省软科学研究计划项目	1
广州市哲学社会科学规划课题	1	国家留学基金	1	中央级科研院所科技基础性工作专项基金	1
中央高校基本科研业务费专项资金	1	福建省软科学研究项目	1	黑龙江省自然科学基金	1
河南省软科学研究计划	1	浙江省哲学社会科学规划课题	1	河南省教委自然科学基础研究项目	1
山西财经大学科研项目	1	湖南省哲学社会科学基金	1	北京市自然科学基金	1

四 "城中村"研究文本分析

(一) ucinet 社会网络图谱分析

运用 Ucinet 建立社会网络图谱需要构建关键词共现矩阵。首先需要通过 Bicomb 导出共现矩阵，然后将共现矩阵导入 Ucinet，转换成 "##h" 格式文件，最终通过 netdraw 绘制图谱（如图6）。

通过 Ucinet 导出的社会图谱可以发现，各个方块之间线条密集，辐射众多，表明当前城中村问题涉及板块众多，在进行研究时需要综合多方因素考量。图谱中"城中村""城中村改造""城市化""改造"等内容在中心位置，符合当前对城中村问题研究的核心和重点是城中村改造这一实际。社会网络图谱的外围分布着"土地利用""利益博弈""空间生产""社会保障"等内容，外围内容反映出当前存在的制约城中村问题研究的因素。结合知网文献，可以将目前学者关注的问题总结为三种类型。

第一，土地利用。要对城中村的土地进行合理利用，首先需要明确城中村土地性质。我国城中村的土地性质主要有两种：第一种是将城中村原住农民转换为城市居民之后，将土地收归国有；第二种是土地所有权不变仍为城中村居民享有。同时，少数城中村还存在集体土地产权不明晰。土地性质限制城中村的产业结构调整。《中华人民共和国土地管理法》第四条明确规定："国家编制土地利用总体规划，规定土地用途，将土地分为

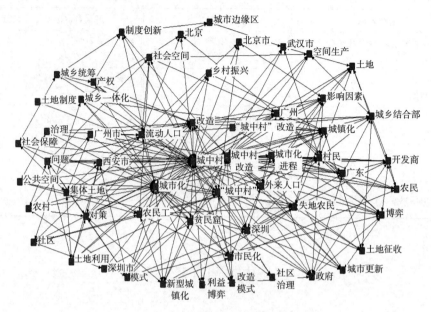

图 6　Ucinet 社会网络图谱

农用地、建设用地和未利用地。严格限制农用地转为建设用地，控制建设用地总量，对耕地实行特殊保护。"其次，需要合理开发，土地与当地生态紧密联系，生态影响人居环境，对城中村改造的初衷是提高土地利用率，从而提高村民生活质量，改善城市布局。各地区城中村所面临的土地问题基本一致。所以，政策层面上加快对于土地性质的界定和对土地利用问题的规范是十分紧迫的问题。

第二，改造安置。目前对于城中村改造，有单主体模式，由政府主导或者企业主导；也有多主体联合指挥，政府和企业联合进行，企业出资进行土地购买，政府出面进行土地征收和人口安置。这一过程中，面临村民不配合、坐地起价、分配不合理、多方权益无法平衡等问题，当前城中村改造中，存在大量结果导向型改造，追求短期成效，快速解决城中村表面问题，忽略城中村深层问题。同时，城中村若发生异地安置，安置过程中防范村民权益受到侵害，安置后失地农民的就业问题，都成为城中村改造后迫切需要解决的难题。

第三，权益互动。当前城中村改造涉及多方利益群体。村民是城中村的主体，通过租赁房屋、开设餐饮等服务型内容获得报酬，形成特有的

"城中村经济"。这一经济模式单一脆弱，容易受到政策的影响。在城中村改造中，村民极易成为无业人员。政府在解决城中村问题中发挥主要作用，政府并不是一味替村民"买单"，也不能站在开发商的角度侵害村民应得利益，而应站在中立的角度，平衡村民和开发商的诉求，争取三方利益最大化。当前多地政府为实现政绩，联合开发商侵害村民权益的行为较为普遍。国家应尽快完善相关机制，及时制止并预防二次对村民利益的侵害。

（二）城中村研究高频关键词聚类分析研究

为更加精准地反映当前我国学者对于城中村问题的研究脉络和研究核心点，对中国知网中目前关于城中村的核心文献进行高频关键词聚类分析（见图 7）。

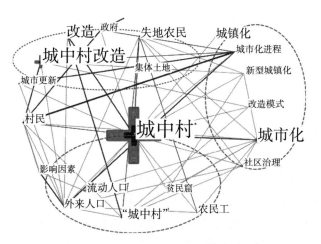

图 7　城中村研究高频关键词共现网络知识图谱

高频关键词共现网络知识图谱，能够直观反映研究重点。图 7 出现了以"城中村"为主的一个大聚类簇，以"城中村改造"和"城市化"为辅的两个中聚类簇。除此之外，还有"外来人口""失地农民""村民""流动人口"等小聚类簇。各聚类簇之间连线紧密，说明我国学者对城中村问题进行研究时涉及各影响因素的考量是全面的。将知识图谱进行整理之后，显示目前关于城中村的研究主要集中于三个方面。

第一方面，集中于城中村改造模式研究。包括城中村模式、新型城镇化以及改造完成之后的社区治理问题。城中村改造是符合城市化的正确选择问题。在此过程中还需要综合考量多个利益主体选择的最优方案。对于城市化的改造，"目前中国特大城市城中村改造的多种模式存在着共性的问题：排斥性、高成本、低效率、逆垄断、不可持续等，中国特大城市迫切需要建立包容性城中村改造模式"①。同时当前公众的参与，在政策决定时起到一定的舆论导向性影响，使城中村改造中"公民个体由于信息的缺乏以及受到自身知识、阅历等的限制，通常只能对一定范围内的部分空间环境进行有效的观察，形成一定的感知，即仅仅能给出各自偏好下的对部分方案的评估序列"②。由此可以看出单方主体的意见具有可参考性，但只参考其中一方或者几方建议有失偏颇。针对城中村改造模式，有学者将其放在新型城镇背景下进行探索，认为城中村的有效改造事关新型城镇的一体化建设。③ 在改造过程中，城中村作为一种"过渡型社区"其治理方式比农村社区治理和城市社区治理难度更大。所牵扯的利益主体又变得多元复杂。④ 在这一方面，城中村改造、新型城镇化建设、社区治理等均属于对城中村这一承载体的研究。针对改造模式的探讨，学者们始终保持着较高的关注度。

第二方面，集中于城中村原生村民权益问题研究。包括集体土地使用、失地农民、政府三方的博弈。城中村初期拥有土地或者宅基地的村民在城中村改造过程中，受到国家土地政策和不同时期政策影响，部分土地丧失，成为失地农民。在城市扩张的过程中，村民的权益并没有随之扩张，相反部分权益受到侵害。如何消解村民对于城中村改造的抵触情绪，以及失地农民的权益保护是政府改造城中村过程中需要考量的因素，如何保障这一部分村民的利益成为当前学者研究的热点，并取得一部分成果。孙锦提出："政府部门要在城中村进行统筹规划，创设农民就业信息服务网络，建立农民就业服务指导体系，同时要在城中村社区拓展农民就业岗

---

① 叶裕民：《特大城市包容性城中村改造理论架构与机制创新——来自北京和广州的考察与思考》，《城市规划》2015年第8期。
② 陶海燕、周淑丽、卓莉：《城中村有序改造的群决策——以广州市城中村改造为例》，《地理研究》2014年第7期。
③ 卢福营：《城中村改造：一项系统的新型城镇化工程》，《社会科学》2017年第10期；李润国、赵青、王伟伟：《新型城镇化背景下城中村改造的问题与对策研究》，《宏观经济研究》2015年第8期。
④ 《聚焦"城中村"改造》：《人民论坛》2017年S1期。

位，为农民提供更多的就业机会。"① 通过促进就业，原本依靠收租生活的村民找到经济来源。刘英泽等提出："逐步建立经济补偿、社会保障、就业服务三位一体的新模式。"② 在促进就业的基础上，增加了对于失地农民的各种保障制度，以此来减弱城中村拆迁改造带来的社会风险。在这一方面，侧重点在于受城中村改造而利益受损的直接主体或者间接主体。如何保护他们的权益目前受到大部分学者的关注。

第三方面，集中于外来人口、流动人口、农民工、贫民窟问题。城中村作为外来人口聚集生活的区域，无论是沿海城市还是内陆城市，城中村房屋租赁价值远低于城市繁华地段，成为城中村人口聚集和房屋私搭乱建的主要原因。对于这一部分流动人口，如何做好管理和使其融入城市，成为部分学者关注的重点领域。郑承智等人通过对于北京地区城中村流动人口职住分离的调查，以期对于北京地区城中村的改造提出具有可行性的建议。③ 对于城中村流动人口的研究一直伴随着城中村问题的始终。相较于超大城市的城中村人口类型复杂，普通沿海城市及内陆城市城中村人口多为务工的农民工、个人商贩和租住人。他们与城中村周围的城市格格不入，无论是住房、医疗，甚至子女的教育都无法得到具体的落实。崔晓黎主张"大中城市郊区农村的村委会可以主动为农民工朋友建立相对稳定的居住社区。一方面可以大大降低农民工居住的费用，另一方面可以大幅度缓解城中村改造的压力"。④ 顾协国认为："政府应通过合理的制度安排，从人本管理、扩大社会保障范围、提倡社会新风尚、增加投入等方面切实解决'城中村'农民工问题。"⑤ 叶继红提出："在考虑外来人口需求的同时，控制城中村流动人口无序流入。"⑥ 通过建立长效机制，能够有效促进本区域内的融合问题。针对这一方面，国内的专家学者们主要关注点在于

---

① 孙锦：《新型城镇化背景下城中村失地农民就业路径选择的思路创新》，《改革与战略》2015 年第 12 期。

② 刘英泽、王慧、赵艳芹、孟文静：《城中村失地居民社会保障问题研究》，《中国农学通报》2009 年第 21 期。

③ 郑承智、张旺锋、武炳炎、梁博：《北京市外来人口集聚型城中村流动人口职住分离研究》，《地理科学进展》2017 年第 4 期。

④ 崔晓黎：《解决农民工居住与城中村改造问题的途径》，《调研世界》2006 年第 2 期。

⑤ 顾协国：《政府的制度安排与农民工问题——以舟山市定海区"城中村"为切入点》，《西北农林科技大学学报》（社会科学版）2009 年第 2 期。

⑥ 叶继红：《城中村治理：问题、困境与理路——以城湾村为个案》，《行政论坛》2016 年第 3 期。

外来人口与原住居民的融合问题，以及如何实现城中村村民和外来人口向城市人口的转变。通过案例分析或者政策分析，由此得出出现差异的原因。当前城中村人口复杂的现象十分普遍，如何促进各种类型的人们的融合与和谐相处也是国内学者关注的重点课题。

（三）城中村问题高频关键词数据分析

为了对当前城中村问题的特征做出判断，通过 CiteSpace 对城中村问题研究领域相关核心文献进行分析、梳理和统计，导出关键词频数分布表，在整理之后得到如表 2 所示的频次前 30 位的高频关键词。根据高频关键词，经过对文献的阅读、梳理和分析后，发现国内学者的成果所反映的城中村问题的演进呈现以下特征。

表 2　城中村问题频次前 30 位的高频关键词

序号	关键词	频次	序号	关键词	频次	序号	关键词	频次
1	城中村	435	11	流动人口	22	21	影响因素	12
2	城中村改造	138	12	农民工	21	22	改造模式	12
3	城市化	87	13	外来人口	16	23	广州市	10
4	改造	43	14	新型城镇化	16	24	政府	9
5	"城中村"	37	15	城市化进程	14	25	深圳市	9
6	深圳	30	16	城市更新	14	26	集体土地	9
7	广州	25	17	社区治理	13	27	社区	9
8	失地农民	25	18	模式	13	28	社会保障	9
9	村民	22	19	"城中村" 改造	13	29	贫民窟	8
10	城镇化	22	20	对策	13	30	社会空间	8

城中村改造的模式不断优化。我国对于城中村的改造大体上经历了三个阶段。第一阶段为 2000 年以前，尽量拆除清理城中村。第二阶段为 2000~2010 年，逐步探索城中村保留治理。第三个阶段为 2010 年至今，保留城中村并建议逐步完善城中村相关配套设施，从而使其逐步融入城市。在高频关键词中"城中村改造"显示频次 138，位居第二，意味着城中村改造在学术研究中一直是一个热点的存在。

对于城中村改造治理模式的探索一直以来都是国内学者致力于研究的对象，叶裕民在特大城市城中村改造治理模式上，提出建立包容性理论框架和实施机制。① 陶然等从土地制度出发，认为在城中村改造时首要考虑因素是土地问题，并提出建立土地公有私用的模式，实现政府、原土地权利人、外来人口，乃至开发商多方的利益均衡。对于城中村的改造模式，地区之间并非完全一致。根据国家宏观政策和各地区不同时期的政策，政府也在不断优化改造治理模式。②

案例分析表明，具体的地域中城中村改造治理模式更加细分化。对于广州地区的城中村研究在过去的 30 年一直占据城中村研究中对于具体地区研究的榜首，且呈现上升趋势。根据中国知网数据，2000~2009 年检索全文涉及广州地区城中村的核心论文共有 702 篇。2010~2019 年截至 8 月共有 2498 篇，数量呈现上升趋势。同时，对于城中村问题具体地域的研究更为细化，不再局限于北京、广州等超大城市，而是开始向北向西转移。李安辉以明末清初名师马明龙的故园武汉马家庄为调研考察地域，对马家庄的社群结构、居住模式等进行考察。马家庄社会文化变迁是乡土个体记忆、民族集体记忆与城市社会记忆的共同见证，是散杂居地区传统回族社区变迁的一个典型代表，也是时代变迁、社会演进、"都市里的村庄"改造与城市发展的一个缩影。③ 张京祥等以南京市江东村为调研考察对象，通过一个全新的视角——空间生产来分析江东村生产的历史性变迁、社会关系的再生产、制造的新空间。研究地域的不断具体化，反映出的是当前城市化过程中各地城中村问题的不断凸显。④ 国内学者们通过对具体地区的城中村治理模式进行分析研究，找出最具效力的改造模式，以期为不同地区的城中村问题的解决找到合理的路径。

统计数字也表明，城中村人口权益问题更受关注。随着我国法律建设和人权建设的不断完善，城中村人口的医疗、教育等权益保护越来越受到

---

① 叶裕民：《特大城市包容性城中村改造理论架构与机制创新——来自北京和广州的考察与思考》，《城市规划》2015 年第 8 期。

② 陶然、王瑞民：《城中村改造与中国土地制度改革：珠三角的突破与局限》，《国际经济评论》2014 年第 3 期。

③ 李安辉：《"城中村"改造背景下民族社区社会文化的变迁——以武汉市马家庄为例》，《中南民族大学学报》（人文社会科学版）2019 年第 5 期。

④ 张京祥、胡毅、孙东琪：《空间生产视角下的城中村物质空间与社会变迁——南京市江东村的实证研究》，《人文地理》2014 年第 2 期。

重视。一方面强调城中村人口和城市人口的融合，另一方面强调对于城中村流动人口的管理和社区建设。汪明峰等提出城中村中影响社会融合的四个维度分别是"社会关系融合、经济融合、心理融合和文化融合"[①]，且这四个维度受到不同因素的影响。在逐渐城市化的过程中，城中村作为城市的一部分，需纳入城市规划中，包路芳认为："推动流动人口融入城市，要逐渐打破制度性障碍，以'城中村'改造为突破口，制定和实施包括外来人口在内的城市规划；融入社区是流动人口最终融入整个城市的前提，要充分发挥社区融合作用"。[②] 对于人口权益的重视一方面保护城中村原住居民的利益，另一方面使外来流动人口的权益在城市中得到落实。

五 城中村未来可能的演进趋势

城中村问题会一直伴随当前城市化进程的演进而表现出更为复杂的趋势。处理好城市与城中村的问题，城中村中外来流动人口和社会的关系，理应由拆变治，疏通关系比拆断联系更重要。

根据当前国内学者对于城中村改造的观点可以看出，当前对于城中村问题研究的重点主要是"改"和"造"的问题。改的是不符合城中村现状的治理方式，比如强制性拆除，造的是新的社区管理方式。《中共中央关于全面深化改革若干重大问题的决定》中明确指出："城乡二元结构是制约城乡发展一体化的主要障碍。必须健全体制机制，形成以工促农、以城带乡、工农互惠、城乡一体的新型工农城乡关系，让广大农民平等参与现代化进程、共同分享现代化成果。"[③] 这一文件可作为政府治理城市城中村的指导方针。对于不同城市的城中村问题，根据具体城市的实际情况作出统筹规划，实现城市空间正义。

运用 CitesPace 对城中村问题的数据样本进行突变词检测（如图 8）。突变词能够反映一定时期学界对于城中村问题的研究趋势。

第一，城镇化问题研究仍将持续受到关注。城中村作为城镇化推进过程中不容忽视的存在，也将持续受到关注。图 8 可以反映出，城镇化突变

---

① 汪明峰、程红、宁越敏：《上海城中村外来人口的社会融合及其影响因素》，《地理学报》2015 年第 8 期。
② 包路芳：《北京市"城中村"改造与流动人口城市融入》，《新视野》2010 年第 2 期。
③ 《十八大以来重要文献选编》上，中央文献出版社，2014，第 523 页。

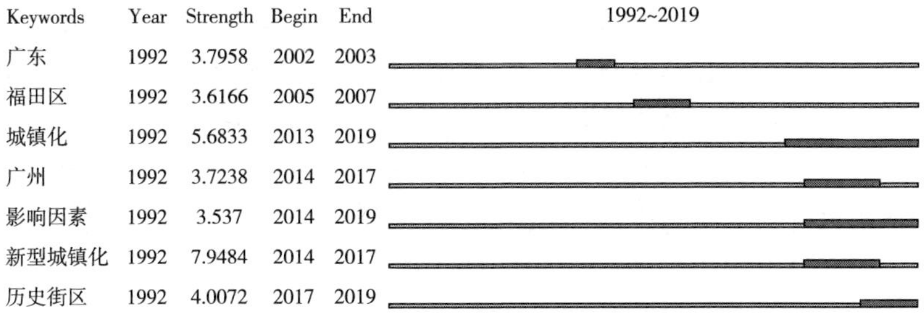

Keywords	Year	Strength	Begin	End	1992~2019
广东	1992	3.7958	2002	2003	
福田区	1992	3.6166	2005	2007	
城镇化	1992	5.6833	2013	2019	
广州	1992	3.7238	2014	2017	
影响因素	1992	3.537	2014	2019	
新型城镇化	1992	7.9484	2014	2017	
历史街区	1992	4.0072	2017	2019	

图 8　城中村研究关键词凸显图

强度为 5. 683。①

第二，强度大。自 2013 年起，城镇化成为研究的热门问题，一直持续至今。城镇化当前是我国改革建设的重点，《国家新型城镇化规划（2014—2020 年）》标志着中国城镇化发展的重大转型，核心是强调人的城镇化，总体要求是"稳中求进"。同时，指出要优化城镇化布局和形态、提高城市可持续发展能力，并着重解决好农业转移人口落户镇、城镇棚户区和城中村改造、中西部地区城镇化等问题。在国家发展改革委关于印发《2019 年新型城镇化建设重点任务》的通知中提及："城市政府要努力改善城乡结合部、城中村等农村贫困人口居住相对集中地区的配套设施。"②在城镇化发展的过程中，要注意避免无序发展，避免城镇化过程中边缘盲目扩张，减少失地农民。随着不同时期城镇化任务的变化，如何对待城中村及融入问题依然成为热点问题。

第三，城中村治理的影响因素成为学界研究的趋势。城中村问题出现的初期，对于城中村问题研究侧重于结果研究，拆除清理违规建筑。随着城市发展，对于城中村的研究不再局限于拆除清理，转向保留城中村，将土地、人口、生态多方面内容进行糅合，对城中村布局进行重新规划，引导其合理有序发展，最大限度地发挥城中村在城市中的优势。事物的发展是曲折前进的，新的城中村问题随之产生。挖掘城中村发展过程中出现的

---

① 突变率保留三位小数。
② 《国家发展改革委关于印发〈2019 年新型城镇化建设重点任务〉的通知》，新华网，http://www.xinhuanet.com/2019-04-08/c_1124338737.htm，最后访问日期：2020 年 7 月 6 日。

新问题及其影响因素成为未来研究的新热点。目前中国知网对于城中村问题的影响因素文献数量持续增长，研究内容日渐细化，多选择以具体的地区为例进行研究。包括开封市原住居民满意度的影响因素，上海地区外来人口社会融入的影响因素，福州市村民对集体资产产权制度改革意愿的影响因素等。随着城中村在一、二线城市逐渐稳定，三、四线城市城中村逐渐形成规模并进入治理常态。对于不同地区的城中村影响因素进行研究变得更具针对性。

第四，历史街区成为新的城中村研究关注点。历史街区并非历史文化街区，历史文化街区是指经省、自治区、直辖市人民政府核定公布的保存文物特别丰富、历史建筑集中成片、能够较完整和真实地体现传统格局和历史风貌，并具有一定规模的区域。而城市的历史街区 20 世纪多作为城市中心存在，大多修建年代久远，建筑物以院落或者低矮的楼房为主，聚集分布，占地面积广。但因城市规划改变，其中心地位开始减弱。历史街区以新的"城中村"模式保留在城市中，区别于传统城中村的高人口密集度和高建筑物密集度。历史街区的人均占有土地面积较大，建筑物利用率低，所面临的问题与传统城中村有所不同。为提高城市土地利用率，部分学者提出对历史街区重新规划建设开发，但历史街区作为载体，承载着城市的历史特色和居民的心理情感，重新规划涉及搬迁安置，复杂程度远高于传统城中村，有学者从保护传统文化的角度表示应保护好历史街区。目前，历史街区面临"传承保护"和"开发建设"两条路径，如何进行这一选择，以及应对新"城中村问题"，将会成为学界研究的热点问题。

结 论

随着城市治理现代化进程的加快，解决城中村问题的科学有效的措施会不断得到落实。我们以中国知网核心期刊文献为基础，借助 CiteSpace、Bicomb、Ucinet 三种可视化软件导出知识图谱，对城中村问题的发展脉络、特征、演化趋势做出梳理分析，为研究城中村改造模式的优化、促进流动人口素质的提高、加强政府投入等提供数据文献支持。相信这将会使城中村改造中的各种问题得到有效化解，让城市更具有可持续的新发展。

The Obstinate Problem in Urban Governance: A Visual Analysis of Research on the Problem of Villages in Downtown

Zhu Li and Feng Xiaojian

Abstract: "Villages in downtown" is a special social phenomenon during the progress of urbanization in China. The emergence of villages in downtown has its complicated historical and realistic factors. There are many problems in this kind of villages, such as dense and illegally built houses, dirty environment, complex population structure, difficult public security management, poor educational degree of most residents, low employment rate and so on. It has been seriously affecting the overall development of urban economy, social harmony and stability, and has become a major problem in urban governance. It has also become the focus of many domestic scholars. This essay is based on the core periodical literature of CNKI, through the knowledge map derived from Cite space, bicomb and ucinet, analyses the development context, characteristics and evolution trend of the problem of villages in downtown. This essay is with a view to providing valuable suggestions for promoting the transformation of China's villages in downtown and solving the problems in the urbanization process under the background of the global economic going downturn, the intensification of various contradictions and conflicts and the acceleration of polarization between the rich and the poor.

Keywords: City Governance, Village in Downtown, Visual Analysis, Transformation Mode

政策试点的局限

——对中国城市生活垃圾分类的个案研究

于君博　张昕婧*

【摘　要】政策试点是中国治理实践中所特有的一种政策测试与创新机制，这种基于"试验"理念的政策制定机制，有利于控制改革风险、降低改革成本、提高改革成功率。其在经济领域治理成效显著，却时常在公共物品供给领域效果不彰。中国城市生活垃圾分类试点于2000年开始推行，2017年出台《生活垃圾分类制度实施方案》，继续以试点形式实施生活垃圾强制分类，这反而说明历行17年的生活垃圾分类试点成效甚微，尚无成熟模式可供推广。本文把中国城市生活垃圾分类作为个案，来探究政策试点的局限，认为政策试点的局限与以下三个因素有关：第一，通过行政发包的方式进行治理；第二，政策试点的供给机制与公共产品的"复杂"性质不匹配；第三，压力型体制对政策试点的影响。

【关键词】政策试点；城市基层治理；公共产品；压力型体制

一　研究问题

政策试点作为一种政策制定机制，其发源于革命战争时期，发展于改

---

* 于君博，吉林大学中国地方政府创新研究中心副主任，教授；张昕婧，中共长春市朝阳区委组织部副主任科员。

革开放时代,① 已有较长的发展过程。作为中国治理实践中所特有的一种政策测试和创新机制,② 政策试点以独有的渐进性转型路径和"摸着石头过河"的思维,有利于控制改革风险、降低改革成本、提高改革成功率。这种基于"试验"理念的政策制定方式,不仅创造了经济领域的"中国奇迹",也成为社会政策领域,如养老、医疗、卫生、社会工作人才队伍建设等制度改革的创新源泉。③ 政策试点也因其"中国式疗法"享有"万灵药"的美誉。

城市生活垃圾分类治理却对"万灵药"提出怀疑。我国城市生活垃圾试点从 2000 年开始到 2017 年 3 月出台《生活垃圾分类制度实施方案》(下文可简称为"26 号文")为止,政策试点推行 17 年,"26 号文"仍强调继续以试点形式实施生活垃圾强制分类,由此暴露出历行 17 年的城市生活垃圾分类试点并未取得预期成效,没有在中央层面形成可复制、可推广的模式,尚未实现"先行先试—由点到面"的固定程式。政策试点在克服意识形态阻力、推进经济领域改革方面成效显著。然而政策试点在处理社会治理领域,如城市生活垃圾治理方面的问题时却捉襟见肘。是哪些因素影响了政策试点在城市生活垃圾分类治理方面的结果,这一问题值得思考。

政策试点是为实现特定政策目标而寻找政策工具的过程。④ 把政策试点和政策过程基本理论进行对接,可以分为"先行先试"(政策创新)和"由点到面"(政策扩散)两个阶段。"先行先试"(即"典型试验")构成了整个政策试点过程的前半阶段,该阶段要经过选点、组织、设计、督导、宣传和评估六个环节。⑤ "由点到面"是在"先行先试"的基础上逐步扩大试点范围。政策试点在经济等领域成效显著,⑥ 这与合理选点密切相关。合理的试点区能预先把政治阻力降到最低,有利于推动政策试点启

---

① 宁骚:《政策试验的制度因素——中西比较的视角》,《新视野》2014 年第 2 期。
② 周望:《中国"政策试点"研究》,天津人民出版社,2013,第 1 页。
③ 郑文换:《地方试点与国家政策:以新农保为例》,《中国行政管理》2013 年第 3 期。
④ 赵慧:《政策试点的试验机制:情境与策略》,《中国行政管理》2019 年第 1 期。
⑤ 周望:《中国"政策试点"研究》,天津人民出版社,2013,第 79 页。
⑥ Heilmann, " Sebastian. Policy Experimentation in China's Economic Rise," *Studies in Comparative International Development* 1 (2008).

动，实现创新。① 其次政策试点具有很强的容错性，政策试点实施方案具有很强的灵活性，宽泛的政策为地方政府提供了自由操作的空间，便于因地制宜地推进政策创新，② 同时利于中央政府提前识别政策执行中的困难，减少"盲目"执行的次数，③ 进而提升体制的整体适应能力。④

就政策试点在公共产品治理方面一再受挫这一问题，学者从以下几方面进行分析。第一，政策试点成效与政府工作人员预期有关。试点"风险"与"政策红利"并存，基于这两者的不同预期，各地方、各部门对政策试点采取不同的治理态度，这将产生不同的政策效果。⑤ 第二，政策试点成效与政策目标及相关主体有关。被搁置的试点往往具有复杂的政策目标，且相关主体存在利益冲突的特点。⑥ 第三，政策试点成效受压力型体制影响。面对繁重的日常工作，被选中的试点政府并没有充足的时间和权限去探索，其所选择的方式多为对既定政策程序的提炼和改进，政策创新成效甚微。⑦ 此外试点经由科层体系运作，内嵌于科层体系，压力作用下的政策扩散和理性选择不一致，⑧ 在政绩产出模糊的前提下，全局推广过程也充满挑战性。第四，城市社会治理领域基层政府的"结对竞赛"，在一定程度上也会成为政策试点扩散的阻碍。⑨

海尔曼（Heilman）虽然看到试点自身的问题是影响政策试点发展结果的重要因素，但就此止步，并未对政策试点在该方面不足的内在根源展

---

① Heilmann Sebastian, "Policy Experimentation in China's Economic Rise," *Studies in Comparative International Development* 1 (2008).
② 宁骚：《政策试验的制度因素——中西比较的视角》，《新视野》2014年第2期。
③ 陈那波、蔡荣：《"试点"何以失败？——A市生活垃圾"计量收费"政策试行过程研究》，《社会学研究》2017年第2期。
④ 王绍光：《学习机制与适应能力：中国农村合作医疗体制变迁的启示》，《中国社会科学》2008年第6期。
⑤ 周望：《中国"政策试点"研究》，天津人民出版社，2013，第81页。
⑥ 张克：《政策试点何以扩散：基于房产税与增值税改革的比较研究》，《中共浙江省委党校学报》2015年第2期。
⑦ 周望：《政策扩散理论与中国"政策试验"研究：启示与调适》，《四川行政学院学报》2012年第4期。
⑧ 熊烨：《我国地方政策转移中的政策"再建构"研究——基于江苏省一个地级市河长制转移的扎根理论分析》，《公共管理学报》2019年第3期。
⑨ 黄晓春、周黎安：《"结对竞赛"：城市基层治理创新的一种新机制》，《社会》2019年第5期。

开必要分析。① 周望虽指出政策试点面对愈加复杂和困难的改革会面临很
多挑战，但并没有详细阐述政策试点在遇到复杂的改革时会产生怎样的结
果，对为什么会出现这种情况也没有做进一步分析。黄晓春等从"结对竞
赛"角度对试点虽好但难以推广这一问题进行分析，但并未阐释政策试点
在"先行先试"阶段的问题。② 学者从不同角度探究影响政策试点成效的
因素，但关于政策试点局限性的研究仍存在补充完善的空间。为什么部分
政策试点实现创新，取得预期成效，而另外一些政策试点却没有取得预期
成效，政策试点成效差异的深层逻辑到底是什么。本文试图从政策试点通
过行政发包的方式进行治理、政策试点的供给机制与公共产品的"复杂"
性质不匹配以及压力型体制下政策试点的局限三个维度对政策试点局限进
行分析，从理论方面进一步探究政策试点治理机制的局限性及它和已有治
理机制间的关系。

二　政策试点的局限：理论分析

政策试点作为"自上而下的政策求解"过程，不同类型的政策试点面
对不同的治理对象，而不同治理对象又有不同的属性，如公共产品/公共
服务的"复杂"性质，会涉及企业、居民等多个主体，对其实现有效治
理，需要多元治理主体协同参与，这涉及国家—社会关系视角。而在国家
治理框架内，政策试点主要解决的是中央—地方之间的关系问题，多缺位
国家—社会关系。为什么会出现这种情况？政策试点在治理过程中，面向
地方政府，不直接面向治理对象。如城市生活垃圾分类试点，其治理对象
涉及多元治理主体、多链条治理过程。高度复杂性的垃圾分类治理，需要
居民、市场深度参与，这在一定程度上超出了政策试点的治理范围。政策
试点不直接面向治理对象本身，公共产品/公共服务需要国家—社会参与，
在一定程度上增加了政策试点的治理难度，加之政策试点运作易受压力型
体制影响，更倾向于行政化操作，只重结果不重过程，在一定程度上影响
政策试点治理的成效。由此本文提出三个维度的政策试点局限构建分析框

---

① Heilmann Sebastian, "Policy Experimentation in China's Economic Rise," *Studies in Comparative International Development* 1 (2008).

② 黄晓春、周黎安：《"结对竞赛"：城市基层治理创新的一种新机制》，《社会》2019 年第 5 期。

架：①政策试点通过行政发包的方式进行治理；②政策试点的供给机制与公共产品的"复杂"性质不匹配；③压力型体制下政策试点的局限。政策试点局限结构分析框架如图1所示。

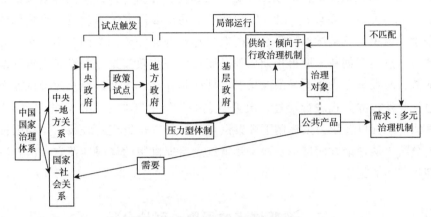

图1　政策试点局限结构分析框架

（一）政策试点通过行政发包方式治理的局限

我国各地情况迥异，地方政府掌握着当地实际情况信息，比中央政府更清楚针对本地实际情况如何运作更有成效。就某些治理难题，中央政府通过政策试点，把地方分散试验和中央选择干预结合在一起，把地方经验有选择地吸收到国家政策中。[①] 政策试点治理从中央到地方的运作属于"下达任务与指标分解且高度依赖地方政府和部门自筹资金"的行政发包过程。中央政府是发包方，各试点政府及其相关部门是承包方。中央政府把具体的治理方式这一任务发包给各试点城市政府，由后者决定如何设置、探索试点内容。中央通过对政策试点结果验收来进一步把控政策试点内容，进一步控制政策试点治理对象，在客观上对政策试点形成督促，故政策试点的局限在一定程度上与通过行政发包的方式进行治理有关。

1. 发包方不直接控制治理对象

针对某一治理问题，"政策试点"于发包方是一次"试错"的规程，

---

① 〔德〕韩博天：《红天鹅：中国独特的治理和制度创新》，石磊译，中信出版社，2018，第59页。

可以控制改革带来的风险和成本。因此发包方在挑选政策试点区时，需要把试点区的经济社会发展状况、改革实践能力等条件都纳入参考范围。发包方通过对试点区的选择性挑选，在具备推行政策试点条件的地区进行政策试点，在一定程度上可以减少改革带来的"副作用"，提高政策试点的成功率。发包方通过下发"试点总体方案"启动政策试点，该方案从指导思想、总体目标、主要任务、试点内容等方面对政策试点提出宏观指导，[①]是各试点地区开展试点工作的计划和指南，也是发包的具体内容，试点地区（承包方）根据"试点总体方案"制订出当地的具体实施方案。同时为保证各政策试点的治理效果，确保各政策试点区的工作进度，发包方还会按照试点总体方案及各具体实施方案，对试点区进行调研，以便及时掌握试点工作进展。当各试点区完成试点任务时，发包方会对各试点区的工作进行阶段性的评估和验收。为保证试点工作的质量，发包方还会根据评估结果对政策试点做出反馈，对政策落实到位、取得较好效果的试验点，给予相应的鼓励和支持；对主观因素导致试点工作进展缓慢、成效不明显的试点地区进行调整和处理。在整个监督评估过程中，中央政府通过对地方政府的奖惩来带动政策试点的运作，中央政府并不直接面向政策试点的治理对象（公共产品/公共服务）本身。

2. 承包方在科层体系内探索政策试点

在接到中央政府推行政策试点的通知后，各试点区政府建立以试点主题为名称的"领导小组""协调小组"，在"试点总体方案"的基础上，结合当地治理对象的实际情况，进一步制定出更加细致的工作计划和实施办法，落实试点工作。然而不同试点区政府对试点项目的"政策含金量"预估存在差异，对试点工作的参与积极性存在差别，由此形成的领导小组级别也存在差异。"试点工作小组"领导级别越高，可以运用领导成员原有的职务权力调动的人力、物力越多，越容易安排试点的推进及在各部门间的分工与落实，易于在规定的时限内实现试点预期目标。然后将具体工作任务以又一级行政发包的方式发包到基层政府。基层政府根据详细的试点实施方案，以通俗易懂、易于接受的语言对该实施方案进行宣传，使当地居民对此次试点工作的主要目的、重点内容、预期结果有一个初步认知和了解，特别是可能会被改革措施影响到的相关群体可以提前做好相应准

---

① 周望：《中国"政策试点"研究》，天津人民出版社，2013，第86页。

备，从而有利于试点工作的顺利展开。

从发包方选择政策试点城市，到试点城市的市政府选择试点区域推进试点治理，政策试点都不直接面向治理对象本身。在发包、承包治理衔接过程中，政策试点一直在科层体系内运作。中央和地方分别作为发包方，中央的主要目标是通过政策试点解决某一治理问题，而试点区地方政府的主要目标是基层政府自身的行政和治理绩效，[①] 两者关注的治理对象的侧重点不一致，所采取的行为会存在差异，由此政策试点在实际治理过程中会产生偏差。

（二）政策试点的供给机制与公共产品的"复杂"性质不匹配

海尔曼通过基本卫生服务这一案例，来阐释政策试点在改善公共产品服务方面的效益不明显。[②] 本文沿袭海尔曼的观点，认为政策试点的局限与公共产品的性质密切相关。奥斯特罗姆认为公共产品的提供效率与利益相关者的参与程度和规模经济有关，公共产品的这种特性一定程度上决定了其需求的治理机制，鉴于这一研究思路，本文认为公共产品的提供者和消费者之间的合作程度会影响公共产品的提供效率。[③] 孙晓冬等认为公共产品的提供效率与公共产品的规模经济有关。对于有较强间接服务的规模经济，可以通过分权治理的方式提供服务。但是，由政府直接提供服务的公共产品，其供给效率还与提供者和消费者间的合作程度有关。所以理想的治理机制需要把规模经济和合作程度这两个影响因素结合起来考虑（见表1），[④] 由此形成四种公共产品类型：高合作、强规模经济型，高合作、弱规模经济型，低合作、强规模经济型，低合作、弱规模经济型。

① 张晨：《"动员-压力-运动治理"体制下后发地区的治理策略与绩效》，《领导科学》2012年第4期。
② Heilmann, "Sebastian. Policy Experimentation in China's Economic Rise," Studies in Comparative International Development 1 (2008).
③ 孙晓冬、宋磊：《产品性质与治理机制：当奥斯特罗姆遇到西蒙》，《北大政治学评论》2018年第1期。
④ 孙晓冬、宋磊：《产品性质与治理机制：当奥斯特罗姆遇到西蒙》，《北大政治学评论》2018年第1期。

表 1 直接服务的四种类型的公共产品

合作程度 规模经济		合作程度	
		高	低
规模经济	强	高合作、强规模经济型	低合作、强规模经济型
	弱	高合作、弱规模经济型	低合作、弱规模经济型

资料来源：孙晓冬、宋磊：《产品性质与治理机制：当奥斯特罗姆遇到西蒙》，《北大政治学评论》2018 年第 1 期。

　　低合作、强规模经济型的公共产品，低合作意味着公共产品的提供者、消费者之间的合作程度对公共产品供给效率的影响比较小，而直接服务的规模经济决定着该类公共产品的供给效率。高合作、弱规模经济型的公共产品，弱规模经济型意味着政府直接服务的各环节所产生的规模经济较弱，公共产品的提供效率主要受高合作影响，公共产品的提供者、消费者之间的合作程度对公共产品的提供效率有比较明显的影响。在我国城市生活垃圾居民分类环节，垃圾的回收率受居民参与的影响程度高，属于高合作类型，需要居民、企业、社会组织参与垃圾分类回收环节。且单个居民分类环节的各工序间并没有较强的规模经济。因此，可以将居民分类环节置于在表 1 中的高合作、弱规模经济型，对于这类公共产品，理想的治理机制并不排除若干不同规模、不同性质的机构共同提供服务，同时包括服务接受者在内的利益相关者的参与也是治理机制的必要组成部分。[1]

　　对于高合作、弱规模型公共产品，其性质决定了提高其治理有效性需要分权型治理机制，即不仅需要满足治理主体的多元化、多层次需求，满足从单一权力向多元权力主体的转变，还需要分析治理主体的结构特点，达成共识与合作，实现多主体共同为治理目标进行协商与合作，需要国家—社会关系广泛参与，形成较强的治理能力。而政策试点在治理过程中，多依靠行政治理机制（中央—地方关系）提供公共产品服务，虽有部分试点地区引入 PPP 治理模式提供公共产品服务，但并未充分调动多元治理主体，因行动者协作能力的高低直接决定着政策试点的不同结果，[2] 故

[1] 孙晓冬、宋磊：《产品性质与治理机制：当奥斯特罗姆遇到西蒙》，《北大政治学评论》2018 年第 1 期。

[2] 刘培伟：《基于中央选择性控制的试验——中国改革"实践"机制的一种新解释》，《开放时代》2010 年第 4 期。

所形成的模式多带有政府有效性的特色。对于需要实现社会有效性的公共产品服务，政策试点成效不明显，社会有效性所要解决的问题不能依靠单一行政治理。①

（三）压力型体制下政策试点的局限

在政策试点治理过程中，中央通过对地方的控制，可以把问题下卸给地方。② 地方在具体推行政策试点的过程中不得不承受由此带来的政策压力，地方政府在具体治理过程中需要对此压力采取相关的应对措施。③ 基于政策试点发起方侧重目标和结果考量，地方政府倾向结果取向治理原则④推进政策试点。政策试点具有基础性权力的性质，需要依靠科层组织及相关的组织资源实现治理意图，同时其治理并非完全按照科层制的逻辑进行，在一定程度上需要打破科层制的壁垒，实现部门间相互协调、通力合作。

政策试点与行政压力相伴，地方政府在推行政策试点的过程中往往会有时间压力、目标压力，迫于绩效考核压力，在政策试点监督考核过程中，中央政府对政策试点的创新核查力度不强，地方政府也就没有很强的积极性进行"真创新"，更倾向于选择行政治理机制推行政策试点，更多以"伪创新"顺利交差。进行"伪创新"，既可以获得相应的政绩，又不需要花费太多的政策试点探索成本，成为多数试点政府的理想选择。相反进行试点创新，需要付出较高的试验成本，更重要的是探索成效不明确，尤其在短期内创新成效不明显。在绩效考核压力下，坚持寻求长期成效的"真创新"不如采用短期策略"伪创新"，这在客观上催生地方竞争越来越趋向短期化，越来越集中于简单的行政治理机制。强调上级权威的压力型体制和强调下级自主探索的政策试点这两个原本自相矛盾的机制，相对比较难自洽地运行于基层治理之中。压力型体制影响下政策试点的结果趋向于"同质化"，这使政策试点的意义大打折扣。

① 欧阳静：《论基层运动型治理——兼与周雪光等商榷》，《开放时代》2014年第6期。
② 刘培伟：《基于中央选择性控制的试验——中国改革"实践"机制的一种新解释》，《开放时代》2010年第4期。
③ 刘培伟：《基于中央选择性控制的试验——中国改革"实践"机制的一种新解释》，《开放时代》2010年第4期。
④ 张静：《基层政权——乡村制度诸问题》，浙江人民出版社，2000，第284页。

中央政府所推行的政策试点，通过行政发包的方式转交给试点政府进行治理，在发包过程中政策试点直接面向试点地方政府（治理主体），发包的具体内容才是治理对象本身。因此在政策试点的具体运作过程中，存在承接发包的问题，中央和地方分别作为发包方和承包方，两者对政策试点关注的目标存在不一致，所采取的行为存在差异，政策试点所产生的结果也就存在偏差。这在一定程度上会削减政策试点成效。公共产品/公共服务自身的"复杂"属性，决定了提高其治理有效性需要分权型治理机制，需要治理主体的多元化，需要国家—社会关系广泛参与，政策试点需要实现多元共治。而政策试点依靠科层体系运行，加之我国基层自治组织的行政化运作，使得社会事务上基本形成基层政府全程参与、全程负责的格局，这使政策试点仍以行政治理为主。① 这在一定程度上加剧了政策试点治理机制与公共产品所需的治理机制间不匹配的问题。政策试点治理又伴随着压力型体制，压力型体制是一种结果导向而非过程导向的权威控制模式，而政策试点的自主性是强调过程的自主性。重结果不重过程的权威体制在一定程度上忽略了政策试点在治理过程中的自主性，会打破政策试点治理的探索规律，会抑制政策试点治理过程中各治理主体的主动性。压力型体制一定程度上加剧了政策试点所提供的治理机制与公共产品所需求的治理机制不匹配问题。

三　政策试点的局限：2000 年之后的城市生活垃圾分类试点

20 世纪 90 年代，北京、上海等大城市出现"垃圾围城"，各级政府逐渐意识到垃圾分类对城市治理的重要性。2000 年中央在北京等 8 个城市开展垃圾分类试点，② 旨在通过试点的方式在全国层面探索出可复制、可推广的生活垃圾分类模式。在垃圾分类试点推行 17 年后，2017 年国家发改委、住建部等部门联合出台《生活垃圾分类制度实施方案》，要求 46 个试点城市推进城市生活垃圾试点。在城市生活垃圾分类试点推行 17 年后，46

---

① 梁玉柱：《压力型体制下基层政府的调适行动与社会治理的行政化》，《社会主义研究》2018 年第 4 期。
② 孟思奇：《我国 8 城市试点垃圾分类 14 年效果不明显》，人民网，http://env.people.com.cn/n/2014/0611/c1010-25132098.html，最后访问日期：2020 年 7 月 1 日。

个试点城市继续推进生活垃圾分类试点，这说明推行 17 年的生活垃圾分类试点没有在全国层面探索出可复制、可推广的模式，没有取得预期成效，存在一定的局限。故本文以 2000 年之后的城市生活垃圾分类试点为个案，探究政策试点的局限。

（一）《生活垃圾分类制度实施方案》出台背景

8 个城市在 2000 年纳入城市生活垃圾分类收集试点后，实行以末端处置为主的城市垃圾分类方式。随着试点治理的深化发展，广州（2011年）[①] 和南京（2013 年）[②] 对之前的垃圾分类方式进行调整，把原来的三分类方式调整为四分类，餐厨垃圾单独设置为一种分类方式。试点城市生活垃圾分类投放情况存在差异。8 个试点城市结合当地生活垃圾产、运情况及试点小区的情况，制定出相应的垃圾分类投放方式。但 8 个试点城市垃圾分类的结果差异化明显，北京市的试点成效最好，基本可以实现垃圾四分类；上海和杭州的生活垃圾分类试点成效次之，虽不同试点小区间存在差异，但试点小区可以做到分类投放；但也有部分地区试点成效甚微，如南京市、厦门市和深圳市，试点小区的分类投放效果不佳，仍以混合投放为主；桂林市仍实行生活垃圾混合收集的传统模式。[③]

试点城市生活垃圾分类收运方式不理想。试点前期缺乏垃圾分类运输车辆，分类投放后的城市垃圾在运输过程中仍实行混合运输。试点后期增加资金投入，调整了运输方式，北京市的生活垃圾由小型人力车进行分类收集，然后转交不同类别的垃圾专用车辆，由其进行分类运输；上海市设置了生活垃圾分类收集的时间告知牌，但不包括有害垃圾，有害垃圾实行单独的收运处理；[④] 其他几个城市仍以混合运输为主。

早期 8 个试点城市的垃圾分类效果不理想。[⑤] 这与居民未能有效参与到生活垃圾分类过程中密切相关。生活垃圾分类是一个由多主体、多环节

---

① 《广州市城市生活垃圾分类管理暂行规定》（2011 年）。
② 《南京市生活垃圾分类管理办法》（2013 年）。
③ 张中华：《我国城市生活垃圾分类的政策工具研究》，硕士学位论文，山东大学，2017，第 16 页。
④ 张莉萍：《城市垃圾治理中的公众参与研究》，科学出版社，2019，第 89 页。
⑤ 孟思奇：《我国 8 城市试点垃圾分类 14 年效果不明显》，人民网，http://env.people.com.cn/n/2014/0611/c1010-25132098.html，最后访问日期：2020 年 7 月 1 日。

构成的复杂系统，分类投放是这个系统的起点，直接决定了生活垃圾治理的成效。8 个试点城市的生活垃圾治理成效不显著，也意味着当地居民没有正真参与到生活垃圾分类治理环节。① 北京市于 2010 年的垃圾分类调查结果显示，已实现分类的垃圾，仍有 75.6% 需要进行二次分拣。② 2013 年，上海市出台《关于优化本市生活垃圾分类减量工作机制若干建议》，强调垃圾分类率的提高与志愿者和分拣员的二次分拣密切相关，有的二次分拣率甚至占到 60%。就早期的试点工作而言，由于居民的垃圾分类意识不强、垃圾分类习惯尚未养成，居民在城市的生活垃圾治理方面的参与度不高。

（二）"26 号文"后的生活垃圾分类试点的发展情况

2011 年以来，中央政府对城市垃圾分类工作的重视程度进一步提高。③ 2017 年 3 月国家发改委、住建部出台"26 号文"，开启新一轮生活垃圾试点。"26 号文"规定：2020 年底前，直辖市、省会城市等共计 46 座城市④ 的城区范围先行实施生活垃圾强制分类。此次城市生活垃圾分类试点呈现以下几个特点。

1. 开展强制分类

"26 号文"之前的城市生活垃圾分类试点以鼓励居民分类投放垃圾为主，⑤ 虽然部分试点区也规定了惩罚措施，但执行力不强。"26 号文"明确提出"46 个城市实施生活垃圾强制分类"。这 46 个试点城市多为省会城市和一线城市，经济相对发达，市民素质普遍较高，且其中一半城市已先行开展垃圾分类试点。⑥ 在一定程度上已具备实施生活垃圾强制分类的条件。"26 号文"还强调了实施城市生活垃圾强制分类的主体。这 46 个城市内的公共机构和相关企业是实施强制分类的主体，这些机构所产生的生

---

① 张莉萍：《城市垃圾治理中的公众参与研究》，科学出版社，2019，第 90 页。
② 郑磊：《北京垃圾分类试点 14 年：七成以上垃圾需二次分拣》，中国新闻网，http://www.chinanews.com/sh/2014/11-17/6781729.shtml，最后访问日期：2020 年 7 月 1 日。
③ 张莉萍：《城市垃圾治理中的公众参与研究》，科学出版社，2019，第 91 页。
④ 直辖市 4 个、省会城市 27 个、计划单列市 5 个、其他地级市 10 个。
⑤ 《国家发展改革委 住房城乡建设部有关负责同志就〈生活垃圾分类制度实施方案〉答记者问》，《中国资源综合利用》2017 年第 4 期。
⑥ 《国家发展改革委 住房城乡建设部有关负责同志就〈生活垃圾分类制度实施方案〉答记者问》，《中国资源综合利用》2017 年第 4 期。

活垃圾范围明确，责任清晰，适宜先行实施强制分类。[①] 第一次明确提出"垃圾强制分类"后，广州率先对城市垃圾分类进行了专门的地方立法，2018 年 3 月 30 日《广州市生活垃圾分类管理条例》出台，该条例对城市垃圾分类的全程管理做出了具体的规定，与之前各大城市出台的规定相比，该条例更强调城市垃圾分类是居民个人的义务和责任，凸显了城市垃圾分类的强制性。[②]

2. 强化政策依据

"26 号文"后各试点城市陆续为城市垃圾分类立法立规，这是生活垃圾分类试点的又一显著特点。46 个试点城市除拉萨、日喀则外均出台了生活垃圾分类法规。从名称上看，《北京市生活垃圾管理条例》《杭州市生活垃圾管理条例》等生活垃圾管理条例属于城市垃圾管理的综合性法规，而《泰安生活垃圾分类管理条例》《铜陵市生活垃圾分类管理条例（草案）》等生活垃圾分类管理条例则是针对垃圾分类出台的专门性法律文件。杭州市、北京市在原生活垃圾管理条例的基础上，结合"26 号文"和当地发展实际出台了新的生活垃圾管理条例。《北京市生活垃圾管理条例》专门设立"减量与分类"一章，《杭州市生活垃圾管理条例》则将"源头减量""分类投放"分设为两章。垃圾分类是当前各试点政府关注的重点问题，部分试点城市把垃圾分类和减量相结合，强化了垃圾分类的政策依据。

3. 引导居民自觉分类

"26 号文"出台之前，城市生活垃圾分类试点运行 17 年，但居民生活垃圾分类意识仍不强。居民垃圾分类习惯的养成是一个长期的过程，不可能一蹴而就。对于城市居民，在法律法规尚不健全的情况下，"26 号文"提倡引导居民参与城市生活垃圾分类，虽未强制城市居民进行垃圾分类，但各城市可结合实际制定居民生活垃圾分类指南，作为引导居民参与城市生活垃圾分类的一种宣传手册。[③] 由此，居民参与到垃圾各分类环节已成大势所趋。

---

① 《国家发展改革委　住房城乡建设部有关负责同志就〈生活垃圾分类制度实施方案〉答记者问》，《中国资源综合利用》2017 年第 4 期。

② 张莉萍：《城市垃圾治理中的公众参与研究》，科学出版社，2019，第 93 页。

③ 《国家发展改革委　住房城乡建设部有关负责同志就〈生活垃圾分类制度实施方案〉答记者问》，《中国资源综合利用》2017 年第 4 期。

4. 完善分类、回收、处理等环节的系统配套设施

垃圾分类涉及多主体、多链条参与，是一项"系统性"工作。前端居民参与垃圾分类的积极性和垃圾分类效果与中端垃圾运输、中转及终端垃圾处理等密切相关。所以建立与分类品种相配套的收运体系属于"末端倒逼"，在收集阶段各试点城市需要改造现有垃圾房、建设垃圾转运站等。在运输阶段要配备与垃圾分类相匹配的专用车辆，规避垃圾混合运输。在处理阶段要完善与垃圾分类相衔接的终端处理设施，尤其要加快餐厨垃圾处理设施建设。[①]

（三）"26号文"后的生活垃圾分类试点治理结果

城市生活垃圾分类试点从 2000 年开始实施，到 2017 年出台"26号文"，再次强调推进生活垃圾分类试点，说明之前推行的政策试点存在一定问题。在实地调研 7 个城市的生活垃圾分类试点后，本文认为"26号文"的生活垃圾分类试点存在试点模式"趋同性"这一明显问题和难以大规模"复制"的风险。

1. "先行先试"阶段"趋同性"明显

从 2000 年开始探索生活垃圾分类试点，到 2019 年在全国地级及以上城市全面开展生活垃圾分类工作，都属于"先行先试"阶段，该阶段试点模式种类增多，但"趋同性"明显。"26号文"颁布后，早期已推行城市生活垃圾分类试点的城市，除非政府官宣试点失灵，大多数试点城市依然推行之前的生活垃圾分类试点模式，并开始在当地进行复制和推广。"26号文"后纳入生活垃圾分类试点的城市，有明确时限要求，需要在 2017年底结合本地实际，制定出台相关办法。[②] 该阶段才开始推行生活垃圾分类试点的城市，由于起步晚、时间节点紧、任务重，多倾向于向试点探索较早、模式"发育"较好的试点"学习"，来形成自己的试点模式。

相比于"26号文"发布前的城市生活垃圾分类试点，社区居民自主进行垃圾分类的试点模式和完全由企业负责的试点模式数量渐增，但这些新纳入生活垃圾分类试点的地区，在向发育较好的试点学习过程中，"模仿

---

① 《国家发展改革委 住房城乡建设部有关负责同志就〈生活垃圾分类制度实施方案〉答记者问》，《中国资源综合利用》2017 年第 4 期。

② 《国家发展改革委 住房城乡建设部有关负责同志就〈生活垃圾分类制度实施方案〉答记者问》，《中国资源综合利用》2017 年第 4 期。

-79-

机制"明显。他们在复制过程中突出强调创新形式上的差异，并未结合当地的实际情况，选择不同类型的社区，因地制宜地探索独有的"新模式"。J市属于"26号文"后推行生活垃圾分类试点的地区，其采用的试点模式是各地方政府比较青睐的PPP模式和"互联网+"的结合，即政府向企业购买服务，企业在小区探索生活垃圾分类治理模式。J市的试点小区共设35个智能干垃圾箱和智能湿垃圾箱，企业为小区住户免费发放生活垃圾分类条码卡和不同颜色的干湿垃圾袋，对居民投放的生活垃圾实行分类编码收集。垃圾箱运用物联网云平台数字技术，对居民投放的垃圾进行智能扫描、智能称重，并将积分通过云平台进行数据传送，结果添加到居民注册的App账户中，居民可通过积分兑换物品。此外垃圾箱还有满载预警功能，可以提醒工作人员及时清理生活垃圾。

J市推出的生活垃圾分类试点模式，是政府服务外包的一种形式。还有不少试点城市和J市一样属于"26号文"后才纳入试点范围的城市，也称找到了适合自己的"新模式"。"互联网+"大同小异，都是智能垃圾箱+积分兑换的模式，只是在智能垃圾箱的款式、颜色等方面存在差异。模仿机制影响下，现有的"双胞胎"型城市生活垃圾分类试点，并非是出于实践检验的"适合"，更多的是基于试点模式种类较少，迫于上级政府的压力，进行的"劣中择优"的被迫复制和移植。由此"百花齐放"的城市生活垃圾分类试点，其实只是从生活垃圾分类试点创新的"面"上来看，试点城市数量增加，更多的社区、企业、群团组织、居民加入到试点模式之中。这种新格局的微妙之处在于城市生活垃圾分类试点看似遍地开花，但试点模式种类突破不显著，试点"趋同性"严重。

虽然部分试点城市的生活垃圾分类采用PPP模式进行运营，企业负责垃圾收、转、运、处理等整个环节，但部分试点区（长春市富豪花园、成都绿色地区）的PPP模式是在目标责任制压力下，以市场机制购买服务的方式体现，这种依靠财政支撑的"社会化"治理并没有脱离行政化的逻辑，依旧高度依赖行政资源推进政策试点，[①] PPP模式在一定程度上异化为行政治理机制。由此试点模式种类在初期就会缩减，甚至会出现仅有几种试点模式的窘境。试点机制的有效性在于先通过地方有效治理摸索经

---

① 梁玉柱：《压力型体制下基层政府的调适行动与社会治理的行政化》，《社会主义研究》2018年第4期。

验，然后借助行政力量加以推广，试点成功推行有赖于试点经验能被科学提炼，并且在推广过程中能保持一定的灵活性。[①] 而这种试点模式在起点"地方有效治理摸索经验"层面已经出现了偏差，后期的推广更无从谈及。

2. "由点到面"难以进行大规模"复制"

2019 年 6 月 19 日，住房和城乡建设部等部门决定在 46 个生活垃圾分类试点城市先行先试的基础上，自 2019 年起在全国地级市及以上城市实施生活垃圾分类，[②] 由此城市生活垃圾分类试点进入"由点到面"阶段。在"先行先试"阶段，46 个试点城市在"26 号文"的基础之上，相继出台城市生活垃圾治理实施方案，并着手推进试点工作。但因不同城市治理"垃圾围城"的迫切程度不同，不同试点城市对城市生活垃圾分类治理的积极性存在差异。迫于"垃圾围城"推进生活垃圾分类治理的城市，其内在治理动机比较强烈，政府注意力分配多，会积极推进城市生活垃圾分类，探索适合自己的模式；而迫于试点城市的政策压力才推行生活垃圾分类治理的城市，其治理动机相对较弱，以 J 市为例，访谈中其基层工作人员指出"在'26 号文'之后，上级政府很快向各基层传达了文件精神，并要求各基层政府积极配合，但之后上级政府对城市生活垃圾分类治理的关注度开始减弱，我们（基层政府工作人员）的积极性日益降低"。内在治理动机强烈的地方政府在探索城市生活垃圾治理模式方面更积极，试点与当地实际情况吻合度更高，成效更明显。所以"先行先试"阶段在治理动机强烈地区形成的试点模式，在"由点到面"阶段，因不同地区生活垃圾在实际产、销方面存在差异，以及不同政府工作人员对生活垃圾治理的积极性存在差异，试点效果的稳固性与持久性无法得到保持，试点模式很难进行大规模"复制"。

牵头部门级别影响政策试点复制。中央政府并未指出将以何种方式对城市生活垃圾分类治理工作进行检查、验收，所以不同试点城市在该方面投入的政府注意力存在差别，由此成立的城市生活垃圾领导小组/联席制度也存在级别差异（见表 2）。盘锦市城市生活垃圾分类领导小组组长由分

[①] 陈那波、蔡荣：《"试点"何以失败？——A 市生活垃圾"计量收费"政策试行过程研究》，《社会学研究》2017 年第 2 期。

[②] 《住房和城乡建设部等部门关于在全国地级及以上城市全面开展生活垃圾分类工作的通知》，中国政府网，http：//www.gov.cn/xinwen/2019-06/11/content_5399088.htm，最后访问日期：2020 年 7 月 1 日。

管副市长担任，长春市由城管委担任城市生活垃圾分类领导小组组长。科层制下横向部门分工清晰，不同部门各司其职，试点城市生活垃圾分类治理的牵头部门级别不高，无法对其他同级横向部门进行综合统筹，不能有效协调各个部门调动相关资源去及时解决试点运作过程中的问题。此外试点城市设置不同级别的领导小组，给基层工作者形成不同的工作导向。一般而言领导级别越高，意味着上级政府越重视，基层地方政府分配给该治理问题的注意力也就越多，政策试点所能调动的人力、物力资源也就越多。因为不同地方政府在推进城市生活垃圾分类治理方面，存在注意力分配不同、差异化创新偏好等问题，所以一类创新模式在"先行先试"阶段可以在某个试点城市落地，到"由点到面"阶段，因试点牵头部门级别不同，试点所能调动的资源存在差异，在其他城市复制成功的概率并不高，移植成功率偏低。

表 2　部分城市出台的生活垃圾分类实施方案

城市	政策名称	出台时间	领导小组/联席制度	牵头部门
北京	北京市人民政府办公厅关于加快推进生活垃圾分类工作的意见	2017. 11. 10	联席会议	市城管委
上海	上海市人民政府办公厅印发《关于建立完善本市生活垃圾全程分类体系的实施方案》的通知	2018. 3. 1	联席会议	市住房和城乡建设局
广州	广州市生活垃圾分类管理条例	2018. 4. 16	—	
成都	成都市人民政府办公厅关于印发成都市生活垃圾分类实施方案（2018—2020 年）的通知	2018. 4. 20	—	市城管委
苏州	市政府办公室关于印发苏州市生活垃圾强制分类制度实施方案的通知	2017. 6. 13	领导小组	—
长春	长春市人民政府办公厅关于推进生活垃圾分类工作的实施意见	2018. 3. 29	领导小组	市城管委
盘锦	2018 年盘锦市城乡生活垃圾分类和资源化利用实施方案	2018. 7. 11	领导小组	分管副市长

（四） 城市生活垃圾分类试点的局限分析

推进城市生活垃圾分类试点已经有近 20 年的历程，仍未取得预期成效，这说明政策试点在解决生活垃圾分类治理方面的问题时存在局限（见图 2）。

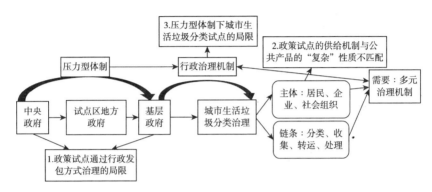

图 2　生活垃圾分类试点局限

1. 政策试点通过行政发包方式治理的局限

发包方不直接面向城市生活垃圾分类试点。2000 年城市生活垃圾分类试点的发包方，即原建设部提出开发生活垃圾分类收集试点，以便总结经验，积极稳妥地推进这项工作。[①] "26 号文" 后生活垃圾分类试点的发包方，即住建部、国家发改委提出 "到 2020 年底，形成可复制、可推广的生活垃圾分类模式且垃圾回收利用率达到 35% 以上" 的政策目标。在生活垃圾分类试点治理方面，发包方的主要目标是通过生活垃圾分类试点区域的自主探索，在全国范围内形成具有普适意义的城市生活垃圾分类治理模式。2000 年城市生活垃圾分类试点以北京等 8 个城市为试点区域，"26 号文" 后的城市生活垃圾分类以 46 个试点城市为该政策试点的试验区，试点区域内的公共机构和相关企业是实施生活垃圾强制分类的主体。根据生活垃圾分类试点的政策内容可以看出，生活垃圾分类政策试点都没有直接面向治理对象，即城市生活垃圾分类，而直接面向的对象是试点城市政府

[①] 《关于公布生活垃圾分类收集试点城市的通知》，中华人民共和国住房和城乡建设部，http://www.mohurd.gov.cn/wjfb/200611/t20061101_156932.html，最后访问日期：2020 年 7 月 1 日。

（即治理主体是地方政府）。两次城市生活垃圾分类试点，发包方分别发布《关于公布生活垃圾分类收集试点城市的通知》① 和 "26 号文"来指导生活垃圾分类试点工作，均旨在依靠试点城市政府去探索生活垃圾分类治理模式。而关于治理对象即生活垃圾分类治理问题，承包方具有很大的自主运作权，在这一行政发包过程中，城市生活垃圾分类试点的直接目标对象是试点城市的市政府（承包方），其为政策试点（城市生活垃圾分类治理）的执行主体，而治理对象（城市生活垃圾分类治理）属于发包的具体内容。

承包方在科层体系内探索城市生活垃圾分类治理模式。承包方（试点区地方政府）在接到发包内容（城市生活垃圾分类治理）后，会在发包方所规定的目标基础上，结合当地的实际情况推进城市生活垃圾分类治理。2000 年城市生活垃圾分类试点以发包方发布的《关于公布生活垃圾分类收集试点城市的通知》② 为指导，推进城市生活垃圾分类。"26 号文"后的城市生活垃圾分类试点以 "26 号文"为指导，结合当地城市生活垃圾特点探索相应的分类治理模式。部分试点城市的市政府把试点模式的具体探索过程下放到区政府，由区政府探索具体分类模式。城市生活垃圾分类试点在基层的运作，也可以看作对其实行的下一级行政发包，市政府是生活垃圾分类的又一级的发包方，基层政府是具体的承包方，具体的承包内容是探索城市生活垃圾分类治理模式。但基层政府任务种类多，突发情况多。其出于"理性选择"，更倾向于选择容易出结果、绩效易于衡量的工作任务。而居民垃圾分类习惯的养成需要一个时间段，城市生活垃圾分类试点想要出结果，耗时长且绩效不易衡量，基层工作人员（承包方）作为理性的行动者，在综合考量下，对城市生活垃圾分类治理投入的注意力会相对比较少。

从发包方选择试点城市推动生活垃圾分类试点，到试点城市的市政府选择试点区域推进生活垃圾分类治理，城市生活垃圾分类试点都不直接面

---

① 《关于公布生活垃圾分类收集试点城市的通知》，中华人民共和国住房和城乡建设部，http：//www. mohurd. gov. cn/wjfb/200611/t20061101_156932. html，最后访问日期：2020 年 7 月 1 日。

② 《关于公布生活垃圾分类收集试点城市的通知》，中华人民共和国住房和城乡建设部，http：//www. mohurd. gov. cn/wjfb/200611/t20061101_156932. html，最后访问日期：2020 年 7 月 1 日。

向治理对象（城市生活垃圾分类）本身。在发包、承包治理衔接过程中，城市生活垃圾分类试点一直在科层体系内运作。中央和地方分别作为发包方，两者对城市生活垃圾分类试点关注的目标存在不一致，两者所采取的行为会存在差异，由此在城市生活垃圾分类治理方面，最终产生的结果会存在偏差。

2. 政策试点的供给机制与城市生活垃圾分类的"复杂"性质不匹配

公共产品的提供效率和利益相关者的参与程度有关，[①] 在分析如何提高城市生活垃圾分类治理的效率时，需要把政府、企业、社会组织和居民行为纳入考虑范围。对于政府提供的具有较强规模经济的间接服务，如引入宣传工作者指导居民进行垃圾分类，二次分拣员直接进行垃圾分类等工作，可以实行服务外包。对于政府直接提供的与企业、社会组织和居民的协作程度有关的城市垃圾分类服务，其服务方式不仅受规模经济影响，还与企业、社会组织和居民的协作程度有关。城市生活垃圾分类治理涉及多主体、多链条，对于城市生活垃圾运输、中转、处理等规模经济比较明显的环节，借鉴孙晓冬、宋磊的观点，理想的治理机制是由高效、大型机构单独提供运输或处理服务。[②] 实现这些环节的有效治理，需要投入大量的成本购置分类运输车辆及不同种类的垃圾处置设施，还需要新建垃圾中转场所、垃圾处理基地等。在相关硬件设置配备齐全后，城市生活垃圾日处理量越大，设施的使用效率越高，投入产出比越优，强规模型经济就越明显。且居民在该环节的参与程度与垃圾处理效率之间的关联度很弱，所以在这些环节协作程度相对较低。对于城市生活垃圾运输、中转、处理等低合作、强规模经济型的处理环节，可以实行集权型治理机制。

但处于治理链条前端的城市居民垃圾分类行为，其实现高效分类，需要居民的高度配合。目前尚没有形成针对居民不分类行为的惩罚机制，混扔者不需要为自己的行为买单，作为理性的个体，小区居民缺乏责任和动力去主动、正确地进行生活垃圾分类。所以城市生活垃圾实现高效、准确的投放，需要每一个居民的大力配合，这属于高协作类型。居民垃圾分类习惯的养成是一个相对较长的过程，这与居民垃圾分类意识的增强密切相

---

① 〔美〕文森特·奥斯特罗姆、罗伯特·比什、埃莉诺·奥斯特罗姆：《美国地方政府》，井敏等译，北京大学出版社，2004，第172页。

② 孙晓冬、宋磊：《产品性质与治理机制：当奥斯特罗姆遇到西蒙》，《北大政治学评论》2018年第1期。

关，与提供垃圾分类服务机构的规模之间并没有直接关联，并不是政府机构提供的工作人员数量越多，居民垃圾分类投放的准确率就越高，所以居民垃圾分类投放行为属于弱规模经济类型。故处于治理链条前端的城市居民垃圾分类行为属于高合作、弱规模经济型，对于这类公共产品，借鉴孙晓冬、宋磊的观点，其理想的治理机制并不排除不同规模、不同性质的机构，而应该鼓励各种类型的企业、社会组织广泛参与到城市生活垃圾分类治理中，实行分权型治理。①

城市生活垃圾分类试点提供单一的治理机制。城市生活垃圾分类试点涉及多主体、多链条治理（见图3），多主体包括居民、垃圾分类企业、政府以及环保类的社会组织；多链条涉及生活垃圾的收集、运输、中转及处理等环节。对生活垃圾分类试点实现有效治理，不仅需要满足不同主体的多元化服务需求，实现生活垃圾回收利用率达到35%以上，还需要突破垃圾分类的地域特性，到2020年底形成可复制、可推广的生活垃圾分类模式；② 更重要的是需要整合政府部门、企业、居民的行为，实现全链条治理。在城市生活垃圾分类治理过程中，治理政策目标多元、技术手段复杂、对环境差异敏感，③ 对于该类复杂政策，"政策制定只是博弈的开始，政策执行才是难点"。④

城市生活垃圾治理前期投入资金高、技术复杂性强、管理精细化程度高，这些特征决定了实现城市生活垃圾分类有效治理，不仅需要调动企业、居民的力量参与，而且需要进行长期持续的监管。然而这样一项高复杂性、高要求的工作目前却没有纳入中央政府的重点考核指标体系内，由此地方政府在推进城市生活垃圾分类治理方面的积极性有待提高。加之政府工作人员对各类政策投入的注意力受成本、复杂性等政策属性的影响，一般而言社会属性强的政策容易遇冷，而城市生活垃圾分类作为一种社会属性极强的公共政策，其公共产品属性决定了其属于投入成本高、相对优

---

① 孙晓冬、宋磊：《产品性质与治理机制：当奥斯特罗姆遇到西蒙》，《北大政治学评论》2018年第1期。

② 国务院办公厅：《关于转发国家发展改革委、住房城乡建设部生活垃圾分类制度实施方案的通知》（国办发〔2017〕26号）。

③ 王蒙：《扶贫开发与农村低保衔接的政策执行偏差及其矫正——基于复杂政策执行的"模糊—冲突"分析框架》，《中国农业大学学报》2018年第5期。

④ 陈家建、边慧敏、邓湘树：《科层结构与政策执行》，《社会学研究》2013年第6期。

势比低且正溢出效应高的政策，[①] 由此地方政府对此类政策的重视度会更加不足。因为我国自治组织主要依赖行政化进行运作，社会权威在公共服务方面相对欠缺，社会事务基本形成基层政府全程参与、全程负责的格局，进一步加剧了基层治理的行政化需求，[②] 这也导致在城市生活垃圾分类治理方面，各试点存在治理主体缺位的问题，居民、企业以及社会组织参与积极性不高，目前各城市生活垃圾分类试点仍然以基层行政治理为主。

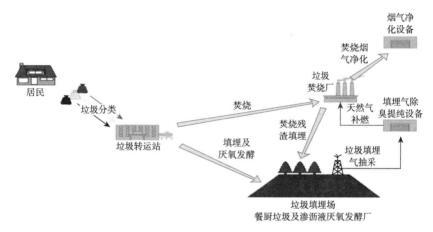

图 3　生活垃圾处理多主体、多链条

3. 压力型体制下城市生活垃圾分类试点的局限

在城市生活垃圾分类治理方面，"26 号文"要求试点区地方政府在 2020 年底完成 35% 的生活垃圾分类目标，并探索出可复制、可推广的治理模式，在这个潜在的行政压力下，地方政府为能如期实现政策试点的目标，行政治理机制"集中力量办大事"的特点深受地方政府青睐。"26 号文"发布后，试点城市开始推进城市生活垃圾治理工作。虽然有的试点成立了城市垃圾治理工作领导小组，也建立了相关联席会议制度。但有些试点领导小组组长行政级别不高，仍存在难以协调各方、调动资源解决问题的困境。城市生活垃圾治理试点因其公共产品性质，涉及多主体、多链条

---

① 周黎安：《中国地方官员的晋升锦标赛模式研究》，《经济研究》2007 年第 7 期。

② 梁玉柱：《压力型体制下基层政府的调适行动与社会治理的行政化》，《社会主义研究》2018 年第 4 期。

治理，面临着技术复杂性的障碍。这种技术复杂性体现在单一部门协调其他部门、调动资源困难重重，科层制固有的部门分割问题，很难解决现有的生活垃圾分类试点技术性障碍问题，此外在依靠行政治理机制运作试点的过程中，还存在行政权力挤占其他治理主体权力资源的倾向，[①] 导致相关企业、小区居民、社会组织等在城市生活垃圾分类治理过程中无法发挥应有的作用。

生活垃圾分类试点的具体运作大多在基层社区，基层工作人员任务范围广、服务对象数量多，人员数量有限，其能调动和利用的资源有限，且经常面临同时执行多种任务的压力。对基层工作人员而言，在压力型体制下，与其依靠各类治理主体去探索治理模式，不如依靠行政体制运行更能掌握主动权，由此城市生活垃圾分类试点总是在行政体制中运行。生活垃圾分类试点一旦被行政体制所捕获，行政体制下政府官员的压力就会促使其更注重短期的"可识别的"效果，从而忽略短期效果不显著的居民自身分类行为养成方面的问题。基于此，很多试点城市更侧重末端处理设施的建设，而忽视通过制度激励去培养人们的行为习惯，这种工作方式很难探寻出可复制、可推广的模式。

四　结论与展望

政策试点的探索性利于解决某些风险较高、需要谨慎对待的问题。如营改增试点，中央政府先指定试点单位，通过试点进行风险评估，进而降低决策风险。其次，便于解决一些影响重大、地方政府不愿意花费太多精力去解决且迫切需要解决的问题。如城市生活垃圾分类治理试点，中央运用行政手段指定政策试点单位，可以在一定程度上推动该问题的解决。最后，政策试点可以发挥地方的创新能力解决社会问题。如服务外包示范城市试点，缺乏可以借鉴的实施经验，中央政府出台指导方案，定下政策试点的基调，给予基层政府较大的创新空间，借助基层地方的创新力量探索最优解。

政策试点在运作过程中，也存在一定局限。

---

① 马雪松、王慧：《现代国家治理视域下压力型体制的责任政治逻辑》，《云南社会科学》2019 年第 3 期。

第一，代表性试点区选择存在困难。政策试点本身的尝试性决定了需要选定少数几个地区进行政策效果测试。而这些"先行先试"的试验效果很大程度上决定了政策试点可行性的整体评估。[①] 针对一些需要在大范围内推广应用的政策试点，试点区域的选择尤为重要，中央政府所选的试点区域要有代表性，要能体现地域的差别、地区经济发展间的差距。同时试点区政府在寻找试点的过程中，既要体现非随机性，又要体现本区域的代表性，由此试点运作的结果才有代表性，才能取得普适性经验，才能把"盆景"发展壮大为"森林"。

第二，政策试点存在"无限期"的困境。政策试点处于尝试阶段，政府工作人员的"预知决策"虽有指导作用，但客观条件在政策试点的实际探索过程中制约力度很强。许多复杂政策试点，如城市生活垃圾分类试点，涉及多主体、多链条、多部门治理，对其进行预判的困难程度很高，且预判结果的可靠性也有待进一步验证。给予政策试点足够的时间和空间去试验、去探索，所取得的治理模式更能顺应公共产品的治理规律，更具有可复制、可推广性。然而有些政策问题亟待解决，这个"期限"给政策试点探索合适方式带上了"枷锁"，使其局限性放大。

第三，政策试点在解决公共产品和公共服务提供方面存在先天不足，公共产品的属性决定了实现其有效治理需要多元治理机制，而政策试点本身在行政体制内运行，其运作过程离不开行政治理机制，在压力型体制作用下，政府工作人员更倾向于依靠行政治理机制解决问题，由此治理机制不匹配的问题使政策试点在解决公共产品的"复杂性"性问题方面存在局限。

中央推行政策试点的本意是进一步完善国家制度体系建设及对社会公共事务进行有效治理，希望在面对复杂政策问题时，政策试点能为上级政府的政策推行提供更为灵活的操作空间和合理性基础，为下级政府提供试错和摸索的空间。[②] 但政策试点由中央选择性控制，中央一方面希望充分发挥地方的创新能力，另一方面又担心任其发展会失去对政策试点的控

[①] 陈那波、蔡荣：《"试点"何以失败？——A市生活垃圾"计量收费"政策试行过程研究》，《社会学研究》2017年第2期。

[②] 陈那波、蔡荣：《"试点"何以失败？——A市生活垃圾"计量收费"政策试行过程研究》，《社会学研究》2017年第2期。

制，因而通过引导和管控的方式总体把握政策试点进程。① 在政策试点目标的压力下，本应以自主动员和有机整合为目标的政策试点会受到干扰，尤其是一些复杂性政策试点，原本需要多元治理，需要社会权威再造、政社之间良性互动的培养以及社会公共精神的塑造等，在压力型体制影响下，对基层政府而言，这种长效机制并非最优选择。② 其更倾向于选择行政治理机制推行政策试点，去解决治理问题。由此从基层政府的视角可以更清晰地看到，政策试点基层治理行政化的逻辑，这种行政化的政策试点运作方式虽然在一定程度上能完成试点目标，但也有自身的限度，会导致政策试点陷入"行政化"循环，难以形成多元治理的格局。③ 因此在公共产品和公共服务提供方面，中央政府通过政策试点治理，虽然在一定程度上可以解决治理问题，但也在某种程度上阻碍了政策试点的作用，其所取得的经验存在难以推广的困境。④

Limitations of Policy Pilot
—A Case Study on the Classification of Urban Domestic Waste in China

Yu Junbo and Zhang Xinjing

Abstract：Policy pilot is a unique policy testing and innovation mechanism in China's governance practice. This policy making mechanism based on the concept of "experiment" is conducive to controlling reform risks, reducing reform costs and improving the success rate of reform. Its governance effect in the economic field is significant, and the problems in public goods / public services are frequent. The pilot project of classification of municipal solid waste

---

① 周黎安：《中国地方官员的晋升锦标赛模式研究》，《经济研究》2007 年第 7 期。
② 梁玉柱：《压力型体制下基层政府的调适行动与社会治理的行政化》，《社会主义研究》2018 年第 4 期。
③ 梁玉柱：《压力型体制下基层政府的调适行动与社会治理的行政化》，《社会主义研究》2018 年第 4 期。
④ 刘培伟：《基于中央选择性控制的试验——中国改革"实践"机制的一种新解释》，《开放时代》2010 年第 4 期。

in China was launched in 2000. The *Implementation plan of classification system of municipal solid waste* was issued in 2017. And the compulsory classification of municipal solid waste continued to be implemented in the form of pilot project, which shows that the pilot project of classification of municipal solid waste in the past 17 years has not achieved prospective results. This paper takes the classification of China's municipal solid waste as an example to explore the limitations of the policy pilot, and considers that the limitations of the policy pilot are related to the following three factors: 1. Governance through the way of administrative contract; 2. The supply mechanism of the policy pilot does not match the "complex" nature of public products; 3. The impact of the pressure system on the policy pilot.

Keywords: Policy Pilots, Urban Grass-Roots Governance, Public Goods, Stress-Based Systems

欠发达地区城市发展与治理研究

——以青海省海东市为例

郑昊霖[*]

【摘　要】欠发达地区城市发展和治理事关重大，党和政府历来重视欠发达地区的城市发展建设问题。新中国成立以来，随着城镇化不断的发展，西部地区发生了翻天覆地的变化，城镇化速度突飞猛进，城市治理成效显著。海东市作为青海省的新兴城市，又是连接甘肃、青海两省份的重要通道，是兰西城市群建设的核心地带，具有巨大的发展空间和潜力。然而受到自然环境等限制性因素的影响，海东市城市化进程较慢，发展动力不足。本文通过对青海省海东市在城市发展和治理方面的研究，发现其滞后城镇化的原因，并为提升民族地区治理体系与治理能力的现代化水平提出一些思考建议。

【关键词】海东市；欠发达地区；城镇化；城市治理

一　城市治理的提出及其概念

城市，根据其字面意思是"城"与"市"的结合，是社会经济发展的产物。英国经济学家 K.J. 巴顿说：现代市场经济社会的"城市是一个在有限空间地域内的各种市场（住房、劳动力、土地、运输、商品等市场）

---

*　郑昊霖，青海民族大学硕士研究生。

交织在一起的网络系统"。① 美国城市社会学者指出："从城市的概念可以进一步的归纳：社会因素是主要的，而且城市是现实（物理、物质）组织，它的工业，它的市场，它的通讯和交通线路，必须是为社会需求所服务。"② 城市产生后，人们在有限的空间和地域范围内进行着经济、人口和生态的再生产，可以说城市是人类社会物质和精神文明的载体。③ 然而，随着城市的发展，人口的增多，城市在承载人类精神文明的同时，也承载了诸如人口膨胀、交通拥挤、环境污染、资源紧缺等城市问题。因此，为了促进城市良好的可持续发展，使人类文明得以有效的传承下去就要治理城市。

现代城市的治理在运用各种手段的同时都需要遵循法治化方针，也就是城市治理与建设法治国家的治国方略相一致。我国长期以来惯用"管理"这一概念，在城市工作中也不例外。随着我国社会主义市场经济的不断发展和完善，民主与法治建设的逐渐深入，在城市工作方面也由原来的"管理"开始向"治理"转变。党的十九大报告指出："打造共建共治共享的社会治理格局。加强社会治理制度建设，完善党委领导、政府负责、社会协同、公众参与、法治保障的社会治理体制，提高社会治理社会化、法治化、智能化、专业化水平。"④ 党的十九届四中全会进一步审议通过了《中共中央关于坚持和完善中国特色社会主义制度、推进国家治理体系和治理能力现代化若干重大问题的决定》，"治理"和"善治"变得越来越重要。在城市工作方面也是如此，"管理"和"治理"虽然一字之差，其内容和含义却大相径庭。从主体上说，管理是一家独大，治理却是多元参与。管理，其主体是政府，虽然也有社会组织和市民参与到当中来，但毕竟只是起到辅助作用，其重心还是依靠政府。治理，其主体具有多元化的特点，不仅有社会组织和市民还有政府和国家，它们的地位是平等的，形成多元化共同参与城市治理的格局。从方式上说，管理是自上而下行政方

---

① 〔英〕K. J. 巴顿：《城市经济学：理论与政策》，上海社会科学院部门经济研究所城市经济研究室译，商务印书馆，1981，第2~4页。

② 〔美〕莱维斯·芒福德：《城市社会学文选》，于海编译，复旦大学出版社，2005，第75页。

③ 蒋晓伟：《城市治理法治化研究》，人民出版社，2016，第3页。

④ 习近平：《决胜全面建成小康社会　夺取新时代中国特色社会主义伟大胜利——在中国共产党第十九次全国代表大会上的报告》，人民出版社，2017，第49页。

式，治理是自下而上协调方式。针对城市工作由原来以上下级的行政手段和行政命令，变成了各主体之间运用法治思维来协调和自治。从内容上说，管理是用计划经济的方式来对城市资源进行配置，治理是用市场经济的方式对城市资源进行配置。

简单来说，城市治理就是通过规划、决策、指挥、执行、安排等手段实现对城市各项工作的协调和控制，从而使各项事务有序开展。随着社会的发展，人们在城市治理方面也积累了各种各样的手段和方法，有经济的、制度的、技术的、教育的等。随着我国经济发展程度的提高，各项基础设施的完善，城镇化进程的不断加速，城市越来越成为人民生活的重要载体，尤其是在中部和东部地区，城市发展和建设已经达到一个较高的水平，随着科技水平的提高和智能化应用的普及，城市运转和工作效率都得以大大提升。然而，在我国的西部欠发达地区，很多城市依旧处于初步建设的阶段，地理和交通的限制，导致其经济发展程度低、基础设施不完善、城镇化速度较慢、人才流失严重等问题，这些问题倘若不能妥善解决，便会反过来又一次制约经济的发展，人民生活水平也无法提高。因此，城市发展不能仅仅关注中东部地区，对于西部地区也不可忽视。对欠发达地区的城市建设，应该发展与治理相结合。需要从该地区的区位环境、设施建设、人才引进、发展规划等方面入手，使其各项工作得到稳步发展，再通过各种机制实现最优治理。

二 海东市发展现状

海东是青海省管辖地级市，因位于青海湖以东而得名，下辖2区4县。于2013年2月经省委、省政府批准，撤地设市，海东市政府由原平安县（今平安区）迁至新成立的乐都区。其作为青海省的新兴城市，在拉动经济发展、促进民族团结、维护社会稳定方面做出了巨大的贡献。自设市以来，随着其城市规模的不断扩大，常住人口的不断增加，城镇化的进程逐步加快，人民的生活水平也得到了一定程度的提高，但是在城镇化的进程中也带来一些问题值得我们思考。

（一）海东市人口概况

人口是一个城市发展的内在动力，也是一个城市发展必不可少的组成部分。人口的增加促使城市规模扩大，从而对城市各项设施的需求也不断增大，这样便会进一步带动城市的发展，从而使得城市规模不断扩大，各项设施不断完善，形成良性循环。

根据青海省统计数据可直观得出，2019 年海东市城镇人口为 46.6 万，占据总人口的 27%，乡村人口为 126 万人，占据总人口的 73%，可以看出海东市城镇居民数量依旧较少。城市治理的首要问题便是人口的治理，海东市就其人口发展状况而言，呈现"新区少，老城多"的特点。乐都区和平安区作为新发展的城区，在人口数量上低于老牌的民和、互助两县。从年内人口流动上看，呈现"迁入少，迁出多"的现象（见表 1）。①

表 1　海东市 2019 年人口数量统计

地区	2019 年末数					
	总户数	总人口			总人口中	
		合计	男	女	城镇人口	乡村人口
海东市	479041	1726313	887335	838978	466000	1260313
乐都区	91161	288040	147588	140452	97122	190918
平安区	41263	127409	64166	63243	54673	72736
民和县	108962	438517	226767	211750	117337	321180
互助县	113551	401659	210015	191644	92751	308908
化隆县	80132	307035	156528	150507	59062	247973
循化县	43972	163653	82271	81382	45055	118598

（二）海东市人均收入水平和相关产业发展概况

1. 人均收入水平

海东市在 2013 年撤地设市，人均收入水平也首次破万元。近些年来，居民人均可支配收入稳步增长，由 2013 年的人均可支配收入 11005 元增长到 2018 年的 17305 元。作为一个由老县城发展而来的新兴城市，各项工作都处于初步发展和逐步完善的阶段，因此在人均收入水平方面，要低于海

① 青海省海东市统计局：《海东市 2019 年国民经济和社会发展统计公报》，海东市人民政府网，http://www.haidong.gov.cn，最后访问日期：2020 年 7 月 2 日。

北州（人均可支配收入 18684 元）、海南州（人均可支配收入 17935 元）和海西州（人均可支配收入 26524 元）等老牌州县。①

2. 人均生活消费支出连年增长，消费潜力巨大

撤地设市的一个重要作用就是可以大幅度吸引外来人员和招商引资，这样或多或少都会促进消费水平的增长。从人均支出水平方面可以看出，撤地设市后，多年来的消费水平呈现稳步上升，而这一现象的背后是海东人民的巨大消费潜力。2018 年的人均消费支出达到了 11653 元，在消费支出方面呈现多元化，由原来的生活资本支出变成了发展资本和旅游资本支出。

3. 相关产业发展概况

海东市第二产业和第三产业有了很大的发展。就旅游人数而言，2016 年 962.5 万人次，2017 年 1161.4 万人次，2018 年 1375.2 万人次。2018 年旅游人次仅次于西宁市和海西州，旅游总收入达 55.1 亿元。② 就第二产业发展而言，企业单位数虽有所增加，但是发展规模小，亏损程度较大。以 2017 年工业规模为例，海东市企业单位 86 个，亏损企业为 26 个，亏损率高达 30%（见表 2）。工业是一个城市发展的命脉和血液，然而海东市企业单位数量少，亏损率高，在一定程度上大大阻碍了其工业化进程。

表 2　海东市规模以上工业企业主要经济指标（2017 年）

单位：个

指标	企业单位数	亏损企业
海东市	86	26
国有控股企业	4	—
轻工业	13	1
重工业	73	25
股份合作企业	1	1
有限责任公司	28	9
股份有限公司	6	1
私营企业	49	14

---

① 青海省海东市统计局：《海东市 2019 年国民经济和社会发展统计公报》，海东市人民政府网，http://www.haidong.gov.cn，最后访问日期：2020 年 7 月 2 日。

② 青海省海东市统计局：《海东市 2019 年国民经济和社会发展统计公报》，海东市人民政府网，http://www.haidong.gov.cn，最后访问日期：2020 年 7 月 2 日。

指标	企业单位数（个）	亏损企业
港、澳、台商投资企业	1	—
外商投资企业	1	1

数据来源：青海省海东市统计局：《海东市 2019 年国民经济和社会发展统计公报》，海东市人民政府网，http://www.haidong.gov.cn，最后访问日期：2020 年 7 月 2 日。

（三）海东市城市规模及地形分布分析

海东市与兰州市毗邻，与西宁市衔接。其作为两个省会城市的连接地带，发展潜力巨大。从地形上可以看出，海东市东西狭长，南北皆为山脉，由于地理环境的先天性因素，不利于城市南北扩张和开发，但其作为连接青海和甘肃的重要枢纽，在未来打造兰西城市群的规划上发挥着不容小觑的作用。

海东撤地设市具有较高的战略意义和实践意义。一个明显的变化就是旅游人次和交通出行人次历年稳步增长，西宁是著名的避暑胜地和旅游文化城市，但是在交通建设方面远远落后于东部城市，选择单一，出行不便，多年来一直是西宁作为旅游城市的软肋。随着海东市的建立和平安机场的落成，交通运输得到了有效的发展，特别是海东市高铁新区的建设，在一定程度使得出行压力得到缓解，近年来游客数量显著增多，旅游所带来的收益也相当可观。

三 海东市发展面临的困境

（一）滞后城市化问题突出，生活未得到改善

人口城市化是农民城市居民化的载体。在城市化的发展史上曾经出现过两种极端现象，即"超前城市化"与"滞后城市化"。超前城市化是指城市化发展速度远远超过工业化发展的速度，造成城市化水平与工业化和经济发展水平脱节的城市化发展模式。① 其带来的后果较为严重，例如，

---

① 杨风：《排斥与融入：人口城市化进程中农民市民化研究》，山东大学出版社，2014，第 67 页。

不利于良好社会生态的形成，造成贫富两极分化，出现"城中村"现象，严重时影响社会稳定，等等。滞后城市化是指城市发展水平落后于工业化和经济发展水平的城市化模式，其后果是大量农村剩余劳动力滞留在农村，无法顺利解决就业问题，农业副业化和工业乡土化严重，导致城市不像城市，农村不像农村。

就海东市而言，是典型的滞后城市化模式，尽管城镇化速度有所加快，但是农村人口依旧比重过高。根据海东市 2019 年人口数量统计，我们可以看出，2019 年海东市非农业户口率远远低于人口城市化率①，这意味着约 126 万海东人民被排斥在市民待遇之外，享受不到城市居民的待遇。城市化滞后发展，即大量农村人口在城市化进程中其身份、地位、权利并未随着地域、职业的转变而发生相应的改变。例如，虽说已经撤地设市，之前的农村人口有了市民的身份，但是在交通服务方面、基础设施建设方面、医疗卫生方面却没有享受到城市居民应有的待遇和福利，很多居民的生活条件也并未得到改善，依旧还是原来的居住环境，只有城市户籍的"空帽子"。很多居民只有城市户籍之名，无城市户籍之实。这组数据也暗示着，撤地设市虽然在一定程度上提高了居民的生活水平，但是对于大多数农民而言享受不到城市化带来的便利和福利。此外，城镇化进程的加快导致大量耕种用地被规划为建设土地，多数农民失去了原有的土地，然而工作问题却没有及时得到解决，造成大量的失地农民出现。以 2018 年海东市为例，乡村农业人数为 133.56 万人，然而乡村从业人员只有 70.80 万人，可以发现，依旧有很多农民处于失业的状态。这些问题倘若不能妥善解决就会滋生社会问题，影响社会稳定，从而不利于城市发展。

（二）城市基础设施薄弱，无法吸引人才

完善的基础设施建设是城市赖以生存和发展的基础，是产生聚集效益的重要物质条件，更是对外开放的物质保证。现代化完善的城市基础设施，对城市的经济、社会和环境发展都有着重要影响，是城市可持续发展的重要物质基础。② 城市化的发展应当伴随着基础设施的完善而进行，甚

---

① 青海省海东市统计局：《海东市 2019 年国民经济和社会发展统计公报》，海东市人民政府网，http://www.haidong.gov.cn，最后访问日期：2020 年 7 月 2 日。

② 张跃庆、吴庆玲编著《城市基础设施经营与管理》，经济科学出版社，2005，第 112 页。

至基础设施的建设速度应当略快于城市人口增长的速度，只有这样才能留得住本地人员，引得来外来人员。否则，便会对本地人员形成排斥力，对外来人员构不成吸引力。

海东市作为新兴发展城市，在基础设施建设方面依旧存在很大的短板，一定程度上制约了城市化的发展。就房屋建筑方面来说，2018 年海东市施工面积为 508.2 万平方米，占青海省施工面积的 20%，竣工面积为 60.5 万平方米，占青海省竣工面积的 19%，房屋建筑面积竣工率为 11.9%。房屋销售面积为 88.39 万平方米，其中住宅面积为 79.21 万平方米，商业营业性用房 7.49 万平方米，仅占总使用面积的 8.47%。① 从道路交通方面来说，按路面类型分：截止到 2019 年末，海东市沥青混凝土路面仅有 2109.433 公里，水泥混凝土路面 7774.045 公里，简易铺装路面 373.471 公里，砂砾路面 984.984 公里，无路面仍有 758.141 公里，远远落后于东部城市道路建设里程数；就文体建设方面而言，截止到 2019 年末，海东市全市有民间艺术团体 75 个，文化馆 7 个，公共图书馆 5 个，博物馆 8 个，广播电视电台 59 座，在满足人民大众的物质文化和精神文化需求方面显得捉襟见肘。在医疗卫生方面，全市医院仅有 56 个，床位 4975 张；乡镇卫生院 109 个，床位 1645 张；社区卫生服务中心（站）66 个，妇幼保健院（所、站）7 个，疾病预防控制中心（防疫站）7 个，存在床位紧缺、就医难、看病难等问题。基础设施的完善程度直接影响人口的迁入与迁出，以人口流动方面为例，2019 年省内迁入 16704 人，省外迁入 2548 人，虽说迁入人口较多，但迁入人员大多为州县退休人员，并不能为城市提供新鲜的活力，其迁入的原因也是其出行较为便捷，房价相比西宁便宜，气候也相对宜人，并不是城市建设方面存在吸引力。2019 年海东市本地迁出到省内其他城市为 20137 人，本地迁出到省外为 3664 人。综合比较发现，人口为净迁出，人员的流失势必导致劳动力的减少和人才的不足，不利于城市的发展。究其根本，还是因为基础设施建设、医疗卫生等方面对本地居民缺乏吸引力。

---

① 青海省海东市统计局：《海东市 2019 年国民经济和社会发展统计公报》，海东市人民政府网，http://www.haidong.gov.cn，最后访问日期：2020 年 7 月 2 日。

（三）城乡生活方式冲突，滋生失地农民

美国学者哈奥哲认为："近代社会中最明显的一种现象就是城市化的发展，即城市人口不断增加。这种现象反映了现代社会的特征，表现了大众社会和城市生活方式的发展，同时，也必须看到这种现象的产生和发展，必然伴随着许多的具体社会问题。"[1] 这些问题一是生活方式的转变，由原来传统的乡村生活方式向现代化城市生活方式的转变；二是身份的转变，由原来的农民身份向市民身份转变。对于欠发达地区而言，城市化滞后，撤地设市导致大量的农民来不及适应生活方式和身份的转变。

随着海东市城镇化进程的加快，大量农用土地被占据，滋生了很多的失地农民，这些农民大多通过房屋置换，居住方面不成问题，但是在生活方面却受到城镇化的影响，尤其是在职业选择方面有了明显的变化。失地农民在职业选择上由于缺乏相应的技能和经验，只能进行粗糙的手工制造业和依靠体力的建筑行业。青海自然和地理环境的特殊性导致其第一产业、第二产业和第三产业与内地相比都不是很发达，但是体制内的收入水平要远远高于私营企业的收入水平。就海东市而言，2018年非私营单位就业人数排名前三的分别是制造业、建筑业和金融业。在城镇化的影响下，农牧业所占比重逐年降低，取而代之是制造业、零售业和服务业等行业的崛起。城镇化进程带来的一个明显的变化便是对人员的技能和要求有所提高，因为新一代"市民"是由原来的"农民"转换而来，所以缺乏一定的文化知识和劳动技能，只能从事劳动强度大、技术含量低、工资薪酬少的工作，在生活方式上出现了很大的冲突（见表3）。另外，身份的转变并未带来思想上的转变。失地农民大多观念陈旧同时深受小农经济的影响，认为小富即安。由于缺乏相关创业经验，他们不能够有效进行自我创业，导致政府给予的拆迁补偿在短时间内挥霍完，然后无法为以后的生活做久远的打算。尤其年龄偏大的农民根本无法顺利找到合适的工作来维持自身生活需求。

---

[1] 〔美〕哈奥哲：《城市生活与城市化》，《美国社会学杂志》1995年第5期。

表 3　海东市 2018 年非私营单位企业和女性就业人数

单位：人

项目	全省合计	海东市非私营单位年末企业就业人数（2018 年）	海东市非私营单位年末女性就业人数（2018 年）
合计	569216	19566	27797
农林牧渔业	9989	4	541
采矿业	39058	81	20
制造业	114548	7887	1845
电力、燃气及水的生产和供应业	30021	592	245
建筑业	66672	4046	412
批发和零售业	31193	1130	553
交通运输、仓储业	48782	833	553
邮政业	2977		174
住宿和餐饮业	8721	267	92
信息传输、软件	8361	231	
和信息技术服务业	12005		1121
金融业	25950	2356	307
房地产业	11791	657	128
租赁和商业服务业	12899	280	795
科学研究和技术服务业	5317	71	
	5168		1191
水利、环境和公共	2500	505	
设施管理业	202		25
居民服务、修理业	412	40	
其他服务业	43245		8665
教育	33592	298	3476
卫生和社会工作	4843		388
文化、体育和娱乐业	50970	288	7266
公共管理、社会保障和社会组织			

（四）地理环境制约，经济发展缓慢

在我国欠发达的西北民族地区，基层金融体系建设严重滞后和资金匮乏，是长期制约其经济发展的重要因素。与经济发达地区相比，海东市由于受到地理环境的影响，经济总量水平低。2019年，全市人均GDP为32806元，仅为北京市GDP水平的1/5。对一个城市发展初期而言，工业化水平的高低直接影响这个城市城镇化进程的快慢。良好的工业发展对经济贡献较大，在拉动居民生活需求方面也有很大的促进作用。就海东市2019年工业发展程度而言，除酒、饮料和精制茶制造业，化学原料和化学制品制造业以及金属制品业等少数产业以外，其余产值皆有所下滑，增长速度为负值，特别是电气机械和器材制造业、非金属矿采选业与上一年相比下降了100%和39.8%。具体参见表4。一个地区经济的健康和平稳运行需要依靠农业、本地工业和手工业的协同发展。工业的增长是吸纳劳动力、解决就业问题的重要推力，然而就海东市第二产业而言，依旧处于刚起步状态，工业发展缓慢，对经济的贡献率较低，工厂发展规模小，就业吸纳水平低，这就大大阻碍了其经济的平稳健康运行和发展。

表4 2019年规模以上工业行业增加值增长速度

行业名称	比上年增长（%）
合计	4
煤炭开采和洗选业	-24.4
有色金属矿采选业	-1.9
非金属矿采选业	-39.8
农副食品加工业	29.2
食品制造业	-32.7
酒、饮料和精制茶制造业	34.6
化学原料和化学制品制造业	24.6
非金属矿物制品业	-0.3
黑色金属冶炼和压延加工业	-0.8
有色金属冶炼和压延加工业	12
金属制品业	27.9
电气机械和器材制造业	-100

四 欠发达地区城市治理逻辑：效益视角下循序渐进发展

（一）加大财政投入力度与发展特色经济相结合

城市经济想要获得发展需从两方面进行，一是通过加大财政补贴力度实现"输血"，二是通过发展自身优势实现"造血"。只有当"输血"与"造血"功能相结合，城市才能获得良性发展。首先，西部欠发达地区受到自然环境和地理条件的双重制约，自然环境特殊性导致自身经济发展先天羸弱，地理条件的限制性导致自身经济发展后天不足。国家为缩小东西部地区发展差异，2000 年在党的十五届五中全会通过了第十个五年计划，决定实施西部大开发的战略，多年来西部地区条件虽有所改善，但是由于西部大开发涉及面广，包括范围多，定点资金较少，对于西北地区尤其是民族地区而言，承惠力度不足。因此，要通过加大财政补贴对西部地区尤其是偏远地区的投入力度，以精准扶贫为突破，针对其薄弱方面给予适当的倾斜和扶持，使其获得一定的启动资金和运行成本，补足短板，从而解决欠发达地区在城市发展方面的先天不足问题，实现外部"输血"。授之以鱼更要授之以渔，海东市是多民族聚集地，自然资源丰富，市场潜力巨大，战略位置尤为重要，未来发展潜力巨大。因此，可以充分发挥具有当地特色的民俗产业，开展具有民族特色的相关活动，让欠发达地区从内部实现"造血"。首先要打好"特色牌"，充分发挥民族特色，将民族特色转换成经济优势。其次要打好"宣传牌"，要充分利用自媒体、短视频等现代技术，做好宣传，打出品牌。最后，要打好"质量牌"，以特色吸引新顾客，用质量保证回头客。外部输血使得城市具备发展动力，内部造血使得城市自我持续向好，只有将外部"输血"与内部"造血"相结合，这样在城市发展上才能形成良性的循环。

（二）完善基础设施建设，打造生态宜居城市

经济的发展将推动基础设施的完善。城市的发展离不开基础设施的建设，基础设施的完善也是打通各城市群协同发展的关键节点，同时也将进一步推动生态宜居城市的建设和发展。2018 年 8 月 31 日西宁市与兰州市颁布了《兰州—西宁城市群发展规划实施方案》，此方案的实施要进一步加大兰

西城市群的建设力度，同时也为周边城市的发展注入了活力。作为连结西宁和兰州的必要通道和兰西城市群的经济交汇点，海东市的基础设施和交通设施不仅要满足本地区的需要，而且其交通设施还需要发挥主干道的作用，满足兰州、西宁等经济区人员流动、物质运输的需求。实现基础设施建设的一体化，对西北欠发达地区而言，能够加强城市群之间的联系，降低运输成本和费用，使得区域内的产业合作、经济合作更加密切，从而促进经济的发展。此外，还要加大对文体产业的投资建设力度，例如逐步增加和完善图书馆、人民公园、歌剧院、体育馆、爱国主义教育基地等基础设施建设，以保证居民物质文化和精神文化的需求得以实现，使得城市在招商引资和人才引进方面更加具有吸引力。加强基础设施的建设势必促进生态宜居城市目标的实现。实现生态宜居的城市目标，首先需要良好的居住和生活基础，其次，需要周围配套设施的完善。海东市地处高原，自然环境的特殊性导致其工业发展起步慢，环境污染程度小。海东市生态环境局空气质量年报显示，2019年海东市两区四县环境空气质量指数（AQI）日均值为39~108，达标率高达95.6%。因此，海东市应在充分利用既有生态优势的基础上，加大对配套基础设施的建设，在城市发展方面坚持生态环境保护优先和协同推进配套设施建设，早日实现高质量发展，创造高品质生活。

（三）加大人才引进，提供内生力

人才是创新的第一资源。[①] 城市治理应当充分发挥人才效益，把实现经济高质量发展作为城市治理的出发点，一方面要把外来人才吸引进来，另一方面要把内部人才培养起来。外部人才的引进有利于激发城市的创新力，内部人才的培养有利于激发城市的再生力。因此，在服务供给上应当有针对性地向高素质人才适当倾斜，发挥高素质人才效益。近年来，全国各地发起"人才争夺战"，郑州、武汉、西安等地更是打出了大学生买房给予政策性补贴、取消落户限制等政策。可见，高素质人才对一个城市的发展是至关重要的。欠发达地区要实现经济发展，基层政府就应当推行人才引进理念，发挥人才效益，以人才促发展。一方面要大力引进高素质人才来提升城市的创新力，通过与中东部地区高校签订人才协议，消除隔阂

---

① 习近平：《在中国科学院第十九次院士大会、中国工程院第十四次院士大会上的讲话》，人民出版社，2018，第3页。

与屏障，提供良好的就业环境和平台，有的放矢地加强对高素质人才的吸引和扶持。此外，还要及时通过对本地区进行定量分析，发现区域内人才存量的分布特点和具体产业人才结构，查找人才紧缺或过剩的行业领域，对紧缺行业的人才大力引进，对于过剩行业人员适当转型，通过高素质人才的流动来最大限度地发挥人才效益。另一方面，要加大对本土人才的培养和失业人员的再培训，为区域发展提供内生力和再生力。通过对教育资源的倾斜，与教育资源丰富地区签订人才培养协议，选派本土人才进行学习，提升自身素质和技能；对于失业的人员要通过技能培训和创业培训，鼓励失业人员再就业，以创业促就业，从而推动社会经济又好又快发展。最后，在制度上给予保障和支持，完善人才保障机制，确保人才"引得进，留得住、用得上"。欠发达地区之所以人才流失严重，除了自身"硬环境"问题，还有"软环境"的问题，部分行业存在对人才和知识的重视程度不够、待遇和保障落实不到位、地区排外思想严重等问题。因此，政府要落实"尊重知识、尊重人才"的方针政策，营造出尊重人才、尊重知识的良好社会风气，逐步提高人才待遇，改善其生活和工作条件，促使其发挥应有的作用。

(四) 加强交流创新，推进治理体系和治理能力现代化

首先，加强欠发达地区与发达地区之间的交流合作，促进各地区之间的高效协同，实现各地区资源的开放共享，形成互利共赢的合作伙伴关系，从而推进治理体系和治理能力的现代化。不均衡发展是我国经济社会较长时间面临的难题，不均衡发展的重要原因除了人才分布不均衡之外，还有区位发展不均衡。区位之所以发展不均衡，很大程度上是由于自身资源的匮乏和交流不足，各地在信息和资源上没有形成开放和共享的机制。因此，要运用协同发展机制，做到信息及时传递，行业坦诚合作，区域协同管理，通过协调各区域之间的资源、人力、信息等要素，确保各区域充分发挥其作用。其次，要加大对高新技术产业的投资力度，打造现代化、智能化发展的样板城市。一个城市的现代化水平和科技水平可以通过其高新技术产业的多少反映出来。高新技术产业、现代服务业等高端、高效、高辐射的产业已经成为支撑和带动城市经济发展的主导力量，对其他产业具有辐射引领和带动作用。[1] 因此，要加大对科技的投入力度，用信息谋

---

① 李程骅：《城市与区域创新发展论》，中国社会科学出版社，2014，第212页。

出路，以科技促发展，用科技创新推动城市治理体系和治理能力的现代化。实行科技创新驱动战略，一要财政支持，通过财政拨款、专项基金等给予其发展和运行的资金，解决建设过程中的后顾之忧。二要人才充足，科技创新的核心是人才，通过人才来激发城市活力，不断推动智能城市的建设。三要制度保障，城市建设制度先行，只有在制度化规范化的前提和保障下，才能保证各项工作的有效运行。最后，要把资源共享和科技建城有机结合起来，在智慧城市建设起步阶段，欠发达地区缺乏经验和技术，可以通过资源共享来对发达地区进行学习和借鉴，从而促进科技建城，科技兴城。发展到一定阶段后，逐步形成自己的特色和创新点，再通过资源共享给予其他城市借鉴和经验，从而形成良性循环。

五　结语

由于自然环境和地理环境的先天限制性因素，西部地区各项发展都远远落后于中东部地区，地理和自然环境导致经济发展的不足，基础设施的不完善导致人才的流失，人才的流失导致一系列问题的出现，形成了发展滞后等诸多社会问题。这些问题很大程度上是自然环境的先天性不足导致的。

发展是第一要义，发展也是优化治理的前提，因此，针对欠发达地区的特殊状况，我们应牢牢抓住时代机遇，求新求变。在城市发展方面，用特色促经济，以人才带发展，实行创新驱动战略，运用协同发展机制，实现科技兴城，在"五位一体"的总布局下全方位推进现代化进程，从而推进治理体系和治理能力的现代化。

Research on Urban Development and Governance in Underdeveloped Areas—A Case study of Haidong City, Qinghai Province

Zheng Haolin

Abstract：Urban development and governance in underdeveloped areas is of great importance. The Party and government have always attached great importance to urban development and construction in underdeveloped areas. Since the founding of the People's Republic of China, with the continuous development and deepening of urbanization, tremendous changes have taken place in the western region, with rapid progress in urbanization rate and great progress in urban governance. As an emerging city in Qinghai Province, Haidong is also an important channel connecting Gansu and Qinghai provinces. It is the core of the construction of Lanxi city cluster and has huge development space and potential. However, due to its restrictive factors, such as natural environment lead to slow the process of urbanization, urban development dynamics is insufficient, through to the qinghai province middle city in the urban development and governance research, found that reasons of the lag of urbanization and for its future development and advancing the modernization level of management system and management ability to make some Suggestions.

Keywords: Hai Dong, Underdeveloped Area, Urbanization, Urban Governance

深化基层社会治理现代化：南京公安民意110的探索与实践

宋雅言　张　练*

【摘　要】为着力解决公安执法服务工作中长期存在的不作为、慢作为、乱作为以及公众参与度较低、认可度不高、获得感不强等问题，南京市公安局探索建立了以民意主导警务为核心的"民意110"机制，建立健全执法服务"好差评"制度，将人民群众具象为每一个执法服务对象，创新了公众参与公安执法和社会治理的路径方式，充分保障了社会公众的知情权、参与权、表达权和监督权，有效提升了警务执行力和执法公信力，形成了基层社会治理现代化的南京样本。

【关键词】社会治理；民意110；公众参与

社会治理现代化是国家治理体系和国家治理能力现代化的重要内容，其旨在用中国的话语来解释中国的社会问题，进行与当今中国社会的发展现状和目标要求相适应、能够为国家改革发展与治理能力现代化提供支撑的实践创新。随着市场经济的发展以及工业化和城市化进程的加速，全面深化改革逐步深入推进，社会治理中的许多新现象、新问题也不断凸显，更多的治理痛点需要在改革创新中进行化解。维护国家安全和社会治安秩序、保护公民的合法权益，是公安机关的重要职责。在进行社会治理过程中，公安机关是维护社会公平正义的重要力量，公安执法服务是社会治理

---

* 宋雅言、张练，南京市公安局警务效能监察支队。

体系和治理能力的重要组成部分，群众参与率较低、认可度不高、获得感不强等问题是社会治理也是公安执法服务面临的共性难题。在社会多元化的条件下，全面深化改革，需要寻求和凝聚社会共识。① 卢梭在《社会契约论》中提出过"众意"和"公意"的观点，认为"众意"是基于私人利益的个别意志的总和，"公意"作为公共意志，则着眼于公共利益。② 但二者的基础都是民意，正确的民意才是社会治理的最高依据。对此，南京市公安局在执法服务过程中把民意作为第一信息源，聚焦民意诉求，落实问题整改，强化建章立制，持续提升警务效能，打造科学、高效、现代的民意主导警务模式，走出了一条尊重民意、汇集民智、凝聚民力、改善民生的新路径，为社会治理现代化中的公安实践提供了南京样本。

一　民意 110 的时代背景与实践需求

党的十八届三中全会首次提出"推进国家治理体系和治理能力现代化"③，为国家治理能力的提高和基层社会治理的发展指明了方向。2015年 7 月，为进一步创新社会治理，南京市公安局按照深化公安改革总体部署，建立了民意 110，使人民群众成为公安社会治理的合伙人、共同体，让治理更加精细、更为智慧、更具质量、更有温度。

（一）民意 110 的时代背景

从党的十七大报告到十九大报告，"社会管理"改为"社会治理"，一个字的变化反映出我党对群众需求变化的认识和重视。中共中央政治局委员、中央政法委书记郭声琨在坚持和完善共建共治共享的社会治理制度论述中提出，我国社会主要矛盾已经转化为人民日益增长的美好生活需要和不平衡不充分的发展之间的矛盾，人民不仅对物质文化生活提出了更高要求，而且在民主、法治、公平、正义、安全、环境等方面的要求日益增长，更加重视知情权、参与权、表达权、监督权，参与社会治理意愿强烈，希望在促进社会发展中更好地实现人生价值。这也符合马洛斯需求层

---

① 周光辉：《推进国家治理现代化需要寻求和凝聚社会共识》，《法制与社会发展》2014 年第 5 期。

② 参见〔法〕卢梭《社会契约论》，李平沤译，商务印书馆，2011。

③ 《十八大以来重要文献选编》中，中央文献出版社，2016，第 817 页。

次理论，当一个人满足了较低层次的需求之后，就会出现较高级的需求。

在当前社会矛盾和人民需求不断变化的时代背景下，现代社会治理不应只是某个单一主体主导，而应是由政府、企业、社会组织、公民等共同协商共同治理来实现的。传统的自上而下的管理学思维不再适用社会治理新要求，基层社会的治理离不开社会组织和广大人民群众的共同参与。在当前中国的政治实践语境下，社会治理是在执政党的领导下，由地方各级政府主导并负责，社会成员和社会组织等多种主体协调参与，共同管理社会公共事务、供给公共服务产品、维护社会秩序、化解社会矛盾和纠纷、满足社会公共利益需要的活动。① 在这个过程中，公安机关扮演的角色，由原来的国家机器重要组成部分，要逐渐转变到为人民群众竭力提供优质高效的公共安全产品和服务，并切实成为社会公平正义的"守护人"。

当前我国正在加快推进社会治理现代化，社会治理要把提升老百姓的幸福感作为最高准则。幸福是指人类基于自身的满足感与安全感而主观产生的评价，习近平总书记也曾强调："人民对美好生活的向往就是我们的奋斗目标，要把人民放在心中最高位置，始终与人民心心相印、与人民同甘共苦、与人民团结奋斗；强调我们共产党人对人民群众的疾苦要有仁爱之心、关爱之心，对困难群众要格外关注、格外关爱、格外关心，千方百计地为群众排忧解难。"② 南京公安民意110，在规范执法服务的同时，扩大公众参与，在提升公安机关参与社会治理能力方面，进行了有益的探索。

（二）民意 110 的实践需求

社会治理创新的实践，必须基于当今国家发展和社会进步而展开。有学者认为"目前我国已经进入超大规模陌生人群治理的新阶段和新常态"，这是理解和分析当代中国社会治理的现象基础。③ 在社会学之父奥古斯特·孔德看来，社会秩序的建立与社会机体各部分的平衡与和谐一致。社

---

① 王浦劬：《国家治理、政府治理和社会治理的基本含义及其相互关系辨析》，《社会学评论》2014 年第 3 期。
② 《十八大以来重要文献选编》上，中央文献出版社，2014，第 471 页。
③ 参见泮伟江《超大规模陌生人社会治理：中国社会法治化治理的基本语境》，《民主与科学》2018 年第 2 期。

会机体本身的庞大、复杂，不可避免地会产生各种社会矛盾。而在以"厌讼"文化自居的中国，老百姓遇到矛盾纠纷很多情况下不情愿去法院，而是往往选择报警求助于公安机关，这些基层的社会治理问题最容易被疏忽，也正是应当引起重视的。

面对矛盾，社会管理者的主要职责之一是将矛盾控制在合理的范围内，维持社会的有序与动态平衡，以保证社会机体的健康发展。① 公安机关作为基层治理的最前沿，执法服务涉及社会活动的各种矛盾冲突，在这个过程中必然涉及用权和监督的问题。孟德斯鸠说："一切有权力的人都容易滥用权力，这是万古不易的一条经验。有权力的人们使用权力一直到遇到界限的地方才休止。"有权必有责，用权受监督，这是公权力运行的基本原则。习近平总书记强调："健全权力运行制约和监督体系，关键是要让人民监督权力，让权力在阳光下运行，把权力关进制度的笼子里。各级执法、司法机关要坚持用制度管权管事管人，加大依法惩治腐败力度，加强执法和司法工作制度化、规范化建设，努力让人民群众在每一起案件中都感受到公平正义。"②

围绕法治南京建设，南京市公安局从主动发现和整改问题入手，认真查找公安工作中存在的短板弱项，总结出以下三个方面的原因。一是执法服务规范化缺少外部评价机制，对工作中的突出问题，过多采用被动式的内部检查整顿解决。二是受理群众投诉监督的部门较多，多头管理、重复办理，监督效率不高。三是考核机制忽略了群众的参与和感受，常常出现业务数据考核成绩很高，而群众的安全感、满意度却不高的现象。面对现实工作中民众需求与警务服务能力不匹配，南京市公安局创新社会治理、深化公安改革，探索实践民意警务，以期实现人民群众满意度、安全感和公安机关执法公信力双提升的工作目标。

二　民意 110 的理念设定

2019 年 3 月 5 日，李克强总理在作政府工作报告时指出，建立政务服

---

① 季卫东、杨力：《大城市治理的主要风险及其法律应对》，社会科学文献出版社，2018，第 153 页。
② 《十八大以来重要文献选编》上，中央文献出版社，2014，第 865 页。

务"好差评"制度，服务绩效由企业和群众来评判。民意110树立用户至上的公共服务理念，把每一次执法服务视作产品，通过回访查找瑕疵，回应群众诉求，再推出更加适应民意的执法服务。南京公安民意110围绕"民意、实战、问题、效能、数据"五个维度，落实了以人民为中心的发展思想，推动了政府职能转变。

一是民意主导，坚持和完善"枫桥经验"。"治政之要在于安民"，习近平在全国公安工作会议上强调：把枫桥经验坚持好、发展好，把党的群众路线坚持好、贯彻好，充分发动群众、组织群众、依靠群众，推进基层社会治理创新，努力建设更高水平的平安中国。[①] 公民参与是民主治理的基础，公民参与程度越高，民主治理的程度也就越高。[②] 自古以来，儒家文化就是中国的主流社会观，在公元前的《尚书·泰誓上》就有提及："民之所欲，天必从之"，反映了儒家汉学文化对人民根本利益与社会发展规律一致性的认识。美国学者亨廷顿也曾明确提出："民意是政府行为尤其是政策制定行为的合法性的来源。"[③] 同样对于公安机关的执法服务，"没有公开便无所谓正义"，[④] 面对公众的需求变化，民意110树立民意主导，把以人民为中心作为基层社会治理的根本立场和价值取向，努力做到社会治理过程让群众参与，成效让群众评判，成果让群众共享。[⑤] 在中国社科院开展的2018年中国警务透明度评估中，南京在全国36个大中城市中排名第一。

二是突出实战，深化警务改革创新。在党的十九届四中全会《决定》中提出，坚持和完善中国特色社会主义行政体制，构建职责明确、依法行政的政府治理体系，必须坚持一切行政机关为人民服务、对人民负责、受人民监督，创新行政方式，提高行政效能，建设人民满意的服务型政府。信息化社会的到来和城市化进程的加速，给新时期的警务工作开展带来了前所未有的挑战，同时也提供了创新的契机。从传统的熟人社会到现代都

① 《人民日报评论员：努力建设更高水平的平安中国——二论学习贯彻习近平总书记中央政法工作会议重要讲话》，人民网，http://theory.people.com.cn/n1/2019/0118/c40531-30575016.html，最后访问日期：2020年7月23日。
② 俞可平：《论国家治理现代化》，社会科学文献出版社，2014，第29页。
③ 〔美〕塞缪尔·P.亨廷顿：《变化社会中的政治秩序》，王冠华译，上海人民出版社，2008，第25页。
④ 〔美〕哈罗德·J.伯尔曼：《法律与宗教》，梁治平译，三联书店，1991，第48页。
⑤ 参见陈一新《推进新时代市域社会治理现代化》，《公民与法》（综合版）2018年第8期。

市的陌生人社会，再到网络上的虚拟社会，信息获取和交流方式发生了巨大变化，高风险社会已经从理论变为现实，平安中国建设面临新形势，面对新挑战。广泛、及时的群众需求信息和反馈，也成为南京市公安局开展警务工作的方向指引和决策依据。这能够促进南京新时期警务工作从事后处理到事前预防，从粗放管理到精准服务，从被动应付到主动出击。

三是面向问题，防范化解社会矛盾风险。改革开放以来，我国社会冲突事件呈现高发、频发和多发的状态，已经严重损害到地方政府的公信力。正如有学者所揭示的那样："在中国，总体上正是一个社会不断从国家中释放出来的过程，并且，在释放出来的社会与国家之间建立何种互动关系，面临着怎样的风险和机遇，则成为中国改革发展和法治建设中的核心议题。"① 社会风险作为习近平总书记强调的七大风险之一，是国家治理过程中基础性、广泛性、持续性的问题。民意 110 创新工作方法，尊重群众的表达权，在倾听诉求的过程中，把矛盾疏导化解在源头；尊重市民的参与权和监督权，把小的不满意在基层一线化解，有效避免了不满情绪和矛盾日积月累而形成的群体性诉求。

四是注重执行力，建立回应型善治政府。随着信息化、城市化的发展，警务工作面临的社会环境、警民互动方式、信息获取的渠道等都发生了巨大变化。建立高效透明廉洁的回应型善治政府，是各级政府转变政府职能、提高服务效能的重要目标。习近平总书记在全国公安工作会议上强调：要着力锻造一支有铁一般的理想信念、铁一般的责任担当、铁一般的过硬本领、铁一般的纪律作风的公安铁军。② 公安机关作为参与社会治理的政府职能部门之一，要把自身高效的执行力转化为看得见的治理效能。按照基层社会治理现代化的理念，要打破市县乡村的层级界限，构建上下贯通的法治监督体系，市级监督部门必要时一竿子插到底，直接受理、处理基层问题线索，努力实现上下贯通。③ 根据这一理念，民意 110 成立由一个处级单位、26 名民警、30 名文员组成的民意跟踪监测队伍，在全局形成上下贯通、职责明确的三级办理责任体系。实现了群众诉求在条线和

① 马长山：《法治社会研究的现状与前景——基于国家与社会关系视角的考察》，《法治现代化研究》2017 年第 1 期。

② 《新华社评论员：锻造公安铁军 建设平安中国》，新华网，http：//www.xinhuanet.com/politics/2019-05/08/c_1124468823.htm，最后访问日期：2020 年 7 月 23 日。

③ 陈一新：《推进新时代市域社会治理现代化》，《公民与法》（综合版）2018 年第 8 期。

属地流转顺畅，确保即时性、便捷性和共享性。

五是数据赋能，助推警务高质量发展。郭声琨强调，科技进步是社会发展的引擎，也是提高社会治理效能的推动力。要善于把大数据、人工智能等现代科技与社会治理深度融合起来，通过现代科技推进社会沟通、改进管理服务，打造数据驱动、人机协同、跨界融合、共创分享的智能化治理新模式。现实警务工作中，出现的民众需求与执法服务回应能力的不匹配、警务工作怠政懒政等问题，都迫切需要通过治理创新来解决。民意110通过四年多的全量汇聚社会评价数据，目前建成了共享共用的南京公安民意大数据库，实现智能分析民意热点，自动生成各级执法服务主体的"民意画像"，并将民意数据同业务、队伍数据关联比对，查找制约警务效能增长的堵点，让民意大数据智能应用成为助推全市公安工作质量和效率提升变革的新引擎。

三　民意110的实践路径和机制保障

党的十九届四中全会《决定》中提出，要优化行政决策、行政执行、行政组织、行政监督体制；健全部门协调配合机制、防止政出多门、政策效应相互抵消。《决定》聚焦制度完善、机制创新，对坚持和完善共建治共享的社会治理制度的重点任务作了具体部署。《决定》提到坚持和发展新时代"枫桥经验"，要想实现"小事不出村、大事不出镇、矛盾不上交"，关键是要把着眼点放在前置防线、前瞻治理、前端控制、前期处置上，通过畅通和规范群众诉求表达、利益协调、权益保障通道，努力将矛盾化解在基层。面对新形势，南京公安民意110改革创新社会治理模式，改变以往监督部门分散、监督方式被动的做法，在工作源头问政于民，全量回访、广泛征集民意，再将民意转化为公安决策的智库和信息源，为警务实践提供行动指南。

（一）实践路径

传统的公安工作模式属于典型的政府推进型，过分依赖国家（政府）单方面的努力，存在先天的动力单一的缺陷，暗含着某种法治的悖论，同时也容易导致"法治共识不足、法律工具主义、制度认同乏力、司法公信缺失等困境"。① 面向新时代，警务工作想要达到社会稳定秩序的构建，需要拓宽利益表达渠道，建立健全利益协调机制。善治是使公共利益最大化的管理过程和管理活动，它的一个非常重要的基本要素是公民参与（civic engagement）。② 为此，在创新公安监督方式、畅通群众诉求渠道、规范执法服务行为等方面，民意 110 进行了探索实践，建立了对时限、目标、考核标准化的流程做法（见图 1），能够更有效地满足社会治理的需要。

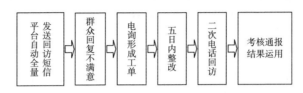

图 1　群众不满意事项跟踪整改流程

一是对执法服务全量访评。根据政府善治的原则，一个科学、民主的政府决策要求实现决策参与主体的多元性，畅通民意表达渠道就成为提高政府科学决策水平和提高党的执政能力的需要。民意 110 建立公安执法服务的"好差评"制度，依托回访平台，对所有报过警、报过案、办理过窗口业务和处理过交通事故的群众，自动全量发送回访短信。对收集到的投诉和不满意事项，逐一询问制作成工单，附带电话访评录音，通过网上办公平台逐级推送到责任单位限期督办。相关责任单位在执法服务过程确有瑕疵的，应主动落实整改措施，并向当事人进行反馈。四年多来，民意 110 依托回访平台，累计发送民意访评短信 2700 余万条，同步电话回访 70 万人次，整改率达 99.86%。

二是整合监督投诉热线。在畅通群众诉求渠道、提升公共服务效能上，南京市公安局归并整合全局 7 项社会评价资源，汇集违法违纪举报、市政务热线、督查投诉、窗口投诉 4 类监督方式，开通民意专线，对群众诉求实行一站式办理。对群众反映的意见、诉求，在 24 小时内形成电子工单，逐级推送至责任单位。热线开通以来，办理群众来电诉求 5.7 万件。

三是定期开展民意调查。民意调查是公共决策民主化、科学化的基本

---

① 参见马长山《法治社会研究的现状与前景——基于国家与社会关系视角的考察》，《法治现代化研究》2017 年第 1 期。

② 俞可平：《论国家治理现代化》，社会科学文献出版社，2014，第 29 页。

前提，是通过了解公众对当前社会热点问题的感受、态度和思想观念来把握民心、民意及其发展趋势的一种调查研究方法。民意110每月定期开展社会治安满意度、公安队伍满意度、社区民警熟悉率调查，全市每个区各抽取200个有效样本，调查人群涵盖不同年龄段的不同行业人员。同时围绕市局重点工作、民生热点问题，开展专项调查，目前已开展了出租房、禁毒、扫黑除恶等工作的专项调查。四年多来，共计开展社会面调查14余万人次，覆盖了南京市常住、暂住和流动人口。图2即为近期开展的南京市创建全国禁毒示范城市专项调查，群众对于南京各区禁毒工作满意度的情况统计。

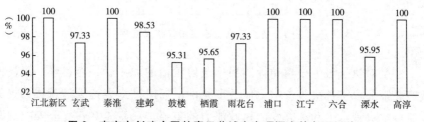

图2　南京市创建全国禁毒示范城市专项调查的各区评价

四是创新公众直接参与的方式。共建的力量来自人民，共治的智慧出自人民，共享的成果为了人民。民意110注重开放共治、协商共建，不断探索公众参与的方式，创新新时代组织群众、发动群众的机制。主要是围绕市局中心工作、专项斗争以及警务工作中群众关注的热点问题、重点领域，依托警民恳谈、"向人民报告"系列活动、大走访等载体，常态化征集、反馈社会各界的意见建议。

（二）保障机制

民意110从规范执法行为、提升服务水平入手，主动发现整改问题，倒逼日常规范养成，以较低的财物和人力成本解决了人民群众不满意的问题。访评过程中，尊重民意但不唯民意，对执法服务过程合乎规范的，责任单位可提出申诉复核。对恶意投诉、诬告诽谤等情况，民意110设置了申请澄清正名的机制。针对疑难复杂事项，建立警种条线的联席会商机制，共同研究解决对策。这些机制为担当者担当，切实打消了执法主体担心被投诉的顾虑。此外，在人员配置、考核奖惩、科技创新等方面，民意 110 经过四年多的探索实践，都总结形成了保障工作良好运行的机制。

1. 聚焦队伍建设，强化行政执行

民意 110 密切跟踪社会治理过程中的新问题、新情况，不断找差距、查问题、补短板。一是谁办理、谁负责，建立上下贯通、职责明确的三级办理责任体系，健全部门协调配合机制。中心为一级平台，将受理的投诉和不满意事项推送到相关责任单位，全程跟踪督办；各部门、分局为二级平台，负责接收推送电子工单，核实反馈整改情况；基层科、所、队为三级平台，负责上门走访群众，落实具体整改措施。二是专业化、常态化，有专门机构、专门力量，所有工作人员都经过了专业化的培训，以具有专业素质的专业人员从事专业性的工作，且全年常态开展、从不间断。三是更规范、更公正，科学设计了回访的问题、提问的方式，制定了规范的流程，特别是下交的不满意工单附有全程录音，对不满意事项允许民警申诉，认真调查核实。

2. 落实考核运用，回应百姓期盼

南京市公安局将民意 110 作为队伍监督的创新手段，让民警当"答卷人"，请群众作"阅卷人"，改变宽泛式、运动式教育整顿队伍的老传统，真正做到精准点穴、靶向治警，实现队伍管理抓在日常、严在经常。一是将群众监督意见挂钩绩效考核。将民意评价结果，赋予 15% 的权重分值，与业务绩效共同纳入全员全员考核体系，以强有力的考核杠杆倒逼全警执法和服务行为规范。二是以群众监督意见作为问责依据。针对群众反映安全感、满意度持续较低的单位，每季度会同纪委监察、督察等部门对单位负责人进行约谈，责成说明情况、帮助分析原因、研究改进措施。三是把群众监督意见纳入执法档案。将每一起群众不满意工单关联到具体责任民警，逐步建立与考核奖惩、职务晋升挂钩的执法服务档案，催生全市公安民警服务为民的内生动力和行动自觉。

3. 科技应用支撑，深化数据赋能

充分发动社会化力量、运用信息化手段、积极打造共建共治共享的社会治理新格局，推进社会治理智能化。将大数据理念深度应用于民意 110 工作，真正将民意民愿转化为公安机关科学决策的智库信息源，转化为南京治警、治安实践的行动指南。一是强化数据整合，努力把准民意。主动打破部门之间信息壁垒，全面导入纪检监察、信访、督察等部门征集的民意数据，实现民意数据全量汇集、深度融合，为警务决策提供最鲜活、最客观的第一手民意资料。二是强化数据挖掘，切实找准梗阻。在分析研判系统内，根据群众反映问题的类型和程度，对每一起群众诉求进行问题标注，以数据形式精确展示共性、突出重点问题，为各级公安机关改进工作提供方向和抓手。三是强化数据应用，实现精准指挥。利用可视化技术，将群众反映的风险信息和短板问题，在研判系统内进行动态化显示和预警性发布，切实构建大数据条件下民意引领警务的新格局。

此外，2018 年 5 月 10 日，江苏省质量技术监督局发布了《警务效能监察工作规范》，标准号为 DB32/T 3393-2018，规定了警务效能监察工作的术语和定义、机构职责、监察环境、监察方式、监察流程、质量控制和结果应用。该标准适用于江苏省由县级以上地方人民政府公安机关设立专门机构开展的警务效能监察工作，其他组织可参照执行。该规范详细阐述了机构职责、监察环境、监察内容、监察方式、监察流程、质量控制、结果运用。

作为一种创新，民意 110 在国内城市中属于率先开展，上述机制和标准也验证了该做法经过实践检验不断成熟，是新时代"枫桥经验"的基层治理样板，为全国形成了可复制、可推广的好经验、好做法。

四 民意 110 的成效与创新

国家安全、社会安定是政府提供的最基本的公共安全和公共服务，群众的安全感、满意度是衡量公安工作和队伍建设的根本标准，也是民意110 的出发点和落脚点。市域层面具有较为完备的社会治理体系和解决社会治理中重大矛盾问题的资源能力，是将风险隐患化解在萌芽、解决在基层的最直接、最有效的治理层级。[①]南京作为长三角地区唯一的特大城市，城市规模和社会复杂程度较高，影响力直接辐射苏浙皖，南京公安民意110 创新运用信息化手段，汇集各类外部监督评价资源，对公安机关执法服务工作进行全方位、全过程监测，及时发现群众不满意问题症结所在，督促问题逐个解决，整改落到实处。民意 110 具有较强的可复制性，创新理念在国内深远传播，安徽、四川、黑龙江、重庆等 10 多个省市已经参照

---

① 陈一新：《新时代市域社会治理理念体系能力现代化》，《社会治理》2018 年第 8 期。

建立民意监测中心并实际运行取得成效。

（一）成效显著

公安机关作为执法机关，直面基层冲突矛盾，受到社会公众的普遍关注监督，是赢得群众认可难度最大的部门之一。党的十八届三中全会在创新社会治理体制问题上提出："坚持依法治理，加强法治保障，运用法治思维和法治方式化解社会矛盾。"① 2019 年，南京大学政府管理学院组成课题组，对南京市公安局的执法公信力进行调查研究。通过建立指标体系分析发现，自 2015 年 7 月民意 110 成立以来，南京市公安局四年执法公信力水平持续提升，一直保持在 90%～95% 的较高水平，南京市公安机关的执法行为得到了南京市民的高度认同。下面这两个实例就表明了这一点。

案例一

某日，居民报警："中学门口很多车辆违停，路堵。"交警及时到场劝离了违停车辆，次日群众评价不满意，原因是路堵问题没有根本性解决。回访平台将意见推送至责任交警大队，大队研究了解决措施，并向群众解释："该路段学校、居民区、企业集中，交通拥堵需由多部门协调逐步解决。"群众表示理解。

一个月后，校门口早晚有交警执勤，安装了抓拍监控，施画了黄色网格线、彩色斑马线，车辆通行明显畅通。群众来电致谢："他们的整改措施我很满意，我感到他们是真的用心在做事！"

案例二

陈某与丈夫赵某系外来务工人员，陈某为全职主妇，赵某贷款跑网约车。某日双方因生活琐事争吵，陈某被打受伤，报警要求追究赵某法律责任。民警对赵某批评训诫，责令其陪妻就医，随后离开。陈某在次日评价不满意，派出所随即进行整改。

民警上门与双方沟通，但丈夫拒不认错，认为老公打老婆是家务事。民警训诫告知赵某根据《治安管理处罚法》《婚姻法》《反家庭

---

① 《十八大以来重要文献选编》上，中央文献出版社，2014，第 539 页。

暴力法》，其对妻子的家暴行为已违法，被家暴人有权要求公安机关处理。经过普法，赵某对妻子诚恳道歉并承诺不再动手，该工单办理最终得到陈某的认可和赞许。

这样的事情每天都在发生。通过这种方式对每一次执法和服务行为进行实时监测，能够及时掌握民意，变被动监督为主动作为。自2015年7月运行四年多来，南京公安民意110督促整改群众不满意事项31万余件，群众不满意事项下降近40%。

在110接处警方面，接警推诿、出警迟缓问题得到根治，全市公安机关平均出警时间缩短30%；在案件办理方面，改革受立案制度，从源头解决了有案不立、立案不查等问题；在窗口服务方面，部分公安窗口态度不佳、效率低下的问题得到纠治，南京市车管所推出通道式上牌，实现了人不离车、半小时挂牌。经过四年多的警务改革实践，多项社会治理基础工作卓有成效（见图3）。

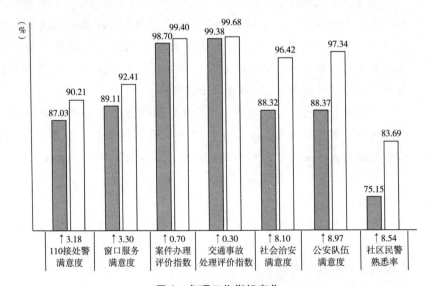

图3　各项工作指标变化

（二）创新突出

郭声琨在坚持和完善共建共治共享的社会治理制度的论述中强调，新时代的社会治理主体从政府主导转向党委领导、政府负责下的社会多元共同治理；治理方式从过去自上而下的单向管理转向多元良性互动；治理目标由过去偏重经济增长转向更加重视推动人的全面发展和社会全面进步。这有利于形成多元主体利益共享、风险共担、协同共进的社会治理局面，有效推进社会治理体系和治理能力现代化。这些论述，在宏观制度设计方面给新时期警务工作指明了方向，民意 110 的改革做法与公安机关传统的回访调查相比，具有三个明显的创新。

一是警务决策从本位主义到民意引领。紧盯影响群众安全感的突出问题，优化巡防体制，地面、空中三道防线纵深布建，刑事发案连续四年大幅下降；全面深化公安"放管服"改革，构建不见面办事模式，南京公安微警务、旗舰店实现 169 项审批服务事项 100% 网上运行。

二是执法服务从靠经验判断到让数据说话。根据群众反映问题的类型和程度，设置 4 个维度 692 个数据标签，对每一起群众诉求进行问题标注，利用智能化技术，发现群众反映强烈的共性、突出、重点问题，探索建立了集主动发现问题、受理投诉、整改反馈、研判问效为一体的智慧民意警务机制。

三是社会治理模式从管理型到服务型。经济高质量发展背景下，社会治理模式如何从管理到服务进而达致善治的转变，是我们必须面对的严峻课题。① 将群众对公安机关的评价意见落到人、见到事、算成分，并与绩效考核、表彰奖励、晋职晋升挂钩，引导全局民警始终聚焦民意、服务民生。

在坚持和完善共建共治共享的社会治理制度大背景下，南京公安将坚持聚焦人民期待的增长点，找准各方利益的结合点，更好满足人民群众多层次、差异化、个性化的需求，不断增强人民群众获得感、幸福感、安全感。民意 110 所采用的创新举措，经过四年多的实践检验不断成熟，对推进社会治理体系和治理能力现代化具有积极意义。先进做法荣获全国机关党建创新成果展示金奖、全国公安机关改革创新大赛银奖、2019 年首届中国城市治理创新奖等系列奖项。当然，由于这种探索实践在全球主要国家和城市中鲜有，在国内城市中同样属于率先开展，所以在运行过程中民意 110 也遇到了一些工作困惑，目前存在刚性监督过重、网

---

① 张康之、李传军：《公共管理是一种新型的社会治理模式》，《行政论坛》2010 年第 3 期。

络民意获取不足、辅助决策效果不明显等问题，还需要进一步的总结和完善。

五　南京公安"民意110"的规划与展望

郭声琨提出，共建的力量来自人民，共治的智慧出自人民，共享的成果为了人民。当前，智慧警务建设已成为新时代公安机关创新社会治理、实现高质量发展的必由之路，打造智能化精细化的民意警务新格局，是公安机关面临的新挑战。在信息化条件、城市化场景、智能化趋势下的探索实践中，民意110明晰了以民意大数据智慧应用为主导的新时代民意警务发展思路。

一是突出智能驱动，打造智慧感知的民意大脑。将督察、信访、12345政务热线、南京公安微警务、网络问政等各渠道民意数据及与其相关的业务、队伍数据实时全量接入平台，建成南京公安民意大数据库。对数据进行格式化、标签化、集约化处理，形成横向关联、条块融合、共享共用的大数据池，为分析研判提供必不可少的数据信息。

二是坚守民意导向，打造精确指导的民意智库。全面建设警务效能监察系统，采用语音转写、热词分析等前沿技术，基于模型和算法对民意大数据开展全要素比对、全维度挖掘。建成南京公安执法服务评价档案，自动生成各级执法服务主体的民意画像，深度解析民意数据背后多元化的群众需求，查找制约警务效能增长的梗阻和堵点，服务领导决策、警务实战和治理实践。

三是扩大社会参与，打造深层共建的民意阵地。探索创新公众参与方式，发动两代表一委员、行风作风监督员、社区干部、专家学者以及优质回访对象等群体，组建治理智囊团。借助微信公众号、二维码门牌等渠道，常态化征集、反馈社会各界的意见建议，建设一个让群众发声、共同治理的家园，真正让人民群众成为社会治理的最广参与者、最大受益者、最终评判者。

Deepening the Modernization of Social Governance at the Grassroots Level: The Exploration and Practice of Public Opinion Surveillance for Nanjing Municipal Public Security Bureau

Song Yayan and Zhang Lian

Abstract: In order to solve the problems of inaction, slow action, disorderly action, and the problems of low public participation, low recognition, poor sense of acquisition in the long-term public security law enforcement service, Nanjing Public Security Bureau has explored and established the " Public Opinion Surveillance " mechanism in which the public opinion leading police service is the core. Moreover, the " good or bad evaluation" system of law enforcement service has also been established and improved, regarding the people as individual object of every law enforcement service. The practices above are innovative methods for the public to participate in security law enforcement and social governance, fully guaranteeing the public's right to know, to participate, to express and to supervise, as well as effectively improving the capacity of the police and the credibility of law enforcement. As a result, a Nanjing Role Model of modernizing grassroots-level social governance is formed.

Keywords: Social Governance, Public Opinion Surveillance, Public Participation

大数据时代城市治理精细化的问题与对策[*]

田祚雄　胡玉桃[**]

【摘　要】大数据技术的普遍运用正在改变着人们的思维方式、工作方式
和管理方式。运用大数据技术能够助推城市治理精细化，城市治理越
精细，市民生活才越舒适，城市生活才更美好。近年来，运用大数据
推进城市治理精细化的实践取得明显成效，但仍然存在治理理念、治
理主体、治理方式、治理能力方面的不足。建议从理念升级、科学规
划、开放共享、细化标准、全民动员等方面采取措施，充分运用大数
据技术，推进城市治理精细化。

【关键词】大数据；城市治理；精细化；智能化；法治化

　　随着城市化快速推进，我国正从"乡土中国"走向"城市中国"。城
市化带来的机会让人们欣喜，但当前日益严重的"城市病"却极大地影响
和制约着人们对美好生活的向往。随着信息技术的迅猛发展，人类社会已
进入一个全新的历史阶段——大数据时代。人们的一切行为都可以数据的
形式被记录、被存储、被处理，人不仅是一切社会关系的总和，更是一切
数据足迹的总和。人们在数字空间的痕迹，不仅创造着新的商业机会和财
富，也对城市治理的精细化、智能化和预见性提出了新的挑战。在大数据
时代，"数据就是流通的货币"，谁拥有数据资源，谁就拥有未来。其实，
拥有数据不是目的，如何运用大数据理念与技术提高城市治理精细化水

────────────

　　＊　基金项目：武汉市社科基金 2018 年度后期资助项目。

　＊＊　田祚雄，武汉市政协委员、武汉市社会科学院政法所所长、副研究员；胡玉桃，武汉市
　　　社会科学院政法所助理研究员，博士。

平，如何用拥有的大数据解决我们所面临的问题、更好地为社会治理和人的全面发展服务，才是摆在我们面前的时代课题。

一 大数据技术在城市治理中的功用

"大数据开启了一次重大的时代转型……就像望远镜能够让我们感受宇宙、显微镜能够让我们观测微生物，这种能够收集和分析海量数据的新技术将帮助我们更好地理解世界。"① 那么，究竟何为大数据（Big Data）？最早提出大数据时代到来的麦肯锡公司认为，大数据是指大小超出了传统数据库软件工具的抓取、存储、管理和分析能力的数据群。高德纳咨询公司的报告则认为，大数据是需要新处理模式才能具有更强的决策力、洞察力和流程优化能力的海量、高增长率和多样化的信息资产。显然，前者更强调数据量的巨大，后者更强调巨大数据的内蕴价值。大数据技术则是基于云计算的数据处理与应用模式，通过对数量巨大、结构复杂、类型众多数据的整合共享、交叉复用形成智力资源和知识服务能力的技术。大数据技术的战略意义在于对海量的数据进行专业化处理，从中发掘出真正的价值。

大数据技术对于城市治理而言，我们以为有四重功用。

（一）赋予人们更强大的认识和治理城市的能力

大数据的最大特点就是"4V"：大量（volume），数据体量巨大，从TB级别跃升到PB级别；高速（velocity），处理速度快，一般要在秒级时间范围内给出分析结果，时间太长就失去价值；多样（variety），数据类型繁多，如网络日志、视频、图片、地理位置信息等；价值（value），价值密度低，以视频为例，连续不间断监控过程中，可能有用的数据仅仅有一两秒，但这一两秒的价值却往往非常关键而巨大。随着物联网、云计算、移动互联网、车联网、手机、平板电脑、PC以及各种各样传感器的普及，人人都是数据制造者和使用者，城市处处都是数据源。通过应用云计算等数据处理技术，对数量巨大、来源分散、格式多样的城市数据进行全时空

---

① 〔英〕维克托·迈尔-舍恩伯格、肯尼思·库克耶：《大数据时代》，盛杨燕、周涛译，浙江人民出版社，2013，第9页。

的采集、存储和分析，能够发现城市海量数据背后隐藏的真正有价值的信息，能够更精准、更直观发现城市运行中存在的供需变化与矛盾、问题及成因，从而为加强城市应对和治理提供可优选方案。

（二）赋予城市治理一种新的思维方式

"一切事物，如果不能量化它，你就不能真正理解它；不能真正理解它，你就不能真正控制它；不能真正控制它，你就不能真正改变它。"[①] 现代城市治理异常复杂，凭经验、拍脑袋决策显然已经过时，循数决策、数驱管理成为必然选择。在大数据时代，万物可数、万物互联，数据成为重要的战略资源，数据不仅成了生产力，更成为一种核心竞争力。城市的人、组织、设施、产业、环境等交互作用，生成一个个立体的大数据生态系统。城市治理主体要转变治理思维模式，在思想意识、思维方式、组织结构、工作流程等方面经历全面的蜕变，善于从这些大数据生态系统中发现真问题、真对策和真规律。大数据必将助推传统公共管理实现转型：从粗放化管理向精细化管理转型，从单兵作战型管理向协作共享型管理转型，从柜台式限时性管理向自助式全天候管理转型，从被动响应型管理向主动预见型管理转型，从纸质文书型管理向电子政务型管理转型，从廉政风险隐蔽型管理向风险防范型管理转型。[②] 技术进步倒逼管理方式转型，根本上是倒逼管理思维方式发生变革。

（三）成为城市治理现代化的重要基础设施

城市治理所需大数据从何而来？当然依赖于信息基础设施建设。其实，前大数据时代，城市运转无时无刻不在产生海量数据，只是因为见识与技术限制，人们无法感知和利用而已。随着现代信息技术的发展，云计算、泛在网络、数据中心、各种智能终端和数据传感器等成为城市治理的信息基础设施，为城市运行数据的采集、存储、传输、分析等提供了承载平台与空间，为城市大数据开发利用奠定了基石。同时，这些基础设施的建设、使用和维护，既能产生大量的就业岗位，又能开拓广阔的产品市场，成为城市经济发展的新增长点。如金融机构、通信公司、跨国企业等

---

① 徐继华：《智慧政府：大数据治国时代的来临》，中信出版社，2014，第 XXXII 页。
② 徐继华：《智慧政府：大数据治国时代的来临》，中信出版社，2014，第 23~25 页。

建立的商业数据备份中心，大型博物馆、档案馆、科研机构等建立的电子化文档数据库，以及大型互联网企业、国家级网络安全基地等，都将为城市就业、发展和治理提供更多机遇。

（四）催生一批新的基础性管理制度

城市大数据资源是宝贵的、敏感的重要战略性资源，其开发、存储、利用等必须有章可循。2012年，《国务院关于大力推进信息化发展和切实保障信息安全的若干意见》中就提出，要建立全面覆盖的社会管理综合信息系统，建设公众诉求信息管理平台，健全网上舆论动态引导管理机制，推动城市管理信息共享，引导智慧城市建设健康发展。2018年6月，国务院办公厅关于印发《进一步深化"互联网+政务服务"推进政务服务"一网、一门、一次"改革实施方案的通知》，要求进一步推进"互联网+政务服务"，加快构建全国一体化网上政务服务体系，推进跨层级、跨地域、跨系统、跨部门、跨业务的协同管理和服务，推动企业和群众办事线上"一网通办"（一网），线下"只进一扇门"（一门），现场办理"最多跑一次"（一次），让企业和群众到政府办事像"网购"一样方便。我国也正在推进集合金融、工商登记、税收缴纳、社保缴费、交通违章、不动产登记等信用信息的统一平台，建立以公民身份证号码、组织机构代码为基础的社会信用制度。同时，人们对网络安全、个人信息保护、数据安全等立法越来越重视、呼声越来越高。这些法制规范的出台和落实必将对政府、社会和市民的生产生活方式产生深远影响。

二　运用大数据推进精细化治理存在的问题及原因分析

近年来，各地在运用大数据推进城市精细化治理方面取得了明显成效，但大数据建设运用和精细化治理程度等仍然存在不少问题，影响了居民生活的便利性、舒适度和幸福感。

（一）大数据时代城市治理精细化存在的突出问题

1. 治理理念：大数据意识与人性化理念不足

无论是政府部门还是社会公众，其大数据意识都还不足以适应大数据时代的治理需要，口号式重视多、实践运用少，公共服务供给侧数据披露少，市民需求侧数据掌握少。有些部门对大数据在城市治理中的价值缺乏足够的认识和重视，循数决策、数驱治理的思维方式和行为方式还未真正实现，对公共数据尚未做到主动掌握、及时更新、依法开放共享和充分有效利用，影响了大数据技术在推进城市治理精细化中的价值实现。城市是人的聚落，无论是治理的信息化还是精细化，最终都要服务于人的需要。"故城市规划建设管理应一切为了人、为了一切人。但纵观一些城市的规划、建设和管理，尚有许多不人本化、不人文化、不人性化的地方，既影响了人们城市生活的质量，也影响了人们对所生活城市的认同感、归属感及主动参与建设管理的积极性。"① 城市治理应始终秉持以人为本的理念，关注公众的切身需求和细节感受。当前我们城市在治理理念上，普遍存在"五重"倾向，即重车辆多于行人，重漂亮多于舒适，重"形态"多于生态，重更新多于传承，重罚款多于服务。② 细节决定成败，态度决定细节，理念决定态度。没有科学现代的治理理念支撑，没有对市民多元需求的精准把握，不可能有精细化、人性化的现代城市治理。

2. 治理主体：多元治理主体的回应性与协同性不够

一是运用大数据对市民需求回应不足。城市治理关系到居民的切身利益和居住生活体验，回应居民需求是治理精细化的目标。回应公民的正当要求是政府的责任。一个负责任的政府，不仅要在公民提出直接诉求时被动作为，更要在公民没有直接诉求时主动作为，创造性地履行其对公民所承担和许诺的各种责任。③ 然而目前政府在城市治理中主动作为仍显欠缺，被动回应的及时性、针对性、有效性也还不够。未能做到充分运用大数据技术精准发现基层问题，对群众诉求进行收集整理和分析研判，并利用大数据将治理手段与资源有效衔接，精准解决城市治理问题。二是治理主体内部及各主体之间协同治理不足。城市治理具有复杂性、综合性和利益关联性等特点，涉及多个区域、政府多个部门的职能权限。大数据时代的精细化治理要求各部门、各环节、各个工作单元之间，能良好地衔接配合、

---

① 田祚雄：《以人为本建设更加人性化的城市》，《武汉建设》2013 年第 2 期。
② 田祚雄：《以人民为中心建设怡人宜居城市》，中国社会科学网，http://www.cssn.cn/zhcspd/zhcspd_yc/201902/t20190218_4827167.shtml，最后访问日期：2020 年 7 月 1 日。
③ 黄卫平、汪成主编《当代中国政治研究报告》，社会科学文献出版社，2004，第 16~19 页。

协同动作，从而提高系统的总体效能。① 但目前城市治理存在部门协同不足和政府与企业、公众之间协同不足的双重矛盾。如河湖水体污染治理，其跨区域、跨部门、跨层级的信息共享和业务协同机制尚不完善；如信访领域中的"三跨三分离"案件，往往存在信访数据共享不够、口径不一、相互矛盾等情况。当前，部门条块分割依然存在，部门间协同水平较低，部分单位出于保密、安全性、权限等原因设置障碍。数据开放标准不统一、数据共享责任主体不够明晰，"数据孤岛"仍然存在。政府、市场、社会组织和公众对数据共享的程度不高，信息不对称，互动不足，利用大数据推进治理精细化的合作机制不健全。

3. 治理方式：数据开放共享与利用的规范性和有效性不足

社会的现代化离不开社会生活的规范化、程序化和合理化。精细化治理要求细致梳理各类治理主体之间的职责权利，建立精细的标准和科学的流程，将精细化落实到城市规划建设管理的全过程。运用大数据技术推进城市治理精细化，同样也要求建立健全大数据相关的法规制度和标准规范体系，但目前在数据采集、存储、开放、共享和利用等数据生命周期各环节中规范性不足的问题仍然突出，仍普遍存在标准化意识缺乏、某些领域标准空白或缺乏科学化与合理性、各个标准体系之间不相协调、标准体系执行力度不够等问题。② 一是数据平台建设运营与服务不够，数据平台建设缺乏统筹规划和顶层设计，数据之间未实现市域联网和行业内联网。城市数字化管理中心在受理案件来源方面还未实现一网受理，同一平台上也没实现并案受理。数据平台缺乏便捷、及时、有效的互动，不利于用户有效获取数据。二是数据质量精准性不够，没有数据、扭曲数据、残缺数据（数据不连续、不全面、重经轻社等）、矛盾数据、私有化数据、神秘化数据等现象还较普遍，数据采集、数据开放、安全保密等关键标准的制定和实施还需要进一步推进。城市管理基础数据的准确性和更新频率不够，尚未建立完备的城市基础数据库，"城市大脑"还存在"脑中无数"问题。三是数据开放与共享不够，部门从自身利益出发"不愿共享"，客观上数据标准不统一导致"不能共享"，担忧数据安全问题导致"不敢共享"等

---

① 陈晨：《城市治理精细化转型路径分析》，《中共珠海市委党校 珠海市行政学院学报》2015 年第 1 期。

② 俞可平：《标准化是治理现代化的基石》，《人民论坛》2015 年第 31 期。

问题普遍存在，数据公开和共享程度低。

4. 治理能力：运用大数据推进精细化治理的能力不足

大数据应用能揭示传统技术方式难以展现的关联关系。大数据的价值挖掘功能能够对数据进行有效的存储加工，提高数据价值密度，降低城市精细化治理成本；高效智能功能帮助处理海量数据，提升精细化治理效率；精准分析功能帮助政府提供因地、因时、因人制宜的城市服务，提升人性化治理水平和效度；模拟预测功能察觉城市运行规律，模拟未来场景，进行风险预测，提升科学决策水平；网络互动功能提供多元参与、优势互补、积极回应、相互监督的环境，将各方主体纳入大数据治理体系，推进城市治理向精细化转型。① 精细化治理必然要求数据化、信息化、开放化，通过建立平台和技术手段开展数据采集、挖掘分析和运用，充分发挥大数据在智慧城市建设中的作用。目前不少城市对大数据治理运用还处于起步阶段，数据多用于查询统计和简单分析、深度分析、趋势研究、预测预警、决策参考和个性化智能服务功能发挥不够。如媒体屡屡报道的"最赚钱电子眼"②"最牛违章车"③ 等，恰恰说明对运用大数据解决问题、提高治理能力还非常欠缺与滞后。大数据治理涉及数据采集、比对关联、挖掘分析等复杂的过程，而目前掌握数据获取、挖掘、使用等方面技术的专业人才严重短缺，熟悉相关业务工作和大数据技术的复合型人才更是匮乏。同时，如何在利用大数据技术推动创新发展的同时，保障数据安全、保护个人信息，也是大数据时代对政府治理能力的考验。

---

① 熊竞：《大数据时代的理念创新与城市精细化管理》，《上海城市管理》2014 年第 4 期。
② 《武汉 "最挣钱的违章电子眼" 位置你知道在哪里吗!!》，搜狐网，https://www.sohu.com/a/169614332_806566，最后访问日期：2020 年 7 月 1 日；《桂林年度 "最赚钱" 电子眼曝光！这些路段稍不留神就挨了!》，看点快报，https://kuaibao.qq.com/s/20190124A1DD4Z00? refer=spider，最后访问日期：2020 年 7 月 1 日；《"最赚钱" 的电子眼，一个摄像头年入 2500 万，被罚车主超过 12 万!》，新浪看点，http://k.sina.com.cn/article_7241721717_1afa3e77500100m95q.html? from=news，最后访问日期：2020 年 7 月 1 日。
③ 刘毅等：《教练车 3 个月违章 80 条扣 260 分 原是老犯同样错误》，《楚天都市报》2018 年 3 月 29 日；叶文波：《武汉这辆车让交警惊呆 违章 487 次罚款比车都贵》，《楚天都市报》2017 年 2 月 20 日；《中国最牛十大违章车辆，最高被扣 4251 分，300 本驾照都不够扣》，搜狐新闻，https://www.sohu.com/a/215766177_475262，最后访问日期：2020 年 7 月 1 日。

（二）大数据时代城市治理精细化存在问题的原因分析

1. 精细化治理文化和大数据公共治理价值观缺失

大数据精细化治理是一种应对现代复杂社会的治理模式，同时也是一种态度、理念、文化和思维与工作方式。我国缺乏"数目字管理"的传统，对精细化治理的需求不是很高，粗放式治理的行政文化传统长期延续，使得城市精细化治理先天发育不足。[①] 城市治理的实践仍然受到传统粗放式管理思维的影响，强调政府强制管理而非人性化治理，重结果轻过程，忽视标准、流程、规则、细节，缺乏精益求精的理念。各方治理主体对于什么是精细化治理、如何实现精细化治理、自身如何参与精细化治理等认识不明。[②] 大数据公共治理价值观的基本要义是包容、自由、开放、分享，挖掘科技应用潜能，促进决策思维模式转变，倡导评估管理模式转型，提升公共治理科学化、民主化、法治化、现代化的深度和广度，使公共治理呈现更有效率、更加开放、更负责任的状态。[③] 大数据技术能不能有效运用于公共治理实践，有赖于大数据公共治理价值观的指导，而目前这种新的治理价值观尚未广泛树立。

2. 大数据推进精细化治理的法规政策支撑力度不足

科学立法是改进城市管理工作的必要手段和重要前提。但现行城管存在非常明显的执法依据不足和执法手段不足等"先天不足"[④]，城市管理综合执法领域的立法工作远远滞后于实践需要。数据法律问题关系到数据主体自身的利益和数据开发者、数据交易者的利益，会影响数据产业的生存和发展。法律对数据的保护需要通过制定一系列制度来实现，涉及数据主体、数据权属、法律责任等内容。[⑤] 目前我国相关法律规范对数据相关的法律关系予以调控，规范了数据采集、开放、共享及使用等行为，促进了数据产业发展，《个人信息保护法（草案）》和《数据安全法（草案）》

---

① 唐皇凤：《我国城市治理精细化的困境与迷思》，《探索与争鸣》2017 年第 9 期。
② 毕娟、顾清：《论城市精细化管理的制度体系》，《行政管理改革》2018 年第 6 期。
③ 许欢、孟庆国：《大数据公共治理价值观：基于国家和行政层面的分析》，《南京社会科学》2017 年第 1 期。
④ 莫于川：《从城市管理走向城市治理：完善城管综合执法体制的路径选择》，《哈尔滨工业大学学报》（社会科学版）2013 年第 6 期。
⑤ 李爱君主编《中国大数据法治发展报告（2018）》，法律出版社，2019，第 12 页。

已提交全国人大常委会审议，并向社会公开征求意见。但关于基础数据建设、数据公开共享、数据权限归属、隐私保护等方面的法律法规还不完善，相关法规制度建设仍然存在系统性、协调性、可操作性不强等问题。

3. 大数据推进精细化治理的体制机制不够健全完善

我国城市政府仍然存在结构科层化和功能科层化的分离，这是精细化治理水平难以提升的结构性约束。法理性权威缺位与非人格化程序缺失，官僚体制内部条块矛盾、机构重叠与职能交错等体制性缺陷，大大限制了行政组织的治理能力。城市基层社会"强行政弱治理"的格局，导致"行政有效、治理无效"，基层社会自组织能力和自主治理能力日益衰败，最终将损害精细化治理的社会基础和绩效。① 当前对以大数据技术推进城市精细化治理缺乏统筹规划的顶层设计，各方协调联动机制、精细化治理的标准化框架体系、治理绩效评估指标体系等尚不健全。基层城市管理执法工作面临身份模糊、编制限制、晋升狭窄等问题，影响执法效能，进而影响精细化治理落到实处。对城市管理的有效投入力度不足，影响城市大数据系统建设和精细化治理的运行维护水平。政府数据开放共享体制机制还存在严重的条块分割、部门利益标准各异等人为障碍，政府与企业、社会良性循环的数据开放共享生态系统还未形成。这都对数据的准确采集、充分流通和有效利用造成阻碍，影响大数据技术促进城市治理精细化作用的发挥。

4. 大数据推进精细化治理尚未形成有效的治理合力

政府、市场主体和公众之间缺乏有效的信息共享、需求传递和服务供给机制，各治理主体之间尚未形成数据开放共享与创新利用的良性循环生态系统。政府没有摆脱全能型政府"行政管控"的窠臼，仍然偏好"自上而下"的管理逻辑，实践中暗藏着"维稳"的隐形目标与"管控"的行为逻辑，忽视"以人为本"的人文关怀，未能将"精细化管理"更好地转变为"精细化服务"。② 在城市治理实践中，政府对企业和社会公众发挥治理作用的重视不够，在大数据平台系统建设和应用开发等方面合作缺乏；对企业大数据应用中的内控制度建设、个人信息和商业秘密保护监管还需

---

① 唐皇凤：《我国城市治理精细化的困境与迷思》，《探索与争鸣》2017年第9期。
② 吴晓燕、关庆华：《从管理到治理：基层社会网格化管理的挑战与变革》，《理论探讨》2016年第2期。

进一步法治化和规范化；对公众获取数据的需求重视不够，也未能充分利用大数据及时发现和解决问题。行业协会等社会组织发育迟缓，自治作用发挥不够，社会组织和公众的公民意识、公共责任较缺乏，习惯于依赖政府，其参与城市治理的方式不多、程度不深、能力不强、积极性不够，未能形成精细化治理多元主体良性互动、协同共治的治理状态。

三　大数据时代推进城市治理精细化的对策建议

国内外先进城市都非常重视通过大数据、云计算、物联化、互联化、智能化等手段，让城市治理变得越来越智慧、越来越智能。如日本于2001年开始分三期启动实施 e-Japan、u-Japan、i-Japan 战略①，从"以人为本"出发，着眼于应用数字化技术，打造普遍为国民接受的数字化社会，典型案例是东京智慧城市建设。新加坡2006年推出为期十年的资讯通信产业发展蓝图——"智慧国2015"（iN2015）计划，力图通过物联网等信息技术，采取完全法治化治理方式，② 把新加坡打造成一个由资讯通信驱动的智慧国家与全球都市，并努力在一些公共服务领域实现从供给方主导向供给方与需求方双向互动的转变，实现从非连续、碎片化的服务向连续性、一体化的服务转变。国内如北京以法治为保障，以精治为手段，以共治为基础，积极推进城市治理精细化，③ 通过强化规划引领、注重规范指导、推进网格化管理、借力科技手段等，综合运用云计算、大数据、物联网等技术，建立智慧城市管理体系。上海出台《关于加强城市管理精细化工作的实施意见》并制定三年行动计划（2018~2020年），提出"一心三全四化"城市治理精细化路径，着力推进"美丽街区、美丽家园、美丽

---

① e-Japan 战略，目标是5年内建成世界最先进的 IT 国家；u-Japan 战略，目标是2010年建成随时随地任何人任何物可连接的泛在网络社会；i-Japan 战略，目标是2015年实现安心且充满活力的数字化社会。

② 张诗雨：《发达国家的城市治理范式——国外城市治理经验研究之三》，《中国发展观察》2015年第4期。

③ 参见刘洋《在精治、共治与法治上下功夫》，中国社会科学网，http://ex.cssn.cn/ddzg/ddzg_ldjs/ddzg_sh/201711/t20171127_3755126.shtml，最后访问日期：2020年7月1日；欧阳晓娟《北京如何推动城市管理向法治精治共治迈进》，千龙网，https://baijiahao.baidu.com/s?id=1590996306136478506&wfr=spider&for=pc，最后访问日期：2020年7月1日；张贵祥、德国洁《街巷长制让北京城市治理走向精细化》，《首都治理》2018年第7期；等等。

乡村"建设。①

综观国内外城市以大数据技术助推精细化治理的做法及经验，有"六抓"值得充分借鉴。一抓理念。大数据背景下的城市精细化治理，必须始终坚持以人为本理念，以市民需求为导向，高度重视市民参与以及与市民互动，充分尊重人情、人心和人性。二抓法治。法治是大数据背景下城市治理精细化的重要手段和有效保障。注重建立健全城市治理法律法规制度体系，充分发挥法治对城市规划、建设、管理和服务的引领、规范、保障作用，通过法治来推进和体现城市治理规范化、标准化、精细化。三抓机制。科学合理的体制安排是大数据背景下城市精细化治理的重要依托。注重全面理顺纵向不同层级、横向不同政府部门的职能及事权财权，打破行政壁垒，弱化利益部门化倾向，建立跨界整体性治理新机制。四抓信息。信息资源是大数据背景下城市精细化治理的重要支撑。注重建设"城市大脑"，实现数据互联互通、有机整合和共享，全面提高城市治理的智能化、智慧化水平。五抓标准。标准化是大数据技术推进城市精细化治理的有效手段，注重建立健全城市治理标准体系，逐步实现城市治理标准的全覆盖、精细化、可测量、高水平，用精细标准推动精细治理。六抓文化。精细文化是城市精细化治理的根本。注重培育、厚植城市治理精细化文化，让精细文化入脑入心，让精致生活成为时尚追求。

城市是一个生命有机体，习近平总书记强调："城市管理应该像绣花一样精细"，"要强化智能化管理，提高城市管理标准，更多运用互联网、大数据等信息技术手段，推进城市治理制度创新、模式创新，提高城市科学化、精细化、智能化管理水平"。② 运用大数据技术推进城市治理精细化是市民享受美好城市生活的内在追求，也是推进城市治理体系和治理能力现代化建设的必然要求。

（一）进一步提升认识、升级理念

理念支配行动，理念差之毫厘，实践谬以千里。大数据时代持续推进

---

① "一核"，即城市治理的核心是人；"三全"，即全覆盖、全过程、全天候，要求把精细化管理覆盖到各个空间、各个领域和所有人群，贯穿到城市规划、建设、管理的全过程，体现一天 24 小时的每时每刻；"四化"，即法治化、社会化、智能化、标准化。

② 《习总书记两会时刻——城市管理应该像绣花一样精细》，新华网，http://china.cnr.cn/gdgg/20170305/t20170305_523637522.shtml，最后访问日期：2020 年 7 月 23 日。

城市治理精细化，必须树立科学先进的理念。一是充分认识城市治理在国家治理中的重要地位。截止到 2018 年底，我国 59.58% 的人口生活于城市，80% 的 GDP、95% 的创新成果、85% 的税收和财富由城市贡献。"城市发展带动了整个经济社会发展，城市建设成为现代化建设的重要引擎。城市是我国经济、政治、文化、社会等方面活动的中心，在党和国家工作全局中具有举足轻重的地位。"[①] 城市的繁荣直接决定着国家的发展，城市治理已经成为国家治理的主要场所。因此，各级党委政府应比以往任何时候都要更加重视城市治理工作，切实将其摆上重要议事日程和工作日程。二是城市治理必须始终坚持"以人民为中心"的思想。习近平总书记指出："城市的核心是人，关键是十二个字：衣食住行、生老病死、安居乐业。城市工作做得好不好，老百姓满意不满意，生活方便不方便，城市管理和服务状况是重要评判标准。"[②] 大数据运用于城市治理精细化，最终都要服务于人满足于人，以人的获得感、幸福感、安全感为前提和归宿。所以，走向以人民为中心的城市治理是我们一切城市工作的根本出发点和落脚点。三是城市治理必须坚持智能化和精细化。时代已发展到网络化、信息化、智能化时代，为大数据技术的诞生和广泛运用提供了契机和空间。城市治理必须完整准确地理解大数据的功用，切忌口号式、标签式使用"大数据""精细化"，必须"真学真懂真信真用"。要精准理解科学理念的含义及其相互关系。比如，城市治理精细化自然离不开大数据的支撑，但用了大数据并不意味着就一定可以推进精细化；智慧化管理不一定能保证精细化管理，但精细化管理一定需要智能化手段运用。无论是推进精细化还是智能化，都需要一定的经济基础和文化基础条件，如果对大数据精细化治理的认识不科学不统一，盲目大量投入智能化设施建设，必将造成极大浪费。

（二）进一步科学规划、增加投入

城市规划是城市建设、管理和发展的蓝本与依凭。精细化管理首先要考虑的就是规划。好的规划当然有助于城市治理水平提升，不当规划势必

---

① 《中央城市工作会议在北京举行》，新华网，http：//www.xinhuanet.com/politics/2015-12/22/c_1117545528.htm，最后访问日期：2020 年 7 月 23 日。

② 习近平：《城市政府应该从"划桨人"转变为"掌舵人"》，人民网，http：//cpc.people.com.cn/xuexi/n1/2018/0209/c385476-29814517.html，最后访问日期：2020 年 7 月 23 日。

会给城市治理带来诸多掣肘和桎梏，低端规划必将整体拉低城市档次、影响城市治理精细化程度与实效。城市规划应力避科学性、前瞻性、特异性、约束性、稳定性和公众参与性"六不够"弊端，力求规划的科学化、精当化。一是尽力提高规划的科学性。规划从来就不是单纯的技术手段，而是带有强烈的价值取向，深受城市文化、历史、政治、经济、自然环境等因素的制约。"新加坡规划之父"刘太格非常强调"城市功能"和"基本需求"的重要性，认为规划者应有人文学者的心、科学家的脑和艺术家的眼。① 城市规划必须处理好共性与个性、传承与前瞻、建设与管理、价值与技术、理念与细节、专家与公众、自然生态与社会生态等相互关系，使城市规划兼具科学性、特色化、操作性和高认同度。二是强化规划的严肃性。要切实维护规划的法律效力，防止公权力对法定规划的不当干涉、肆意扭曲和恶意弃置。规划的变动不居造成了诸多社会矛盾，规划部门应主动带头维护规划方案，防止被攻关、被围猎、被俘获而随意调整规划。三是加强法治、投入等专项规划建设。无论是大数据基础设施建设、数据采集挖掘分析和动态更新，还是精细化治理的深入推进，都离不开政策规划、法治规则和投入规划的支撑。应进一步强化"城市大脑"规划建设，避免各自为政、各自为战的大数据平台重复建设，既造成极大浪费又增加兼容交互障碍；应进一步提高城市治理的法治化水平，努力实现技术力量与行政管理的有效衔接，特别是对大数据的数据质量、数据安全、数据独裁、数据产业等如何规制，急需从法规政策上进行明确界定。

（三）进一步打破壁垒、开放共享

一般实体物品是"物以稀为贵"，故物品的拥有者往往不愿意与人共享；而大数据时代，根据麦特卡尔夫定律，数据遵循"物以多为贵"法则，越共享越能实现其价值最大化。故信息（数据）资源的拥有者采取破壁开放的态度才是最理性的选择。但实践中，因为思想认识、权限范围、利益观念、标准体系等存在多种差异，不少部门仍不太愿意开放共享数据资源，多重投入、多套系统、多个平台彼此隔离形成诸多信息孤岛，极不经济，效益低下。一要切实解放思想，保持开放心态。要让人们更加充分

---

① 刘太格：《把城市功能做好，想不国际化都很难》，和讯新闻，http://news.hexun.com/2018-10-30/195038593.html，最后访问日期：2020年7月1日。

认识到大数据时代的特点，因势利导、与时俱进，主动以理性开放态度拥抱新时代，切忌自我封闭、画地为牢。二要加强制度建设，推动数据共享。真正打破部门垄断，遵循公开为常态、不公开为例外原则，严格落实政务信息公开制度。要加强部门协作与信息平台对接和兼容，切实让非涉密数据流动起来，努力让数据价值得到最大化体现，智慧政务服务得到最大化实现，从而节省大量社会运行综合成本。三要加强大数据统筹管理机构建设力度。随着人们对大数据时代认识的提升，广东、浙江、贵州等省率先设立大数据管理专门机构，广州、成都、沈阳、兰州等城市的大数据管理机构挂牌运行。新一轮党政机构改革方案显示，不少省市也新成立了大数据管理局，但机构运行成效如何尚待观察。应进一步增加大数据管理局统筹协调、标准衔接、分析发布、督导考核等相关功能，解决没有数据、数据不准、数据打架、数据隔离等问题，提高大数据使用的可靠性。

（四）进一步精细标准、心中有"数"

城市精细化管理其实是科学管理，是基于精密、细致的研究和测量来实施的管理。我国城市精细化管理才刚刚起步，当前以大数据技术推进我国城市治理精细化需从以下几方面着手。一要更加重视标准化建设。精细化离不开标准化，必须用标准化来衡量治理精细化的程度。要着力解决城市治理标准化缺失、标准化水平不高、标准化执行缺位、标准化考核薄弱等问题。标准化设置应紧紧围绕"安全、整洁、生态、舒适、美好"等关键价值和优序权重，全方位、全覆盖"衣食住行、生老病死、安居乐业"等各个领域。要包含城市所有的公共空间和设施设备，从颜色、规格、位置、时序、功能等城市硬件，到管理主体素质、执法规范、考核办法等城市软件，都要进行细化、量化，确保标准科学清晰，可测量、可考核。二要扎实建好城市治理基础数据库。人工智能的关键在于云计算、大数据和算法三大因素，其中云计算是前提，大数据是燃料和基础，算法是灵魂。快速发展的人工智能都是靠大数据驱动的，可以说"无数据不智能"。要管好城市，必须对城市的"家底"一清二楚，心中无"数"、数据匮乏恰是我们目前的短板。建好城市治理基础数据库，从地上的各种设施部件，到地下的各种管网线路，从街商户地址、经营类型、人员信息等，到道路桥梁、建筑场馆、山水资源等，所有城市设施设备及资源的数量、位置形成"一本账"，才可能建立快速发现、快速反应、快速处置的动态治理机制。三要切实加强大数据开发利用。数据无时无刻不在产生，关键在是否被注意、是否及时采集；数据价值内蕴于海量数据中，关键在是否被及时开发、被合理利用。大数据技术说到底是个工具，只有合理利用才能够实现其价值。因此，要力避赶时髦、口号式使用大数据概念，培养大数据开发使用人才，让大数据技术在城市治理中真正"用"起来，让数据思维、循数决策、数驱治理成为常态。

（五）进一步强化宣教、全民参与

"人民城市人民建，建好城市为人民。"生活于城市中的每个人，都既是城市治理的主体，又是城市治理的客体。一要强化宣传教育，增强市民的主人翁意识。市民只有把自己当成城市的主人，才可能对生活的城市倍加爱护和珍惜。人人都是数据的生产者也是使用者，唯有人人合理使用数据、参与城市精细化治理，城市治理水平才可能真正得到提高。要从市民最关注、最易突破、涉及面最广泛的问题入手，通过举办各种市民喜闻乐见的活动，增强市民对所生活城市的认同感、荣誉感和自豪感，努力实现从"要我参与"到"我要参与"的转变，不断提高市民城市生活的安全感、获得感和幸福感。二要着力弘扬工匠精神和精细文化。城市治理应弘扬追求卓越的创造精神、精益求精的品质精神、用户至上的服务精神等工匠精神和一丝不苟、追求极致的精细文化，自觉摒弃"马虎相、凑合用，差不多、将就过"等粗陋文化。比如，城市空间保持干净、平整、安全、有序，这些基本要求为什么难以达到，既有法规制度为何总是执行不到位，貌似是我们的标准低、考核软，实则是我们精细文化缺乏，满足于勉强过得去，不求过得硬。三要迅疾开展一场"全民除弊"大清查行动。号召城市居民对身边的不精细、不科学、不人性化的地方进行搜集、反馈，供各职能部门汇总、研判，发现大数据背后的规律，并限期整改问题。所谓城市管理应像绣花一样，要的就是精细的追求、精益求精的态度。如果人人参与、个个出力，如果时时、处处精细，城市自然就精细化了。

当然，大数据技术也是柄双刃剑，关键看人如何使用技术。过度依赖数据（无数据便不会管理）、过度利用数据进行监管（危害公民基本权利）、个人信息保护不力、信息保密安全薄弱、非法利用数据技术等，也是大数据时代推进城市精细化治理中非常值得警醒的问题。

Problems and Solutions for the Refinement of Urban Governance in the Era of Big Data

Tian Zuoxiong and Hu Yutao

Abstract: The widespread use of big data technology is changing the way people think, work and manage. The application of big data technology could promote the refinement of urban governance and therefore we will live a better life . In recent years, there have been remarkable achievements in using big data to refine the urban governance. However, there are still deficiencies in the governance concept, governance subject, governance mode and governance capacity. We suggest that measures be taken to promote the refinement of urban governance from five aspects, that are the upgrading of concepts, the scientific planning, openness and sharing, the refinement of standards and the mobilization of the whole people.

Keyword: Big Data; Urban Governance; Refine; Intelligentize; Rule by Law

城市3.0：AI+时代城市治理的价值维度和实现机理

吕玉雪*

【摘　要】随着 AI+时代的到来与 web 3.0、生命 3.0 的渐进，作为复杂有机体的巨系统——城市也必将随之进入更高阶的阶段：城市 3.0。城市作为一个"生命有机体"，与人工智能技术具有多重耦合性，智能智慧、以人为本、宜居善治将是 3.0 版本城市的核心内容。在新技术的发展推动下城市治理有望突破传统治理模式的困境，实现面向未来、面向人本、面向可持续的价值趋向，并进一步革新城市治理的思路、升级城市治理手段、细化城市治理领域、优化城市治理决策，推动城市治理能力和体系的进一步现代化。

【关键词】城市治理；人工智能；城市 3.0；系统论；生命体论

一　引言

城市治理的每一次推陈出新几乎都与科学技术的发展紧密相关，在马克思看来，科学是一种在历史上起推动作用的、革命的力量，科技的每一次跃进都会深刻改变社会格局。信息环境和数据基础的变化不光为人工智能的发展突破奠定了基础，更是助推了经济全球化和政治多极化的进程，

---

* 吕玉雪，青岛大学政治与公共管理学院硕士研究生。

民族国家作为经济和政治单元的地位开始下降，城市及其治理的作用与影响日益凸显。出于历史原因而错过第一次、第二次工业革命发展良机的我国城市治理，长期困囿于陈旧的治理理念与模式中，虽经历了第三次工业革命的洗礼，但各种"城市病"层出不穷，参与全球城市治理之路仍任重而道远。伴随着人工智能的热议，第四次工业革命正在悄然而至，有别于先前单一学科发展对城市治理的推动，人工智能技术从全方位、多领域革新了城市治理的理念、模式、手段、产业运作方式和市民生活习惯，成为城市治理创新、治理现代化的重大历史机遇。2017 年，国务院发布《新一代人工智能发展规划》，提出以人工智能"推进城市规划、建设、管理、运营全生命周期智能化"的要求①，正式将以深度学习和机器学习为代表的人工智能纳入我国城市治理领域。在 AI+时代背景下，城市治理必将迎来多重创新发展，实现从"总体—支配型"到"制度—技术型"再到"系统—协同型"的转变，达到"善治"乃至"善智"。因应人工智能时代的发展，了解人工智能对城市发展带来的改变，实现城市治理模式创新、治理能力现代化具有重要的理论和实践意义。

二 城市 3.0：概念与内涵

时代的变迁与科技的变革会引发城市的革新，并催生新的城市结构与相对应的治理模式。城市作为一个具有主体性、自组织性的有机体，其治理模式与本土化技术的互动必然会促使其进行版本的升级。

（一）理论支点

从系统论的角度来看，城市是一个物理存在、开放复杂、快速进化、自然系统与人工系统相覆合的巨系统，是由多种类、多量级的子系统聚合而成的复杂有机体（如图 1）。这个有机体高度聚集了人口、政治、经济与文化，不光能与外部环境进行物质、能量与信息的交换，还能协同内部要素的竞争与合作，具有自适应、应激性、新陈代谢、生长发育和遗传变异等"生命体"特征。因此，在认知城市治理问题时，首先应将城市看作一

①《新一代人工智能发展规划》，人民出版社，2017。

个"生命有机体"①，认同它具有自我完善的取向和生命演化的规律。

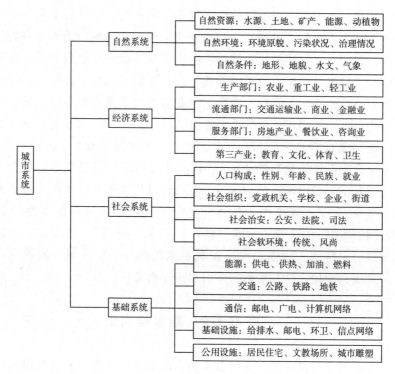

图 1　城市系统结构

　　基于"城市生命体"的认知，从系统关联的角度来计算分析城市问题而非单一系统视角也就更为合理。迈克尔·巴蒂（Michael Batty）指出"城市呈现出多方面复杂性，体现在：城市是由世界各地的联系网络所组成的，包括贸易、社会交往，甚至包括以互联网传播而变成全球性的知识网络"，并运用基于元胞自动机的动态计算模型来诠释城市系统与外界的关联和城市生命的演化。② 在复杂性理论视角下，城市犹如生命体一般由多系列共生的子系统构成（如图 2），每个子系统都包含完整的结构：节点（Node）、网络（Network）和流动要素（Flow），同时又通过协同合作支撑

---

① 1967 年埃罗·萨里宁（Eero Saarinen）提出"城市是个有机体"的观点，此后用生命体征诠释城市现象理念开始发展。

② Batty M., *Cities and Complexity： Understanding Cities with Cellular Automata, Agent-based Models, and Fractals*, Boston：The MIT Press, 2007.

起了城市生命体的正常运转。

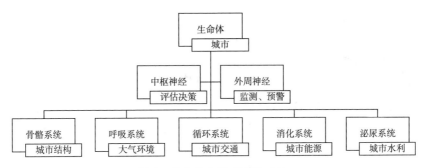

图 2 生命体与城市系统对比

如前文所述，在耗散性结构理论和协同理论视角下，城市有其自演化性，作为一个"生长"着的有机体，其功能和形态都是动态发展的，除了"身体"——基础设施、能源交通水利等——的发育需求，也必然会有"智力"——指挥决策等——的成长需要。随着时代的进步，人工智能技术的突破为城市的"智慧""智能"提供了可能，城市在不断地进行转换升级，其概念与成分也被不断改写，数字城市（Digital City）、智慧城市（Smart City）等新的概念不断涌现。但是，"城市病"也在不断地升级，除却污染、拥挤、贫富差距、犯罪等痼疾，数据爆炸、技术歧视、信息污染等"新症"开始蔓延，这也使城市治理更为复杂艰巨，辅助技术的突破成为需求。而要将人工智能技术融入城市治理体系，则必然要进行相应模式的转型与适应性调塑。这样在城市自身所具有的自主演化性、城市治理和技术相互促进的情态下，城市的结构与治理模式必将在 AI+时代进行全方位、深层次的转换升级，"城市生命体"也会逐步进入更智能的高级阶段。

（二）概念释义

依据工业革命的时间线为城市治理的阶段进行划分看似准确合理，但我国城市化进程起步较晚，城市治理与技术变革的历史轨迹不尽相同，因此应从本土化认识城市 3.0。城市 3.0 是基于 AI+时代，适应于政府 3.0，是相对于城市 1.0、城市 2.0 而言的。事实上，尚无学者明确对城市做出1.0、2.0 和 3.0 版本的划分，但基于生命 3.0、web 3.0、政府 3.0 的出现，城市 3.0 也应运而生。虽然大部分领域都是基于 web 3.0 来界定何为

3.0 版本，但城市的运作和治理并不仅局限于技术，技术万能和技术替代制度只是科技浪潮下的幻象，需要我们审慎地思辨，所以对于我国城市版本的分析也要超脱于技术轨迹。

迈克斯·泰格马克作为未来生命研究所的创始人，提出了"生命 3.0"这个概念，以崭新的角度对生命进行了重新定义：生命是具有一定复杂性的系统，[①] 并依据其复杂程度进行了 1.0、2.0 和 3.0 的划分：生命 1.0 处于生物阶段，依靠进化获得改变；生命 2.0 处于文化阶段，依靠进化获得硬件但能自己设计出软件；生命 3.0 就是科技阶段，可以自己设计硬件与软件，但这在地球上尚不存在。基于先前所探讨的"城市生命体"的认知，借由迈克斯的生命阶段划分来理解城市的生命周期也并非无稽之谈。在新中国成立初期，城市治理整体呈现一种刚性、静态的"总体—支配"结构，高度集中的制度构架下不能脱离"计划"自主发展，只能依靠阶段性的"运动式治理"来得到改变，这正如"城市 1.0"阶段；改革开放后，信息技术在我国进入快速发展阶段，整体社会实现了结构性过渡，粗放、笼统的城市治理模式随之转型，步入虚拟与现实交织、空间与时间压缩扩展、主体与多元统一的新阶段，与此同时，根据 Web 2.0 的网络特点，蒂姆·奥莱利提出了政府 2.0（Government 2.0）的概念，指出政府从条块分割、封闭的架构迈向一个开放、协同、合作的架构，[②] 但此时城市治理依然缺少智能化，这也恰如生命周期的"城市 2.0"阶段；迈克斯的生命 3.0 目前尚无法触及，但城市 3.0 却在 web 3.0 与政府 3.0 的加持下有迹可循。

查尔斯·兰德利将创意城市划分为了四个版本：历史上的城市 0.0，比如紫禁城；由政府主导，按部就班、思维守旧的城市 1.0；交互性更强、更智慧也更注重城市居民需求的城市 2.0；更开放、更适于人类居住、企图突破时间空间桎梏的城市 3.0。查尔斯更多地从人文环境上来关注城市的版本，强调城市的创意水平和创造力，更像是对于城市发展的愿景规划，而没有与大数据、云计算、人工智能等技术紧密结合，只在侧面为城市的版本升级揭开了一角。但正如查尔斯所言，"3.0 版的城市应该是一

---

① Tegmard M., *Life 3.0: Being Human in the Age of Artificial Intelligence*, New York: Knopf Doubleday Publishing Group, Knopf, 2017, p. 58.

② 转引自孟庆国《政府 2.0：电子政务服务创新的趋势》，《电子政务》2012 年第 11 期。

个更开放的概念，任何人都可以参与到城市中来"①，人是贯通社会系统和自然系统的关键桥梁，也是实现城市治理的出发者和目的者，Web 3.0 指向在交互的基础上为用户提供个性化服务，政府 3.0 倾向于以人为核心实现公共治理的价值，这两者与城市治理的发展趋势不谋而合，最终的落脚点都在于"人"。

此外，IBM 公司提出以"感知—互联—智能"为核心的"智慧地球"（Smarter Planet）构想以来，② "智慧城市"所引发的热度也经久未消，2012 年中国工程院在重大咨询研究项目"中国智能城市建设与推进战略研究"中正式提出智能城市的概念，包括城市建设的智能化发展、城市信息的智能化发展、城市产业的智能化发展及城市管理的智能化发展四个部分。③ 王众托等认为当代城市在根本上是一类由物理系统、社会系统和信息技术系统耦合而成的开放式复杂巨系统，④ 而人工智能技术毫无疑问是提升城市各方面"心智"，促使各系统智能交互的有力助推器，并一步步实现城市 3.0 每一处的应有之貌。

综上所述，随着 web 3.0 的发展与推广、城市本土理念与结构的转型、AI+时代下人工智能技术的跃进，城市治理理念、路径和形态都将发生巨大的改变，城市 3.0 就是在此基础上，遵循以人为核心，充分运用人工智能时代的新技术，致力于打造宜居善治可持续的"智能城市生命体"的创新型治理模式。

三 城市 3.0 的价值取向

（一）面向未来

如前文所言，城市有其自组织性与自演化性，其本质是不断发展与自我完善的，城市 3.0 版本也必将沿袭此特性。人工智能技术作为城市 3.0

---

① 金元浦：《创意城市的 3.0 版本：中外城市创意经济发展路径选择——金元浦对话查尔斯·兰德利（二）》，《北京联合大学学报》（人文社会科学版）2017 年第 1 期。

② Palmisano S. J., A Smarter Planet: The Next Leadershipagenda, http://www.ibm.com/ibm/cioleadershipexchange/us/en/pdfs/SJP_Smarter_Planet.pdf, 2008.

③ 潘云鹤：《中国的智能城市和城市大数据》，《中国信息化周报》2014 年第 35 期。

④ 夏昊翔、王众托：《从系统视角对智慧城市的若干思考》，《中国软科学》2017 年第 7 期。

的重要组成部分，是一门现在式与未来式共存的学科。从宏观层面来讲，人工智能实质上就是自动化的过程，人类依托于工具实现各种生产活动来解放劳动力，但复杂的工作必然要使用复杂的工具，使用复杂的工具就需要掌握更多的技能，如此与最初的需求相悖，因此人们希望有能够自我运转的工具，也就是黑格尔所说的"自在自为"①。所以，智能机器的诉求早已浮现在历史长河里，而现在，人工智能早已实现自动化模式，甚至在某些领域智能程度已超过了人类（比如2017年Alpha Go击败了世界围棋冠军柯洁），其未来的发展将会与更多领域融合，并挑战人类的传统认知（如表1）。因而，城市的发展会在人工智能的推动下结合更多的时代潮流与未来元素，将这些新的因素，比如智能化政务、智能交通系统、智能医疗队伍、终身教育体系等引入城市治理的框架中。

表1　人工智能的未来趋势

类型	现有基础	方向	未来发展方向
大数据智能	知识表达技术、大数据驱动知识学习	从数据到知识、从知识到智能行为	连接多领域知识中心，实现跨界融合
跨媒体智能	视觉、听觉、文字等分类型数据处理技术	跨媒体感知、学习、推理和创造	建立和研制智能感知、跨媒体自主学习与推理的模型
人机混合增强智能	智能机器人	类智慧与机器智能系统的高水平协同融合	混合型增强智能的新计算形态，实现人机、脑机协同的情境理解、问题求解、调度与决策
互联网群体智能	网络智能	基于互联网组织群体智能的技术与平台	群体智能及其在互联网上的协同、秩序、安全、演化、学习与进化的机理及平台，以及相关产业动态
自主智能系统	机器人	自主智能系统的技术、架构、平台和设计标准	形成各种机械、装备和产品的自主智能载运平台、自助生产加工系统和智能调度监控系统等

资料来源：潘云鹤：《人工智能走向2.0》，《工程》（英文版）2016年第4期。

　　人工智能+城市治理，既是现实发展的需求，也是面向未来的进步。

---

① 〔德〕黑格尔：《精神现象学》上卷，贺麟、王玖兴译，商务印书馆，1981，第260页。

目前，新一代 AI 技术与城市治理的交互已初现端倪。依托人工智能强大的分析能力、精密的逻辑推理和迅捷的信息流反馈，城市治理的相关要素和权重以前所未有的清晰形态呈现，通过模型构建来分析综合这些因素，继而利用 City Scope 平台①以及 PSS 系统②等进一步辅助城市的规划与决策行为，通过大数据、云端算法和智能网络来实现城市的智能化与现代化，借助人工智能赋予城市治理新的活力。相对应的，基于城市治理的应用反馈与进一步需求，新一代人工智能技术也会在反复实践中实现简单智能向复杂智能的过度，为未来的智能城市、感知城市、虚拟城市等提供一系列的技术支撑。

（二）面向人本

美国《外交政策》杂志、A. T. Keamey 咨询公司和芝加哥全球事务理事会在 2011 年联合推出了城市指数，基于对 24 个度量方法的评估大体分为 5 个领域：商业活动、人力资本、信息交换、文化体验以及政治参与。城市是人的存在的集合，其英文"city"出自拉丁文"civitas"，字根指向"公民"（citizen）聚居之所，其发展、建设与治理基于"人类结社之愿"，如亚里士多德所言，"结社是人类天赋的冲动"（The impulse to political association is innate in all men）。人类通过每个人的参与和投入组建了生存的群体环境——城市，同时，群体的力量也能更好地实现每个人的诉求，实现个人与群体的相辅相成，也即上海世博会的"城市，让生活更美好。"毋庸置疑，以人为本才是城市最终的价值取向，但月满则亏，过多的人口会造成城市系统的沉重负担，尤其是在交通、经济、信息技术较为发达的当下，各种沉疴新疾层出不穷，这又导致城市的人本服务品质逐步下降，与其面向人本的初衷相悖。因此，如何解决人口负担带来的城市系统过载，实现城市资源均等化是学界一直探讨的难题。但随着人工智能技术的发展，各种资源的智能化分配趋势逐渐显现，城市的智能化程度也逐日加深，以人为中心的"自由人的联合体"之城未来可期。

---

① 一个为了让专家和非专家都能参与到易用的、协作的、循讯的城市决策过程中来的动态的、证据辅佐的城市决策辅助系统。参见张砚、肯特·蓝森《City Scope——可触交互界面、增强现实以及人工智能于城市决策平台之运用》，《时代建筑》2018 年第 1 期。
② 宋彦、李超骥、陈炎等：《规划支持系统（PSS）在城市规划与决策中的应用路径——美国的经验与启示》，《城市发展研究》2017 年第 10 期。

对现代化的城市而言，开放性与参与性是不可或缺的要素，但中国当前城市治理依然没能完全走出政府包揽一切计划的阶段，公众参与也更局限于事后的、被动的参与，真正符合现代化的公众参与机制仍未成型。但新一代通信技术和网络服务正逐渐改写这种局面，为大众参与提供了更广阔的平台。比如美国德克萨斯州马诺尔与斯坦福大学、Spigit 科技公司合作推出的网站——"马诺尔实验室"，可以收集居民对于城市改进的建议并进行投票。[①] 在人工智能技术的深入融合下，自由型城市和开源型城市已有迹可循。自由型城市体现为集体智慧的凝聚和应用，公民可以了解使用数据、质疑城市治理的制度实践，并通过维基、微博、Fab Lab、Living Lab 等沟通形式强化个体参与；开源型城市体现为公众参与的有效性，通过合法机构的沉浸式对话、众包、集体协商等，构建参与式、开放式平台，来引导和推动城市的发展，保障城市的开放性、无障碍性，保障"城市人"的参与性。

（三）面向可持续

城市的"生长"是受多种因素影响的复杂演化过程，是各种要素相互博弈与协调的成果，但由于传统的认知与技术水平的局限，这一显著特点成为"盲点"。传统的城市治理倾向于设计的单一化，只注重成果而忽视过程，甚至于为何以及如何达成目标也缺乏科学解释，更遑论如何协调城市治理的各要素以达成可持续的良性循环的研究。而随着人工智能技术的导入，机器的深度学习可以从城市数据以及复杂现象中挖掘总结规律，对城市发展中的各要素、动力、现象和结果进行指标分析并构建新的数据与模型。比如通过预测城市发展的城市动力学模型（Urban Dynamics，UD）[②]等数学模型，将城市各系统之间的复杂关系剖析出来，提取出变化机制，并借由 AI 技术、相应的历史规律，将其中的各节点与要素进行模拟推演，刻画并了解城市内部复杂的生态，为城市的可持续发展提供帮助。

传统城市的发展离不开工业化，工业的发展极大推动了经济的发展，提高了生产力水平，同时为城市提供了丰富的物质资源。丰富的资源也激

---

① 张小娟、贾海薇、张振刚：《智慧城市背景下城市治理的创新发展模式研究》，《中国科技论坛》2017 年第 10 期。

② Forrester J. W., *Urban Dynamics*, Productivity Press, 1969.

发了市民的消费需求，推动了工业的进一步发展，形成了生产—消费的双向促进关系。但资源生产的原料毕竟是有限的，且工业大生产往往伴随着"竭泽而渔"的生态破坏，无限发展的结果只能是人类自身的毁灭，因此，保持城市的活力与可持续性是客观需求。城市 3.0 是人工智能时代下的新模式，除了固有的物理空间，还有基于物联网、互联网、云端设计、大数据等新技术所塑造的"虚拟空间"，城市的治理系统可以抽象为现实与虚拟交互的复杂网络模型。在这个模型下，资源节点的分布几乎一目了然，物质资源、治理资源与产业资源的调配便会更加智能高效，经济发展与生态维护的悖论有了突破的可能。比如 AI 技术的伴随产物之一——共享理念，其内核便是可持续，共享单车、共享汽车、共享充电宝、共享洗衣机等产品涉及社会生活的方方面面，实现了资源的节约与有效使用。总之，3.0 版本的城市治理指向通过 AI 技术和各方资源的合理配置，实现产业结构转型和工业升级，继而实现城乡统筹发展、生态协调发展，保持城市的"生长"活力与可持续性。

四 城市 3.0 的实现机理

(一) 创新城市治理思路

城市的发展是一个自然的演化过程，有其特定的推演规律，但传统的城市治理往往忽视这一点，更青睐于"设计"特定的发展蓝图来统筹城市治理的方向，对城市问题往往过于"简化"，这也是"城市病"不能痊愈的原因之一。但人工智能催生了全新的认知体系，城市 3.0 的治理核心趋于智能化，通过 AI 技术的计算和区域 DNA、CA 等模型的推演（如图 3）来预判未来城市发展阶段可能出现的场境，实现了城市规划、管理、交通、教育、医疗、公共安全和公共事业等领域的智能、互联和高效，在一定程度上革新了城市治理的思路，推动了城市治理各层面的智能化转型。

首先是城市规划的智能化。城市规划是一个研究历史悠久的领域，但人工智能在城市规划领域的应用并非新生事物，事实上，自人工智能诞生以来，两者就呈现密切的互动趋势，在过去 30 年已诞生了多种智能规划技术，包括但不限于计算机辅助设计技术、城市定量分析技术、城市动态模拟技术及城市智能交互技术。目前，AI 技术主要应用于城市生长规律和空

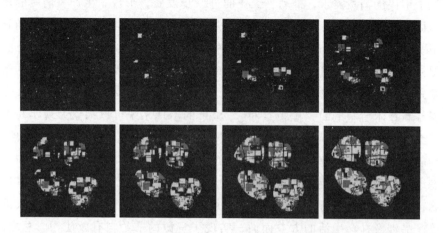

图 3　城市个体的推演的理论过程

图片来源：甘惟：《城市生命视角下的人工智能规划理论与模型》，《规划师》
2018 年第 11 期。

间规律的机器学习（Machine Learning）与深度学习（Deep Learning）等方
面，比如龙瀛、沈尧提出的为规划设计的全过程提供数据实证与支持工具
的数据增强设计（Data Augmented Design）①，姜鹏、徐飞提出的针对不同
人群需求的洞察的度量体系（Citizen Based Metrics）等。② 甘惟等学者指出
"城市智能规划的技术应具备大数据、自动化、交互性、复合性和生长性
五项基本特征"③，新一代的 AI 已非"吴下阿蒙"，在丰富的数据库、强大
的算力和先进算法的协助下，人工智能可以逐渐摆脱对于人工编程的依
赖，通过学习来直接处理大量实例。正如吴志强院士提到的"以城市规律
为导向编制城市规划"④，实现城市规划的智能化指日可待。

　　其次是政府的智能化。政府作为城市的重要组成部分，是城市治理中
的中流砥柱，其智能化是实现城市智能化的充要条件。赫拉利在《人类简

①　"数据增强设计"，https：//www. beijingcitylab. com/projects - 1/17-data-augmented-design，
　　2018。
②　姜鹏、徐飞：《基于 150 亿条数据的通州城镇化规划研究》，第二届数据增强设计学术研
　　讨会，2016。
③　吴志强、甘惟：《转型时期的城市智能规划技术实践》，《城市建筑》2018 年第 3 期。
④　吴志强：《人工智能辅助城市规划》，《时代建筑》2018 年第 1 期。

史》中指出"科学革命"的历史是科学、政治和经济结合的历史，[1] 科技发展与政治密不可分：科技不断创新发展，促进政府治理模式的变迁进步；政府借助科技手段，探索政治行政发展规律，主导技术理性，推动社会发展。[2] 人工智能技术在政务领域的应用虽然尚处起步阶段，但不可否认的是 AI 技术的不断成熟与应用使得政府治理进行优化升级如虎添翼，缩减开支、提升能效、细化治理等方面有了技术支持与操作性保障。以大数据为凭据，借强大算力与核心算法搭建政务智能平台、系统、模型等是实现人工智能政治扩散的结果形态，通过经验学习模型（例如 Decision Tree）、深度学习模型（例如 ANN）、感官学习、自我调节模型、复杂适应系统（CAS）等对政府治理中的过程与现象进行抽象数学表达，人工智能已在解放（relieve）、分解（split up）、取代（replace）、增强（augment）等多方面为政府治理提供服务，并依据政务需求搭建了诸多政府智能系统，比如智能在线客服、GPS 公车定位、无人化政务服务等，为人工智能在政府治理领域的应用提供了可靠的实践支撑，也为进一步的智能政府建设探索了前路。

当然还有其他领域的智能化，比如城市智能交通管理、智能医疗队伍、智能垃圾分配、智能教育体系等，在此不再赘述。总之显而易见的是，在 AI+时代，3.0 版本的城市治理思路已大大不同于传统的治理思路，是一个更开放、更创新的概念。

（二）升级城市治理手段

不可否认的是，人工智能技术的飞速发展极大扩展了城市治理的路径与手段，AI 技术的升级，城市治理方法也随之跃迁，数据驱动（Data-driven）、平台驱动（Platform-driven）和模型驱动（Model-driven）三位一体（如图 4）。

首先是数据驱动。舍恩伯格曾经敏锐地指出：在大数据时代，人们处理数据的思维方式将会发生重大的转变，即要全体而不要抽样，要效率而

---

[1] 〔以〕尤瓦尔·赫拉利：《人类简史》，林俊宏译，中信出版社，2017，第 236 页。

[2] 王啸宇、王宏禹：《DT 时代的治理模式：发展中的数字政府与数据政务》，《河北大学学报》（哲学社会科学版）2018 年第 4 期。

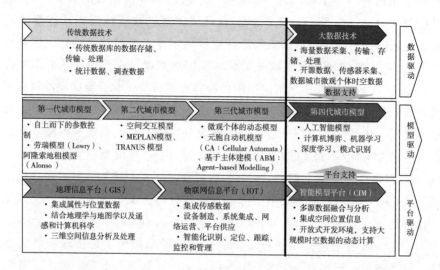

图4　城市治理手段的技术内核

图片来源：甘惟：《城市生命视角下的人工智能规划理论与模型》，《规划师》
2018年第11期。

不要绝对精确，要相关而不要因果。① 诚然，大数据是AI+城市治理的必要
条件，也在很大程度上改变了传统的治理思维模式，收集并从多个数据库
进行数据的抽取、转换、清洗、集成成为城市3.0运作的逻辑起点，友好
的数据生态也是实现全国甚至全球城市协调一致发展的前提。而在实践
中，大数据的应用也极大提升了城市治理的能力：通过技术分析，能实现
数据从无序到有序、由静态到动态、自隐性到显性的转变；海量、动态的
数据能集成有效的信息资源，还原社会危机发生的真相；数据的归纳整合
能最大限度地解决城市治理主体主观世界与城市客体世界之间的信息不对
称问题，打破数据的孤立与分散局势，推动城市治理实现现代化。

　　其次是平台驱动。在传统的城市治理中，由于管理资源与渠道的有
限，信息的处理与传递面对极大阻碍，"信息孤岛"的现象并不罕见。因
此公共信息平台的建立至关重要，它是搭建政府与公众之间信息桥梁的保
障，是实现城市之间管理部门内部、城市内部管理部门与相关公共服务组

① 转引自陈万球、石惠絮《大数据时代城市治理：数据异化与数据治理》，《湖南师范大学
社会科学学报》2015年第5期。

织之间迅捷沟通协作的基础。其次利用 AI 技术构建的平台也可以实现城市治理信息的公开，将政府官员与决策议程进行精准的记录与收集，供民众与监督部门查阅，最大限度地避免腐败贪污的产生。比如眉山市东坡区，建构了惠民大数据监察平台，通过惠民资金、惠民项目、惠民政策、三资公开四个项目将政府的决策信息有序展现在民众面前。此外，智能平台也能对城市内部的关系进行梳理与剖析。比如朱钥和李琦教授的团队，通过以 GIS 技术为基础的城市空间智能计算平台的构建，统概了经济问题、社会问题及环境问题与空间活动模型之间的关系，对城市的空间活动进行了分析与计算，为解决城市复杂问题提供了科学支持。[①]

最后是模型驱动。有赖于人工智能技术的飞速发展，城市的计算模型得到了新的提升，改变了过去必须手动输入参数与规则的方式，实现了模型的自动化计算。另外，智能化城市模型还可以实现自主化学习，其计算结果能作为新的数据库样本进行循环迭代，有能力覆盖过去城市治理模型力所不能及的场域。在智能模型中首要的便是深度学习模型，通过人工神经网络（ANN）将基础模型连接起来组成不同的网络，再加上日趋成熟的语音识别、图像识别等来感知城市，实现对城市隐藏信息的系统、深度挖掘；其次是自我调节模型，通过城市生命过程的模拟与计算，诊断甚至预判"城市病因"，实现城市的关键要素调节与合理配置；最后就是各种子系统运转模型，比如智能政府决策模型、智能交通模型（ITS）、CA 模型、CAS 建模工具和 Holodeck 模拟器等，这有助于实现城市治理中各领域的自主运转。

（三）细化城市治理领域

在治理新格局下，城市发展的外延不断扩大，尤其是在数字化变革之后，物理城市、社会系统和赛博空间[②]相互叠加，传统的治理模式很难做到"抽象而全能"，在此条件下，精细化治理应时而生。但城市作为"系统的系统"，其治理难度可想而知，但正如前文所言，人工智能技术的发展升级了城市的治理手段，由功能分区治理到要素分配治理的精细化转型

---

①　朱钥、李琦：《城市空间智能计算平台研究》，《地理与地理信息科学》2011 年第 1 期。

②　由计算机生成的景观，是连接世界上所有人、计算机和各种信息源的全球计算机网络的虚拟空间。

有了技术保障。大数据技术的发展和计算机性能的增强为城市精细化治理提供了适宜的环境，能够完成以城市微观个体要素为研究对象的复杂计算，以元胞自动机模型（Cellular Automata，CA）、基于主体建模（Agent-based Modelling，ABM）为代表的空间动态模型构建取得较大的进展，实现了由静态到动态的突破。

首先，人工智能不光能够通过多种渠道收集清洗社会数据，而且能够通过数据互联打破地域与时空的限制，破解城市之间、城市子系统之间的数据壁垒，使碎片化的社会信息像网格体制化转变，便于整体性态势的宏观掌握与微观治理。比如美国迈阿密，通过大数据和云计算对迈阿密市戴德县进行分析，获得了一个关于该县的较为全面的"情报信息"，在充分利用水资源、减少交通拥堵、解决突发事件和维持公共安全等方面取得了有效成果。① 北京东城区在整合自然属性数据与社会属性数据的基础上，进一步关联聚合了人口、地理和管理等信息，根据"人—户"情况，实时了解空巢老人和残疾人的居住和活动情况，实现精细化、个性化的人口服务管理工作。②

其次，人工智能基于其强大的算力和算法，能生产许多特定领域的智能专家系统，比如机器律师、机器分析师等，在社会治理、教育管理、司法服务、城市运行、环境治理等领域发挥针对性、精细化的作用。例如基于 Multi-Agent 的交通情景动态集成模拟系统，融合了交通社会学与交通工程学，应用交通行为理论和人工智能技术，致力于解决复杂的城市交通拥堵问题。还有上海在大数据信息库的基础上启动"医联工程"，为每一位病人自动生成电子健康档案，建立了电子健康档案信息库和 PB 级医学影像档案库，医生能够根据病人的病史做出更加精准的诊断；病人则会根据数据库的提示做出合适的就医选择；政府则可以提高对疾病和疫情的预测和处置能力。③

最后，借助智能感知技术对城市生命体的样本数据进行采集，并应用人工智能技术——诸如各种模型和专家系统——从数据中学习规律。例如

---

① 谢然：《大数据应用案例 TOP100》，《互联网周刊》2015 年第 6 期。
② 陈之常：《应用大数据推进政府治理能力现代化：以北京市东城区为例》，《中国行政管理》2015 年第 2 期。
③ 九三学社中央大数据课题组：《大数据，给政府治理带来什么？九三学社"利用大数据技术提升政府治理能力"调研侧记》，《中国统一战线》2014 年第 6 期。

CA 模型，能够敏锐地模拟城市流变过程中的宏观变化与微观变化，精准识别出城市各区域要素的流动与分配，以及密度和数量上的差异——即对城市演变有重要影响的区域 DNA，从而实现城市每一寸土地的精准计算、精密部署和动态调节。再比如美国一位程序员发明的 SeeClickFix 的应用程序，可以通过民众的拍照上传，再进行相应的图像识别，将乱涂乱画、交通灯损坏、排水管堵塞、安全井盖缺失等各种问题分类发送到相对应的公共事业部门，实现自下而上的精细化治理。

（四）优化城市决策模式

决策是城市治理系统中至关重要的部分，是一定时期内城市发展和建设的依据，同时，决策活动也是一个动态过程，是因时因事而变的。在 AI+时代，城市治理的决策模式也理所当然地进行了优化，依托大数据、人机共智、场景模拟等基于知识的决策支持系统，大幅度提升了决策模式的确定性、科学性、民主性和动态性。

首先是大数据智能的支持。AI 技术可以实现多个数据源的管理分析与挖掘。获取真实、全面、有效的信息，并精准识别其"轻重缓急"是进行城市治理决策的重要前提，但在传统的决策模式中收集处理信息需要投入大量的人力与时间，且难以保证信息的全面与真实，在此基础上的决策结果往往面临诸多不确定性与风险性。相比之下，人工智能在数据领域有天然的优势，它可以通过对多个数据源 ETL[①]、清洗、集成完善数据获取流程，并通过设定源数据与目标数据的对应关系，自动生成抽取数据的代码。比如天津市人大常委会法制工作委员会通过北大法宝智能立法支持平台，待审查文件、法律数据库与"敏感词词库"三者可以形成对照组，只需标注出特殊的"敏感词"，就会自动呈现与之相关的法律规定，相关工作者可以进行下一步的对比考察。[②] 另外，人工智能也可以通过深度学习，以"过往经验"为蓝本，建立智能监测平台和智能预警系统，基于大数据对城市问题的概率与分布进行风险预测，将相关资源与侦察频率进行合理

---

① 即抽取、转换、转贮。
② 高绍林：《人工智能如何辅助地方立法》，搜狐网，https://www.sohu.com/a/215288081_671251，最后访问日期：2020 年 3 月 21 日。

分配①，比如美国纽约市长办公室的数据分析系统，与城市消防部门合作利用机器学习来决定应派遣建筑检查员的地点。②

其次是人机共智。借由 AI 技术来辅助决策活动确实能极大提高决策效率与质量，但目前的 AI 和 ES 远非真正的智能，在自主自动方面仍有较大的不足，尚不能由机器单独完成所有的决策行为。且城市治理中的决策活动也不是利用单独的一种技术就能完成的，而是要依靠多项技术的组合，这在短时间内仍处于探索阶段。此外，过于依赖数学分析，而脱离人的经验判断与推理思维，难免会落入"量化陷阱"，使城市治理的人本气息荡然无存。所以技术的不足仍需要人类智能来弥补，在较长时间内人机共智（Man-machine Hybrid Intelligence）仍会是城市决策系统的主流。人机共智的决策具体有三种表现形式：一是通过人的训练，使机器能够认知、判断，比如麻省理工学院媒体实验室（Media Lab）研发的 City Scope 项目；二是人发布命令，机器进行执行与反馈；三是基于机器的学习与分析结果，人来完成决策制定。这样通过人与机器的有效互动，能制定出更科学、更准确的决策方案，实现决策模式的优化。

最后，AI 技术可以通过场景模拟实现城市决策的成本预测与效果评估。客观世界的场景可以在智能世界里拆分为时间、空间、语义和语境四个要素，③将这些要素通过实时数据、属性测量、符号分析、环境分析等运作虚拟还原物理世界，能够实现待决策问题的场景化模拟。此外，人工智能系统具有"天赋的"多学科交叉的优势，将特定学科的理论与 AI 技术相结合，构建基于领域本体特性基础层、智能查询与动态集成的方法和多 Agent④ 协同模型的多层次模型，通过输入特性属性与要求来进行针对性的场景模拟，能够评估各项政策方案会带来的成本、社会影响以及预期效果，研判复杂的社会现象与措施行为后果，为政策的制定与修改提供参考。这样，城市的决策系统可以在最大限度上节约人力、时间与经济成本，并契合准确的时机点，避免实体"试点"中无法挽回的失误。

---

① 徐骏、苗运卫：《智能辅助：破解环境刑事司法证据困局之匙》，《常州大学学报》（社会科学版）2018 年第 2 期。

② 转引自 Cary Coglianese & David Lehr, "Regulating by Robot: Administrative Decision Making in the Machine-Learning Era," *Georgetown L. J.* 105（2017）: 1161.

③ 朱琳等：《全局数据：大数据时代数据治理的新范式》，《电子政务》2016 年第 1 期。

④ 特指角色 Agent，即模拟参与者。

City 3.0: Value Dimension and Realization
Mechanism of Urban Governance in Intelligent Age

Lv Yuxue

Abstract: With the advent of the intelligent era and the gradual progress of Web3.0 and life 3.0, as a giant system of complex organisms, city will also enter a higher stage: City 3.0. As a "living organism", city has multiple coupling with artificial intelligence technology. Intelligent intelligence, people-oriented, livable and good governance will be the core content of version 3.0 city. Driven by the development of new technology, urban governance is expected to break through the dilemma of traditional governance mode, realize the value trend of facing the future, people-oriented and sustainable, and further innovate the idea of urban governance, upgrade urban governance means, refine urban governance areas, optimize urban governance decisions, and promote the further modernization of urban governance capacity and system.

Keywords: City Governance, Artificial Intelligence, City 3.0, System Theory, Life Body Theory

Collaborative Governance in Post-disaster Housing Reconstruction: A Case of Nepal 2015 Earthquake

Raunab Singh Khatri*

【Abstract】 After the event of disaster, rebuilding of damaged houses constitutes as one of the most important conquest for the government and other stakeholders for reconstruction efforts. In case of Nepal, much government efforts, social organizations and aid-donors have helped finance significant portion on housing reconstruction. This paper analyzes the effect of governance effectiveness on housing reconstruction. The author analyzed the role of state, social organizations and citizen's in participation for effective housing reconstruction. The research was conducted with a view that despite much emphasis placed by aid-donors, communities, NGOs and governmental institutions, the recent experiences show that such commitments haven't really been translated into reality at grounded level. This case study was done from period 2015-2017, two years since April 25th 2015 earthquake. The case study reveals that the state capacity, coupled with its collaborative efforts among other actors of governance is low when it comes to post-disaster reconstruction of private housing in Nepal. Some considerable measures have to be taken on monitoring and coordination

* Raunab Singh Khatri, 北京大学燕京学堂 (Masters in China Studies, Yenching Academy of Peking University)。

mechanisms to speed up the reconstruction of private homes and yet more concrete efforts in increasing effectiveness of aid delivery and mobilizing local resources are required for reconstruction.

【 Keywords 】 Post-disaster Reconstruction, Housing reconstruction, Nepal, Urban Governance

1. Introduction

Natural disasters like earthquake, floods and landslides come in occasionally all over the world. A natural disaster in a vulnerable area may have different type of consequences including fatalities, injuries and property damage. [1]For a mountainous country like Nepal, the risk of encountering such disasters is eminent. Nepal is ranked 4th, 11th and 20th in terms of climate change, earthquake and flood risk countries of the world . [2] The aftermath of such events presents that post-reconstruction of man-made destroyed infrastructure becomes politically challenging and economically expensive. In any event the government faces daunting challenges in distribution of aid and relief materials effectively that is required to rebuild traditional heritage sites, private houses of the affected households, and public infrastructures. The resilient infrastructure coped up with sound policy can mitigate the adverse consequences of such kind of disruptions. Responding to disaster requires a policy network of inter-dependence among government, social organization and the private sector. How well the disaster management framework prepares the authority to manage emergency crisis and how the governance mechanisms can quickly adapt to complex circumstances to meet people's needs determine the efficiency of post-disaster reconstruction.

---

[1] Sebastiaan, J., Maaskant, B., Ezra, B., & Levitan, M. L., " Loss of Life Caused by the Flooding of New Orleans After Hurricane Katrina: Analysis of the Relationship between Flood Characteristics And Mortality," *Risk Analysis* (2009) .

[2] Dhungel, R., *Disaster Risk Management: Policies and Practices in Nepal*, Retrieved from http: //www. adrc. asia/countryreport/NPL/2011/FY2011B_NPL_CR. pdf (2011).

The April 25, 2015 earthquake of 7. 8 magnitude scale was the biggest in the country after 1934 earthquake. ① The earthquake resulted in 8, 857 deaths and 21, 952 injured and over 498, 852 houses destroyed. ② The damage was eminent in both urban and rural areas of 16 districts of country. Nepal was set with a major task of rebuilding and relief efforts at worst affected areas by the earthquake. The coordination of disaster risk management is overseen by Ministry of Home Affairs (MoHA), however with the scale of operation required, the need of separate institution (National Reconstruction Authority) was realized which took 9 months to get established. Coped with political instability③, leadership④ crisis and the absence of comprehensive disaster management act, the authority had a troubling time in engaging operation. The pressure to provide basic needs to victims along with providing shelters to the victims are of highest priority and comes with enormous pressure. Furthermore, during this period, the government concluded International Donor's Conference on July 2015 A. D. that pledged $4. 1 billion dollars for relief and reconstruction efforts. How well the government will be able to utilize the funds for post-reconstruction will depend upon its state governance and the urgency to complete post-reconstruction within completed time of 5-years.

---

① Lacey-hall, O., *Nepal Earthquake: Challenges to Disaster Response?* Retrieved March 06, 2018, from The Huffington post: https: //www. huffingtonpost. com/oliver-laceyhall/nepal-earthquake-challeng_b_7421856. html (2015, May 22).

② More information from: http: //drrportal. gov. np, the official disaster risk reduction portal from the Government of Nepal and from "Post Disaster Needs Assessment" (NPC, 2015)

③ The earthquake occurred at a time when government was preparing to promulgate its constitution since it's federalism. After the International conference pledging $4. 1 billion, the country announced it's new constitution, which paved way for economic disruption through political reasons. See, Montano, S, *Blockading Nepal's Earthquake Recovery*. Retrieved April 28, 2018, from Disasterology: http: //www. disaster-ology. com/home/2016/1/19/blockading-nepals-earthquake-recovery.

④ Leadership of NRA was put to crisis with changes overtime. Govinda Raj Pokharel initially led the authority for two weeks only to know that the bill required for gaining legal status of NRA wasn't passed and the authority was dissolved. Two weeks after that, Sushil Gyawali of Town Development Fund (TDF) was elected for a year which was again replaced by Govinda Raj Pokharel. After 7 months, Govinda Raj Pokharel quits the authority to contest for elections. NRA has seen change of leadership 4 times within 3 years. Now Yuvaraj Bhusal heads it.

In this research paper, the author examined the challenges in governance of post-disaster urban housing reconstruction. As public reports and citizen's opinion ventured with personal experiences flashes out, it becomes inevitable to assess the governance mechanism of the institution. It begins with a brief discussion of aid-governance and governance mechanism in Nepal followed with institutional framework. From then, the author analyzes the present status of disaster governance in Nepal and provide that disaster governance has resulted in aid-ineffectiveness in post-disaster reconstruction.

1.1 Need to Understand Disaster Management

It is well known that some countries have successfully operated post-disaster reforms while others have lagged behind. The 2011 Global Assessment Report concluded that "aside from reducing disaster mortality, existing risk governance capacities and arrangements generally fail to achieve their aims". [1] In this regard, little attention has been given at the process of governance such as formulation of policy, roles of different stakeholders. [2] How the disaster governance fits into the broader landscape of local development requires significant research. [3] Shrestha, Alhers, Bakker and Gupta[4] have provided comprehensive view of disaster management framework of Nepal. However, previous scholarly research has shown that there is limited research over state's capacity to operate such mass-scale relief works. With a still bureaucratic framework and limited flexibility, [5] the rigid governance system becomes non-

[1]   Cutter, S. L., & Nguyen, K., *Governance in Disaster Risk Management*, Integrated Research on Disaster Risk (2014).

[2]   Samantha Jones, K. J., " Governance Struggles and Policy Processes in Disaster Risk Reduction: A case study from Nepal," *Geoforum* 10 (2013).

[3]   DIIS, *Towards "Good Enough" Climate and Disaster Risk Governance Emerging Lessons from Zambia, Nepal, Viet Nam and Uganda* (Copenhagen: Danish Institution for Inernational Studies, 2014).

[4]   Shrestha, R. K., Alhers, R., Bakker, M., & Gupta, J., " Institutional Dysfunction and Challenges in Flood Control: A Case Study of the Kosi Flood 2008," *Economic and Political Weekly* 2 (2010).

[5]   Marks, D., "Introduction: Decentalising Disaster Governance in Urbanising Asia," *Habitat International* 52 (2016): 1-4.

adaptive and responsible enough to respond to complex emergencies due to their political budget, bureaucratic framework and rigid organizational hierarchies. The overall narrative of this paper is to understand the state-governance collaborative efforts with local institutions on reconstructing damaged private houses in Nepal.

A second focus point in the needs assessment and rebuilding efforts is the aid-effectiveness. The reconstruction process started after the International donor's conference that pledged $ 4.1 billion dollars on relief efforts. It is widely accepted that aid and reconstruction efforts need to be participatory and community driven approach, a goal that was always not met. [1] Developing countries like Nepal-those that lack accountable, inclusive and effective governments-are unable to be resilient in the face of disaster. [2] Further, there are considerable evidence-based literatures that aid flowing to governments implementing inefficient policies is wasteful. [3]Building settlements with prolonged disaster resiliant features is a common policy shared by stakeholders and the purpose of aid. Thus, post-reconstruction housing (dependent variable) relies heavily on government's capacity (independent variable) for efficiency aid-effectivness. The relationship between governance and their service delivery has yet to be interpreted among Nepali academic scholars, which presents a major challenge for post-reconstruction housing after the disaster of 2015 A. D.

1.2 Disasterand Aid Governance: A Historical Review

Nepal is one of the most vulnerable countries in the world for disaster. This notion has led pathway for establishment of legal and policy environment for disaster risk reduction in one form or another in Nepal since 1982 and has

---

[1] Daly, P., & brassard, C., " Aid-accountability and Participatory Approaches in Post-Disaster Housing Reconstruction," *Asian Journal of Social Science* (2011).

[2] Lindborg, N., *Rebuilding Nepal, from the Government Up.* Retrieved April 2018, from Foreign Policy: http://foreignpolicy.com/2015/05/07/rebuilding-nepal-from-the-government-up-earthquake.

[3] Kaufman, D., *Aid Effectiveness and Governance: The Good, The Bad And The Ugly*, Brookings Institution, 2009.

regularly been reviewed. [1] Also, following the Hyogo Framework, GoN had initiated National Strategy for Disaster Risk Management (NSDRM) in 2009 with support from UNDP and the European Commission. In order to make Nepal more disaster resilient country, National Disaster Response Framework (NDRF) was introduced in 2013 A. D.. [2] The government has recently endorsed the bill to enact the New Disaster Management Act.

However, even with such framework, the governance of disaster risk reduction remains a critical point of effectiveness of such programs. From the world perspective, through 6 decades of aid intervention, the concept of "good governance" in aid effectiveness was finally realized during start of 1990s. Alongside the deepening patters of poor governance, the political difficulties for reforms become challenging resulting in aid ineffectiveness. Indeed, for efficient disaster management, the role of the government is crucial. However, mitigating disaster is a global agenda, which is being driven in disaster prone countries funded by the UN and other international agencies. Nepal, as an aid dependent country and aid contributes to an average 6% of the GDP. [3] Ever since receiving official development assistance since 1952 A. D. [4] there has been a continuous influx of aid development assistance to Nepal on an average of 6% . However, with constant political turmoil, [5] the narrative has shifted from "decades of

---

[1] With the launch of first 5-year plan (1956 – 1961), Nepal joined the league of countries on receiving aid. A substantial portion of development expenditure, amounting to around 55% has been financed through foreign aid.

[2] MoHA., *National Disaster Response Framework*, Government of Nepal, Minsitry of Home Affairs (2016).

[3] Khadka, N., "Foreign Aid to Nepal: Donor Motives in the Post-Cold War Period," *South Asian Survey* 11 (1997): 1044–1061.

[4] Nepal received its first development assistance in 1952 through the Colombo Plan for cooperative, economic and social development in Asia and the pacific Wikipedia (2018). The government, in 1976 came up with "Nepal Development Fund" to channel all the foreign aid related activities. As of 2010 – 11, 55% of all foreign aid disbursements have focused on nation wide development activities (disaster management programs being one of them) .

[5] Ever since overthrowing 104 years of autocratic Rana regime in 1951 A. D., Nepal for decades have been inflexed with constant geo-political crisis from establishment of democracy to Panchayat system, to re-establishment of multi party democracy, civil war and overthrowing of Monarchy.

development" to "*decades of doubt about development*".[1] This characterization of unstable political situation can often create obstacles to the effective utilization of aid assistance not only after the disaster, but also in the pre-disaster situation.

There is an old saying in the military, "Your success at war depends upon your preparations during peace".[2] In the context of disaster management, it means to establish proper legal framework, institutional capacity and preparedness all of which are to be pre-installed before the event. Disaster in Nepal have been managed on an ad-hoc basis and attended to only during the time of their occurrence. This paramount's risks of getting overloaded with post-reconstruction management complexities dealing with multiple stakeholders with crisis in governance. In Nepal's case, in spite of millions of rupees poured into humanitarian aid, there is little assurance over whether the money will be responsive to their needs. The next section of the theoretical study analyzes the aid effectiveness in post-disaster contexts and its key challenges in ensuring its effectiveness.

2. Aid-Effectiveness in Post-Disaster Context

In the same year of the occurrence of earthquake in Nepal, Asian Developoment Bank stressed on strong accountability for greater political oversight and greater assurance that relief efforts will continue on time. In other words, it calls for aid effectiveness with a mandate that development goals can be achieved not just by the quantity of aid presented but, in the manner, it was given. Historically, in Nepal's context, aid effectiveness has been of what author Malla describes as "nobody's concern". Despite spontaneous flow of aid, administrative lethargy and inefficient aid analysis were considered as an important factor for foreign aid misuse. When Paris declaration for aideffectiveness[3] OECDwas

---

① Hayes, L. D., "Political Development of Nepal," *The Indian Journal of Political Science* 2.

② Taken from the book written by RadhaKrishnan Pillai *Corporate Chanakya on Leadership*, p. 46.

③ Paris Declaration was held on 2nd March 2005 A. D. to take far-reaching and monitor able actions to reform the ways in which the developed and developing countries deliver and manage aid. It consists of 5 fundamental principles for effective utilization of aid.

signed, Nepal became one of signatory nations. In the declaration, foreign aid effectiveness was at the cornerstone. One of the agreements was based on periodical publication, allocation and expenditure of development to enable more transparency of aid allocation. Subsequent literature has proved that aid effectiveness will take place with inherent parameters of aid process. [1]Alongside, getting transparency requires for efficient monitoring of aid related projects that allows for two-way information exchanges.

OECD (2008) has stressed the importance of monitoring and evaluation as nation's top priority for donor's proper usage of funds. Following the drawbacks of Paris declaration[2] Nepal's inability to effectively utilize was apparent. The coordination between aid-implementing institutions like NRA towards the needy people depends on extensive monitoring mechanism. In one of the districts, the NRA has guidelines to establish "post-disaster resource center"[3] in order to facilitate local projects for speedy recovery. When visited the affected area in 2017, there has been found no evidence of facilitating such centers to cadre the needs of the post-earthquake victims. Malla has a term for scenarios as "aid-indigestion" -incapable of absorbing aid amount into the concerned projects. The capacity of countries like Nepal to make effective use of aid after post-disaster context has been of contentious issue. Strong absence of fully functional government (both in central and local level)[4] can slow down aid-rescue process aftermath of the disaster.

---

[1] See Winters, M. S., "Accountability, Participation and Foreign Aid Effectiveness," *International Studies Review* 2 (2010): 218 - 243. Torrente', N., "The Relevance and Effectiveness of Humanitarian Aid: Reflections about the Relationship between Providers and Recipients," *Social Research* 2.

[2] Glennie provides description of Paris decleration meeting only one out of the decleration's 14 indicators of aid effectiveness. Roberts argues that because the decleration is technical oriented, it doesn't take into political dimensions and thus only guides development assistance providing little support on relief efforts.

[3] National Reconstruction Authority.

[4] Central government is heavily influenced by frequent change in political leadership (1 term period being average 9 months), and misunderstandings between parties while the elections for local governments were held after 2 decades on 14th May, 28th June and 18th September 2017 A. D.

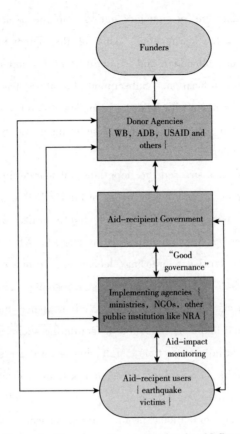

Figure 1　Two-way communication in aid-flows

Source: Diagram is author's own.

One example to add a note to the above point is the evidence at Maujua village.[①] Due to its geographical location and owing to the absence of local ward units, the relief aid was dispatched only 2 months after the disaster. The relief operation was mostly coordinated between local NGOs[②] with limited accountability towards local/district offices. With delayed establishment of NRA and arrival of winter prompted many NGOs to swiftly diversify their housing re-construction

----

① Maujua Village is located on point of Naubise, Dhading that is 3 hours drive from capital city Kathmandu. The village is situated 2 hours upstream from the Dhading Chautari base.

② This documentation is based on author's relief work experience in Maujua, Dhading during May 2015 A. D. Maujua is surrounded between.

Figure 2   An aerial view of Maujua village after the April 25th earthquake
Source: Author's own.

activities after post-earthquake event. According to Sager Acharya[1] "NGOs have constructed houses but the district treasury controller doesn't hold those records" which has a lot to do with limited presence of government at the local level. At central level, there have been no official mechanisms to monitor the transparency of NGOs as the anti-corruption agency (Commission for investigation of abuse of authority) only monitors the activities of the government Manandhar. Relatedly, for gaining aid effectiveness, policymakers need to repeatedly refrain from actions whose results are individually negligible but collectively devastating. In Nepal, there is a common tendency of high political meddling over resource allocation and desire for power which has resulted in a constant struggle for workable and stable political institution.[2] Bell reports that as soon as $4.1 billion was pledged at the International donor's conference, politicians switched their attention to "power politics" which gave both donors and implementing agencies a splitting headache during the period.[3]

---

[1]   Sagar Acharaya is chief of National Reconstruction Authority's Secretariat district coordination committee of Dolakha (Rastriya Samachar Samiti, 2017).
[2]   Hayes, L. D., "Political development of Nepal," *The Indian Journal of Political Science* 2.
[3]   Bell, T., *What's Really Holding Back Reconstruction in Nepal*, Retrieved January 5, 2018, from Aljazeera: http://www.aljazeera.com/indepth/opinion/2016/04/holding-reconstruction-nepal-160424075649714.html.

Incidents like above-where implementing agencies are questioned on their effectiveness in aid-implementation both from donors and the end users' beneficiaries-is somethingthat Wildavsky refers to "holding the grip".[①] He argues that main complaint of effective aid implementation in Nepal is the policies prepared by specialized bodies[②] still have to rely on central government for its final decision. The heredity still persists, as there is not a separate funding source directly under supervision of Reconstruction Authority. The government established "reconstruction fund" which channels all financial resources received in Prime Minister's relief fund. [③]Due to the changes in the government and political wrangling in the competition over resources, the bureaucratic process halts the efficient usage of the funds that have been disbursed. In the eyes of donors, it creates clouds of doubt and careful awareness before disbursing the amount.

Table1 Status Of Funding's from International Donor Conference 2015 from Bilateral Sources

Bilateral Sources	Announced (NRs Billion)	Committed (NRs Billion)	Received (NRs. Billion)
India	140	100	0
China	76. 69	76. 69	1
Japan	26	24. 70	4. 9
USA	13	15. 97	0. 0143
European Union	11. 74	11. 18	3. 28

① Wildavsky, A., " Why Planning Fails in Nepal," *Administrative Science Quaterly* 4 .

② These are agencies that direct the government towards policy planning process and includes institutions like National Planning Commission (NPC). NPC is also an advisory council to National Reconstruction Authority (NRA).

③ Prime Minister disaster relief fund (DRF), different from what it sounds like, is coordinated by the vice-chairperson of the National Planning Commission along with 8 Secretaries unanimously nominated. It is different from Prime Minister "Assistance Fund" which is controlled by Prime Minister and is not audited. Prime Minister DRF is a means of "fast-track" method to channel aid effectiveness against procedural delays in a slow bureaucracy.

Bilateral Sources	Announced (NRs Billion)	Committed (NRs Billion)	Received (NRs. Billion)
UK	11	16. 55	0. 990
Germany	3. 35	3. 40	0

* World Bank and ADB have disbursed only 6. 61 billion and 2. 58 billion respectively.

* Out of \$4. 1 billion, only NRS. 75 billion is spent on post-reconstruction housing, Baral.

* The dataset is based until 2017.

Data taken for two years period 2015-2017 A. D.

It is the underlying fact that any attempt to improve aid effectiveness thus lies in the complete rethinking of not just policy agendas associated with the aid but in the nature and relationship between the donor and the recipient. In Nepal, policy at disaster management is heavily centralized leaving little room for aid accountability and upholding capacities of local government to effectively handle aid. In such scenario, Jacobs critically encapsulates more strong relationship through dialogue and nature of issues faced and appropriate responses through potential interventions with local partners. [1] It is so because for Nepal, as one of the observants responded "receiving money is the easiest part, its what happens after that which disrupts the reconstruction processes".

3. Institutional governance in post-disaster context

Among its many definitions, the term "governance" captures a variety of ways in which society is not simply acted upon by the state, but has actively shaped the actions and outcomes of the state activity. This is supported by Haggar[2] and Evans[3] who have converged to idea that society provides crucial elements of support to the state for its effectiveness, and that a state is critical to collective action in society. Another solid reasoning for this argument by World

---

[1]　Jacobs, A., "Listen First: a Pilot System for Managing Downward Accountability in NGOs," *Development in Practice* 7 (2010).

[2]　Haggar, S., *Pathways From Periphery*, NY, USA: Cornell University Press, 1990.

[3]　Evans, P., *Embedded Autonomy*, Princeton, NJ, USA: Princeton University Press, 1995.

Bank is that merely allocating public resources for production and consumption might not bring desirable outcomes if institutions involved in execution and monitoring are malfunctioning. Therefore, the effectiveness of state is determined through its governance practice. There are various interpretations about governance, but for this paper, I focus on governance as an attempt of the state, social organization, and the citizens in general, for rational decision-making and allocation of resources that cadres the needs of society. Overall, governance is concerned with how societies, governments and institutions are managed. Governance can have a different meaning based on the terminology we apply towards its study. Daniel & kay state that if all the interactions, layers and applications are to be taken into account, then it diminishes the idea of governance as an effective organizing concept. Prof. Ruth Dixon[①] also state that the idea of governance is about state's effectiveness on delivering services to its people. Fukuyama research centers with notion that governance is government's ability to make and enforce rules regardless of its structure. In that essence, it becomes vital to place the role of government as an important point to research conclusion. In this section, our prime analysis will focus on role of government coupled up with evaluation of role of citizen's and social organization in rebuilding urban housing. This will be presented by describing the short comings based on findings through 3 key actors of governance: State, social organization and citizens Lil, Witt, & Bilau, Meerman.

3.1   Role of State

From the state point of view, disaster response is mitigated and managed by a sole agency, the Ministry of Home Affairs. It's role has been characterized by coordination malfunction and lack of precise line of authority definition. The recent volume of 2009 NSDRM[②] articulates the authority to be chaired by Prime Minister, with vice-chair being the Ministry of Home Affairs along with 19 other

---

① Prof. Ruth Dixon, Research fellow at Blavatnik School of Government gave a lecture at School of Government Peking University on 26th March, 2018 A. D. on citizen's satisfaction with the government of UK lecture. The above text is based on informal conversation with the author.

② National Strategy on Disaster Risk Management.

ministries, chief of Nepal Army as well as 4 other NGOs (representing women, Dalit, and other backward classes) and a few disaster management experts. With division of labor, the coordination has at times become a major obstacle in relief and rescue efforts. MoHA is on the same hierarchy level as other respective ministries so is equipped with limited authority over other departments. In their investigative report, Fuady Bisri (2016) advocates that of the 62 mandatory emergency response service activities, 30 were completed based on NDRF (National disaster risk framework) timeline, 17 were implemented with some negative consequences and mostly through outside sources and 15 were not even implemented at all. A contributing factor have been cited to be government's weakness in reporting the disaster responses and that it did not had its own mechanism while covering humanitarian relief.

Despite some leverage was provided to the district offices to coordinate relief efforts independently, the absence of " local resource center " (providing resourceful information regarding post-reconstruction efforts) in each of affected districts prove lack of coordination among central and the local level in post-disaster response. In this regard, Mr. Drona Koirala[1] argues that "*At the local level, we do not have the equipment for removing the debris caused by earthquake in spite of the fact that government had committed to deliver the same on time.*" Upon initial phase of recovery, many volunteers argued that there was haphazard distribution of aid relief in the beginning resulting in unequal distribution, duplication of relief required and lack of coordination with central and local government. One donor representative says

"There are lot of I/NGOs because there is lack of state capacity here. If there was active government participation, we would have been working for government".

To put more salt on the wound, the absence of local government was seen as a big barrier in relief efforts. Provision have been made in Local Governance act

---

① SAIS, (May).

1999 about capacity development of local institutions towards such calamities but it was never put into force without elected bodies representation.

Furthermore, considering the analysis of the present situation and the role of government, some respondents argue that granting authority to MoHA does not justify prevention of disaster risks and that *"Home Affairs Ministry is not focused on basic development activities and there should be a separate fully autonomous authority to oversee the disaster risk management activities"*. The NEOC (National Emergency Operating Center) was faced with tumultuous times facing political uncertainty and lack of preparedness resulting in overlapping and duplication of work among the existing policies Environment friendly and local governance (EFLG), Local adaption plan of action (LAPA), Local disaster risk management plan (LDMP) and Minimum Conditions and Performance Measures (MCPM) (SAIS, May). After the disaster 2015, the initial oversee of disaster management related activities was conducted solely by disaster management division under Ministry of Home Affairs. After an initial phase, the coordination was performed on a large scale with coordination between Ministry of Federal Affairs and Local Development (MoFALD), Ministry of Urban Development (MoUD) and Ministry of Home Affairs (MoHA) until the National Reconstruction Authority (NRA) was formed. Daly, Duyne, Ninglekhu, & Nguyen (2017) state that during this time reconstruction largely stalled due to lack of bylaws and reconstruction policy, new building codes for designing private houses all of which required homework from the government. This is common among most of the ministries in Nepal as there is uncomfortable coordination outlook between the departments. In an instance, the design of building codes and purchase of land are crucial to providing earthquake resilient buildings. From Nepal, construction of buildings for government offices falls under Ministry of Urban development while construction of schools falls under Ministry of Education and similarly, for hospitals under Ministry of Health. As these institutions have been severly damaged, there is confusion among who to take responsible action to reconstruct the buildings. The NRA was no exception in this regard that its very establishment was poised by political dillydallying that hindered the reconstruction process. Furthermore, for construction of private homes, the US $3000 is widely

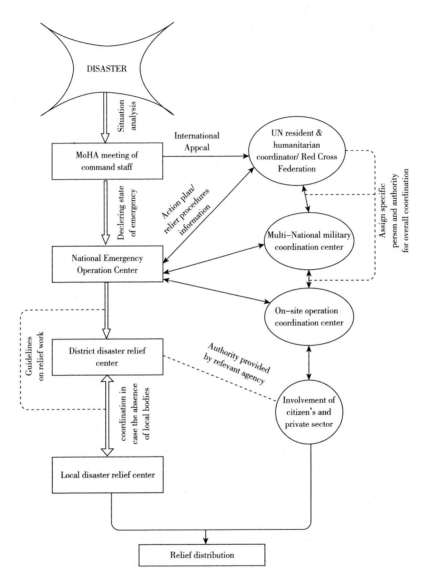

Figure 3   Coordination process among government/social organization after the post-disaster 2015 in Nepal

* Diagram is Author's own with inputs from Pal & Chatterjee, and MoHA.

seen as inadequate for rebuilding homes in Nuwakot where the building costs could surge up to around $15000. NRA believes the relief amount is a small compensation to incorporate all household victims to set a base for people to "build back better". The notion of equal distribution for all has been backfired on many grounds. *"How can me, a victim from a very remote village in Nuwakot get equal compensation as to a victim in wealthy Kathmandu? They have extra additional money to build house themselves. I do not even enjoy such privilege."* (Nuwakot resident). In this regard, Govinda Raj Pokharel[①] says *"I can only coordinate and collaborate"* in that households should be more engaged in rebuilding efforts over criticisms. From its initial phase, the surveying of households for relief distribution took a lengthy turn. In Nuwakot, respondents argue that survey procedure started at least a year after the earthquake which means a year delayed already in reconstruction efforts. Upon further interviewing, an official criticized government's preparedness and decision-making ability *"where allocating the relief amount was priory set before surveying the damaged households / victims"*. As reconstruction process got delayed, so got many sectors affected. In most sectors of Nuwakot, monitoring was lethargic with survey team initially involved in evaluating the post-disaster damage outcomes. However, an engineer reported that some of his co-workers left abroad for future prospects amidst to lower wages and benefits. Usually the engineers were provided with sum of NRs 8000 ($ 80 approx.) a month for going to villages in reconstruction efforts. This excluded their travelling expenses. This had halted the distribution of relief amount as prior engineer's approval are required to get the relief amount. Monitoring mechanism isn't the first time the government has been accused of. In 2008 Koshi flood, the Ministry of Home Affairs (MoHA) then admitted that *"Nepal was not prepared for, nor had adequate resources to manage during this sort of disaster"*.[②] Chetteri had put forward analysis that except for weather forecasting, there was no proper early warning system for disaster problem solving

---

① Rai, 2017, Govinda Raj Pokharel was the then CEO of NRA durin the survey. He has been replaced by Yuvaraj Bhusal as the new CEO making him the 4th change in leadership in NRA during a period of 3 years.

② Shrestha, R. K., Alhers, R., Bakker, M., & Gupta, J., "Institutional Dysfunction and Challenges in Flood Control: A Case Study of the Kosi Flood 2008," *Economic And Political Weekly* 2 (2010).

in Nepal. ① 17 years later when monsoon flood struck on southern plains of Nepal, while the early SMS warning on flood control was kept in place, the displacement brought in possibility of major humanitarian crisis IRIN (2017). With rapid uncontrolled urbanization, fast growing cities of Nepal in particular have seen limited open space. Upon personal reflection, aftermath the 2015 earthquake, due to limited public open area, a lot of people had to take shelter into their neighbor's residence for open and safe space.

3.2   Role of Social Organization

One of the features of the authority is its feasibility to collaborate with non-governmental institutions to deliver effective relief efforts NRA (2016). However, even prior to the establishment of reconstruction authority, national/international social organization played an important role in relief efforts. While the district/local authorities were granted some authority in managing relief efforts, post reconstruction activity isan issue of funding. In developing countries like Nepal, disasters usually exceed the coping capacity of local government so they rely on external sources for financing Ikaputra (2012). With provisions of relief-rebuilding efforts at local level, it can get pretty complex when INGOs are involved. INGOs at first are required to register themselves under Social Welfare Council (SWC)② . National NGOs on the other hand register with their respective district government. The SWC is generally involved in carrying out local DRR projects but, it can incorporate INGOs economic assistance even if approval has been given at only local level. In case of post-disaster reconstruction, INGOs and NGOs often want to work independently on a politically instable countries like Nepal, bypassing the government institutions. In some VDCs of Nuwakot, some respondents replied that NRA officials have encouraged not to take donations from external sources apart from their $3000 grant to built houses based on their building codes. Also, there was no

---

① Chettri, M. B., *Nepal Country Report* 1999, Government of Nepal, Ministry of Home Affairs. Kathmandu: Government of Nepal, 1999.

② Social Welfare Council.

establishment of training programs to aware locals about disaster management prevention. Ayush Baskota, a civil engineer working as a district coordinator for Nuwakot district states "This *is the first-time engineers have come to the village and trained the local masons*". ①While the training programs were facilitated by National Reconstruction Authority, it wasn't without the support of the non-governmental institutions financing such projects. In that regard, many NGOs in Nepal have been criticized for functioning more like a business that competes for massive funding from donors than less of social service and less of "social organization". On the other hand, there has been no local elections in Nepal for the past 20 years. So, with lack of elected representatives combined with weak local-authorities functional capacity, there were significant unawareness about topology, households, damage done and the like. As a result, when international aid givers, NGOs arrived on the scene, they frequently lacked data on damages, contextual information, and well-organized, knowledgeable local partners onto whose capacities they could couple into providing a foundation for coordinated action Manandhar, Vraughese, Howitt, & Kelly (2017). While some authority was provided at the district level for coordinating relief efforts, the reports of duplication, inefficient distribution of aid had caused the government to enact "One-door policy②" where all the distribution of relief materials would be channeled through the government source. Previously, the INGOs would require approval of their projects through the district offices while reporting to them simultaneously about their work efforts. However, with the new policy enacted from August 4, 2017 A. D. the district government would be in charge of all relief activities that placed the relief operation activities of many such institutions under halt. "*The INGOs in Nepal cumulatively can only support a minority of victims. Say 90% of work government will have to do from its part*", an INGO informant replied. One of the key issues of collaboration has been on facilitating technical know-hows and skills. Some NGOs had started providing trainings to

---

① World Bank, 2016.
② This policy was enacted during August 2017 A. D. aftermath the increased flood in the southern plains causing death of 141 people and over 1.5 million affected.

local mobilizers in Nuwakot based on the design curriculum provided by DUDAC① prior to the establishment of NRA but with its central role, many such institutions working in different districts had to reshuffle their working mechanisms that came with limited availability of information at first place. Also, with the absence of "local resource center" comprised of technical staffs to provide expertise on mobilizing resources for reconstruction, there was severe lack of coordination among these avenues for efficient coordination. In Nuwakot, there was no evidence of NRA officials providing technical and vocational trainings to the local administration to sharpen the disaster risk reduction management skills. In that regard, the challenges are enormous in bureaucratic hurdles for implementing a project under consideration from NRA. At the beginning, the institution who wish to contribute to post-disaster reconstruction efforts require a certificate of understanding from NRA. It contains NRA's mission, plans, financial management and mobilization of resources guidelines. Then the organization prepares a proposal including the local level government it wants to work with and its collaborative procedures. This process follows a hectic bureaucratic process as it has to get consensus from at least 2 ministry department and is finally send to NRA for approval. The challenges are enormous and this process might take a tedious time. As a consequence, many social organizations in Nuwakot have been more focused on providing awareness campaign for future prevention of disaster management rather than getting involved in the re-construction campaign.

> " Creating *awareness is the foremost responsibility for disaster management. As it goes that prevention is better than cure. There is no guarantee that money provided will let people build safe buildings if they are not aware.*" (Informant from UN)

---

① Department of Urban development and Building construction (DUDAC) is responsible for house design catalogue, curriculum for different trainings and implementation and follow up on building code in the construction houses.

Such institutions have established the concept of "build back better" by organizing awareness campaign in form of general assembly, radio programs, street performance, and even through entertainment means like TV shows. In some societies, households have become self-reliant because of the social cohesiveness through positive social interactions they have implanted among each other despite of significant damage. In one case, the village of Maujua in Dhading district which is completely inaccessible from roads and other infrastructures, people have started building houses themselvesfrom their available resources rather than some places with accessible roads waiting for relief materials.

3. 3　Role of Citizens

The vertical "top-down" nature of government decision and its political turbulence over the years has sometimes proven problematic for citizen's "opinion" in a way that at one level, local government has very little decision-making capacity while on the other level, there was no local elections held for last 20 years. Most people are skeptical of the design building codes that NRA have provided to then and wish to construct building in the design they prefer in statement that cites the lack of presence of the government in their district. It has hindered the public awareness to most extent of the people of Nuwakot that people have very little awareness of prevention method during disaster occurrence. From institutional perspective, the bottom up approach was at times a tedious process. With little framework on handling complaints from citizen's, government officials didn't seem considerate enough for local wards level resolution process while the local officials remain skeptical of central government's assistance. According to an NRA engineer, the official process of handling complaints would start after the grant distribution have completed, while the same question forwarded to other local officials in Nuwakot, they remain unanswered. There is a lot of confusion about how to handle citizen's complaint in this regard. There was also major confusion about designing building codes information awareness among citizens. Most of them believed that the cash money distributed is for relief materials purchase and merely constructing building as per NRA mandate. As one volunteer responds *"Unless the community understands how this is going to be carried out, the reconstruction process won't turn out smoothly"*. Upon a personal reflection, on our volunteering to Nuwakot a month after the earthquake, we were stopped at the middle of the road by local official. Demanding our details of relief materials to the locals, the official said to *"either bring enough for all the households or do not bring it at all"*. However, of the three, the private and citizen's sector has been the most effective including training and operational management schemes and transfer of technologies. Also, most of the respondents have a vague way of addressing the problem by referring it to the politicians instead of a specific department or area. While the political leaders and their parties where actively involved in the post-disaster relief efforts, their role got diminished due to political uncertainty, external aggression and importantly the take over by NRA and establishment of District Coordination Committee (DCC). However, some victims still look upon the politicians as their last savior to meet the ends. The degree of citizen's engagement is associated with religious beliefs, societal understanding and public awareness. Most of the victims consider the damage done to be the act of god or the consequences of the sin they committed in the past. Also, the design structure of most of the building's dates to years back before universities in Nepal formally trained civil architects to design houses of earthquake resistant. Furthermore, with only $3000 available, Nuwakot has some high terrain with people living up on the hills, for whom transportation materials costs more than the relief amount itself. Upon interview, some officials said that it was confusing at times because some of those very old houses were not registered (*land ownership certificate*) with current government system and were not included in the CBS data. The CBS and government authorities had to create a provision for beneficiaries to register their land ownership certificate for which they had to move back and forth the municipality time and again delaying the process to further extent. This vicious process of trial and error have proven tedious in disbursement of grants. An engineer replied that some beneficiaries were unable to withdraw the money because their name on the citizenship and CBS survey data were not matching and that the bank had denied access to grant the relief amount to the beneficiaries. *"If we can properly educate the citizen's about disaster management and the government relief methods after post-disaster efforts, then 50% of the work can get completed before the occurrence of the disaster only if citizens are accepting government's way of doing work"* (an informal student *from Nuwakot*). Most of the social organization institutions and government officials realize that awareness to the community is the very essence of providing disaster relief.

4. Conclusion

Within a small survey respondent representing similar backgrounds and livelihoods, the capacity to deliver the reconstruction efforts were largely differentiated. Two years after the earthquake, some of the poorest households would be seen using everything at their disposal placing it to rebuild their homes while some middle-income families where still to be in despair with the tumultuous disaster waiting for government grants to get their homes re-built. Yet, the concern remains the same of not just rebuilding homes, but in a manner that can withstand future risks. The research provides some challenges encompassed by the stakeholders in providing reconstruction efforts and in between government, the social organizations and international assistance. Most of the issues raised have been about coordination efforts and the role of state in maintaining accountability. Good governance requires that there exists an "above threshold" relationship between state, civil society and its citizens and how well the state implements the derivatives it has prepared, matters a lot to the efficiency and effectiveness for the housing reconstruction after post-disaster of April 2015. The research was set out to identify the governance status of Government of Nepal on rebuilding efforts. During the process, it has sought to identify the relationship between aid and housing reconstruction and the process of governance associated with it. The study finds that while moderate efforts, the externality and slowpoke process of on the ground relief efforts have hindered the governance of the authority in speeding up the reconstruction of private houses. Nepal, 11th in riskiest country for earthquake requires more relevant discourse on mitigating disaster risk management to avoid catastrophe in near future.

From this research study, there are number of areas which can be further delved into for study purpose. Firstly, there is a need to understand rise of NGOs in Nepal coupled with little economic progress and the aid that flows through them. Secondly, there is a need to study government's structure and working mechanisms, decision making on relation to disaster management policies and ministries responsible for such actions. Thirdly, more focus has to be given on the coordination mechanisms from top-down approach where separate ministries oversee separate aspects of DRR, it becomes more complex and requires rigorous evaluation of previous policies.

Urban Governance and Culture: Care for the Urban Way of Life

Alan Blum *

【Abstract】 Cities are exemplary of constant worldly change. This paper offers a critical analysis of the relationship between urban governance and culture. It first treats urban governance as a social relationship, tying together two important concepts: governance and culture. It then addresses the dialectic between urban governance and culture through the lens of the art of care, requiring seeing the detail of a city as reflections of the particular character of a person. The paper goes on to dissect the relationship between soul and the change in cities, particularly focusing on the globalizing forces of gentrification. Qualitative interviews were conducted with local Venetians regarding their attitudes and feelings about Venice being transformed into a global tourist city, driving out local residents and fundamentally altering its social environment. It concludes that cities are often viewed as maintaining itself thought adaptation, exhibiting not only theatrical change but also dramatic ways of learning modernity and the phenomenon of self-governance.

【Keywords】 Urban governance; Culture; Urban change; Gentrification

I am pleased to participate in this forum and want to raise as an opener the

---

* Alan Blum，多伦多城市文化研究中心/社会创新研究中心执行主任。

question of the relation between the interest of the forum in urban governance and my interest and history of research in the culture of the city. In other words, just what kind of relationship do we hope to develop between governing the city and culture? It is this interaction at this intersection that is my problem.

Urban Governance as a Social Relationship

Note that urban governance is connected to methods for organizing the social order of the city to make it more efficient, to strategies for planning such an order, to ways and means of making and designing a better city. How does my interest in culture relate to such a project? This invites us to reflect on how two concepts—governance and culture—are tied together and I affirm the legacy ofKarl Marx here by saying that these two concepts must not be treated not as opposites but dialectically as corelated in decisive ways.

Care: the Dialectic between Urban Governance and Culture

First I suggest that the notion of governance as making and designing a city not only presupposes its own beliefs and values as to what is the best way of making such a thing but assumes that the city can betaken as a thing, rather than as a human association that exceeds such boundaries, and so might be ruled by an algorithmic vision of making. But note that making a city not only creates something new but must remake something handed down in a way that shows how urban governance as a desire to innovate is between a past that is inherited and a future that is not yet. So we see several things about the concept of urban governance with which we begin: it is a social relationship to time, oriented to making something new and modifying something old, making use of concepts such as heritage and innovation (two concepts that are in vogue today and that I will discuss eventually). This shows that urban governance as a practice is in the words of Max Weber, "oriented to an order and governed thereby in its practice". This begins to alert us to the cultural component of urban governance as a relationship grounded in interpretations and a belief system. Once we understand this, we see that urban governance does not just deal with congestion, transportation, crime control and such matters as these but with a relationship to values of which such matters are indications. But to appreciate the cultural character of urban governance as more than a philosophy or ideology of making and planning we need to rethink the notion of culture. Only then can we begin to formulate the dialectical relation between these notions.

Now, as I use the notion of culture, it does not refer to the customs of a people or city or society such as hospitality, food, manners, and the like because these are surface indications that we need to "read" and interpret, to move beyond, in order to discern their cultural aspect. This requires what the philosopher Wittgenstein called an aesthetic attitude or art: he said art is not a product simply such as painting ormusic but a relationship that can see something-as something. In other words, art exists in seeing-as, in seeing, say hospitality or food habits, as something else, insofar as this capacity for analogy or figurative language (seeing one thing as another) is the foundation of art.

So, my message at this point is that all of these facts, these details connected to culture as customs and to urban governance as planning, regulation and policy, need to be seen-as something else, as if they are images or reflections of a social relationship.

So, I propose that our rethinking of both of these notions, urban governance and culture, involves seeing them as expressions of a relationship that joins them in ways that allows us to see governing as cultural insofar as they are tied together by the notion of care. Governing a city is, in a sense, showing care for its specific and particular character and such character has been described typically as its identity, identity used in this way as a designation of what culture is. So governing is care and care is one aspect of culture. Note that to care for something is not just exemplified by showing care for people but, as I take it, care for quality, i. e., care for the quality of a city, care for the quality or identity of China, and as I am trying to show here, even care for the quality of language (of concepts such as governance and culture). I take care to be that kind of relationship. Note also, this concern for quality is itself an art, an aptitude that many cannot do (US example of teenagers and robots caring for the elderly). If to care for quality is to be attuned to its special character, such an aptitude or ability to "tune in" and listen to the inner voice of the population is itself a part of culture.

The Art of Care

I say the art of care requires seeing the detail of a city as expressive detail, that is as reflections of the particular character of a people, not just its themes in the way an anthropologist must classify a population (optimistic, ambitious etc.) but as indications of a particular angle of viewing the world, what the Greeks call the bias or stigma of a people, the relation that seems to make them different. And if sociologists have talked about values here, a philosophical tradition, especially Hegel, says that what we are dealing with is something like the spirit of a people, an "object" that can only be measured or treated denotatively at risk of simplifying it out of existence. The spirit of a people is definite and immeasurable, but can be represented and discussed, brought to view in dialogue. Though not an "object" such a connotative surfeit can be engaged in conversation. As Gertrude Stein said, a name like China is depleted when it is used as a common noun without care for its quality; such care is designed to bring the noun to life as a name with special character. This works best when we design or find situations in the everyday life of a city when conflict over this very question—what is the identity of the city (or any category) comes to view. In the US we see this around gender, race, the meaning of the country as a legacy, all situations that elicit conflict and as such become research opportunities for us. The question for us: howdo we gain access to the spirit of the city since it is unmeasurable, and how on earth can we care for such spirit if it is hard to capture or pin down? We look at attempts.

If we listen closely to the literature, research and common speech, we can appreciate the notion of the city as an object of desire. Though many are thrown into the city through the accident of birth, more seem to be lured to the city, drawn to it because of what it seems to offer in the way of its promise of a better

life or sweetness of living. The city seduces us to taste its wares and then to
accept the consequences of this encounter.

Spirit as the Spice of Life

In his desire to recover the quality obscured by quantitative approaches to
the city and the urban as an object for analysis, the sociologist Louis Wirth
wanted to develop the difference between what he assumed to be insignificant and
essential in any such formulation of the city and so was at the same time
concerned to discriminate between such conditions and another "object" of
analysis, the relationship to the urban that appeared to exceed the functional
engagement with conditions, a kind of affective immersion in these conditions.
Thus, if the city seems first and foremost a mix of disparate influences, people,
groups, and interpretations of this and that, perhaps the quality of the city is
disclosed in how it engages this mix. In this way, the question of the identity of
the city could be heard as shifting from a concern with material conditions to
thequestion about the emphasis a city can be seen to place on material life, how it
engages materiality itself, revealing materialism as a social relationship always
and everywhere. Of course the city must prioritize the activities of settlement and
its routinization in work, domestic life and private sojourning. In this way the city
must provide a framework for a functional relationship to life, always creating
patterns and opportunities for doing survival, to make possible something like an
infrastructure of niches of survival, not just as an opportunity structure but as
grounds for an art of survival that seeks to invest such a functional network with a
degree of meaning that must desire to do more than survive in life, to spice it up
so to speak. So the urban way of life is embodied as a functional association and
as something more, perhaps oriented to ethics and to overtones of life that seem
aesthetic. Any dialogue on the city must capture these differences voices.

In this sense the urban way of life, identified prosaically with the "buzz" of
the city, is connected to the spirit and jouissance of city living, both positive and
negative, but in ways that cannot be concretely determined or measured,
disseminating an aura that seems intangible to empiricists but definite despite its

indeterminacy. To paraphrase Wittgenstein, the urban way of life is not a thing but it is not nothing either. This permits Clement Rosset to say of any relation to the Real that it is both definite and ambiguous, that it is definite in the sense of beingsomething or other but not something in particular, that its unambiguous existence as something or other discloses its Grey Zone as definitely indefinite, as fundamentally ambiguous. Applied to the urban way of life, to paraphrase Rosset, we can say that its intangibility is tangible to the modern subject, something not to be determined obsessively but (in his words) savoured as and for what it is (Rosset, 1989, 5-21). As an example of such an urban tone, both definitive and yet ineffable, note the way Larry McMurtry depicts Houston and its inspirational force for him.

"Houston was my companion on the walk. She had been my mistress, but after a thousand nights together, just the two of us, we were calling it off. It was a warm, moist, mushy, smelly night, the way her best nights were. The things most people hated about her were the things I loved; her heat, her dampness, her sumpy smells. She wasn't beautiful, but neither was I. I liked her heat and her looseness and her smells. Those things were her substance, and if she had been cool and dry and odorless, I wouldn't have cared to live with her three years. We were calling it off, but I could still love her. She still reached me, when I went walking with her. Her mists were always a little sexy. I felt, in leaving her, the kind of fond gentleness you're supposed to feel after passion. It was the kind of gentleness I never got to feel with Sally. Its expression might be stroking a shoulder, or something. I had had such good of Houston, she had dealt so generously with me, always, that I walked andstroked her shoulder for an hour or two, in the night. Then, when she was really sleeping, I went home. I wanted to be gone when she woke up. "

We see that the notion of the urban way of life must begin to represent the way a city gets embodied in its subject, gets under its skin in specific ways, leaving sensual vestiges in its capacity to touch, to be tasted and savoured.

Therefore, the convention of identifying the city with the market place and the ruling motif of materialistic interests is intelligible as a gloss that always requires more in the shape of a formulation of the kind of spirit such an emphasis makes possible. Thus, the posit of materialism as a beginning invites us to inquire into the imaginary relationship it must assume as an oriented relationship to the world, to objectives, time, space, and human desire and its conditions. I have noted that the sociologist Louis Wirth recognized the insufficiency of this gloss as a final interpretation and its value as a beginning provocation when he used the cliché as an opportunity to analyze the urban way of life.

Wirth recognized how description of the city must make reference to a notion of a way of life that reaches beyond the recitation of demographics, conditions of affordable housing, congestion, sprawl, and social determinants, not by disavowing such factors but by making reference to the way such conditions influence and presuppose an infrastructure of interpretation, idealization, and imagination relating to ways and means of bearing life and of handling itspleasure and pain. Part of this dialectic between pain and pleasure makes reference to the need and desire to do more that endure the functionalist requirements of urban life. In this way Wirth recognized that as a way of life any attempt to study the city must reveal some sense of the city as an object of desire or a relationship to value, what Simmel called the Ought, as an engagement that is fundamentally ambiguous.

Soul, Authenticity: Change in the City, Losses and Gains

When we began the Culture of Cities project, the context of our initiative was ruled by the image of a world in flux characterized as such through the rubric of globalization. We neither accepted this cliché unreservedly nor rejected it because it was a shibboleth: for our work it simply stood as a powerful indication of elemental collective representations that could be taken up and investigated, a social phenomenon registered in language as a conception of the world and of its divisions that is of currency. In particular, while some were chanting anti-globalization mantras and most were enrolling as cheerleaders for this new market and the so-called freedom of its deregulation, for us, the relevance of globalization for the project resided in its character as a stimulus to rethink the notion of local identity, for it seemed in the popular imagination that the world was being transformed to the extent that cities were viewed as only points in mobile circuits of influences, repelling and attracting the movement of capital, people, and information, in ways that seemed to compromise the particular identities of cities as they had beentraditionally conceived. For in such a borderless world, cities appeared almost interchangeable, losing their special character or aura, functioning instead as destinations of convenience, happenstance, accident, and opportunism.

What we recognized at this point was that if cities were thought in such ways, in being treated as sites that simply make the most of such opportunities, there could be both economically successful and (we might say) socially unsuccessful cities because the cities that seem to grow or prosper economically might be the most indistinct cities. Since we also knew that the social existence of cities, their force in everyday life and collective imagination, rested on claims to distinctness, singularity, and a kind of uniqueness, we wondered how such claims (and so, such cities) could survive under these conditions of interchangeability. This posed an interesting problem to the extent that cities might be seen to grow economically at the same time as they appear to become indistinct. In a certain sense, cities could become successful and unsuccessful at the same time, two-sided, in ways that were not merely curious to me but might cause anyone to think through the notion of what makes a city "successful?" This might be the important problem to put on the agenda, a conceptual rather than an economic problem pure and simple.

At the time of our project, the intellectual environment was characterized by a mix of speakers (political economy, geography, urban sociology, architecture, environmentalism) alladdressing the global city as an emergent phenomenon. This mix consisted of an array of views, each advancing a particular position but none really interdisciplinary. These fruitful approaches, tending to be positive and quantitative, were necessarily silent about many important facets of urban life that they could not quantify, facets pertaining particularly to the distinctive effervescence and tone of the city that appeared to provide for its quality and unique voice. This meant that in order to address the questions of interest to us we needed to develop a fluency in thinking about matters not immediately accessible to quantification, questions making reference to the quality or spirit of the city and that seemed to require the intuitive capacity of judgment.

Such a capacity or inclination enabled us to identify cities and distinguish them from organizations, families, and societies as we all do, and it often but not exactly enabled us to delineate boundaries showing where a city begins and ends vis-à-vis suburbs, hinterlands, region, state, and where one city starts and ends in relation to others, and what can be taken as Chicago over and against Philadelphia, and what kinds of conditions compare and contrast cities such as restaurant prices, taxi fares, unemployment figures, crime statistics, or numbers of thises and thats, each and all of great importance but only when formulated in relation to whatever gives them significance. Such conventions forced upon us this truth and no more, leading us to accept the givenness of the name of the city as a façade of individuality, as a verity, as true, but leaving us with the what of the city and its configuration of variables, and not its who. And without some sense of more than a recitation of variables and coefficients (and even to understand those at best or to speculate on them) we could not develop this sense as robust enough to empower us to face important questions concerning the city, its value for people, whether or how it is changing, and the like. In other words, without developing our sense of thge city as a social form we could not engage all of the questions of life and death, ethics, aesthetics, and judgment that we need to face, and we certainly could not come to terms with the question of the city as a human association.

So all questions of relevance to us—are cities good for people or not; what makes cities special compared to other kinds of collectives; are cities changing and in what respects, indeed, how is one city different than another—seemed to require interpretation and judgment in excess of the prosaic limitations of common sense, and they seemed to rest upon some notion of what all cities share and how they differentiate this share.

Name and Life

By focusing upon the tension between a name and a life, approaching the city as a life beyond its name, captured in the convention of culture as the signature of a collective, we followed the Greek notion of identity as what we might call the bias or stigma peculiar to aperson or collective, and in this case, the particular slant of a city. Identity is then somewhat like a distortion or particular accent on reality presented and coming to view by a city or people.

In this way, we can posit that Philadelphia is not simply a place different from Chicago, but a manner of being. The circumstances that seem to mark a city as particular make reference to a history that is somewhat like *poesis* as a kind of formative process integral to its name. The formative process, as *poesis*, is not uniform and linear but an irregular trajectory marked by contingencies, ruptures, and discordances that extend and perpetuate the persistence of the name in the circumstances that disrupt it. The name remains as the voice that digests the extenuating circumstances of influences. These circumstances that I called after Diderot "little adjacent alterations," mark the city's preservation of itself as something other than these influences as if it maintains itself *in* these influences and retains these influences in itself as a sign of appropriation. In the struggle with their generality as a city, Philadelphia and Chicago make throughout their history "little adjacent alterations" in the very notion of a city, still sustaining and redeeming that notion in their distorted shape as the city they each seem to be. In relating the name of a city to its life, we become engaged in addressing the peculiarity of the city.

It then appeared to us that what cities have in common *and* what differentiates cities is one and the same, and that the condition, a kind of effervescence, tone, or quality gives meaning to cities in ways that are distinctive and particular to each city. So if the identity of a city is like its stigma, a symptom as we would say for an individual, this stigma is simply one particular way of working out the character of all cities, making each and every city seem comparable and yet different. But if each city is stigmatized or symptomatic in a different way, how can we determine a path of inquiry so opaque? And then again, when cities change as they must like all mortal beings, how do these changes relate to transformations of their stigmata? Can these questions even make sense or be anything but idle? We needed a method, a vocabulary, a model.

We began by examining a process that seemed to occur in ways affecting all cities, so-called globalization, in order to begin engaging the question of how different cities were handling such a problem, and what we discovered was that everyone and anyone was saying the same, that cities were becoming gentrified. We ask the question, what happens to the symptom of the city under the weight of globalization as a force?

The cities in our research project certainly seemed to be examples of the globalizing force of gentrification, whether Dublin as Celtic tiger, Berlin's architectural renovation frenzy, and Toronto's celebration of its diversity and sanitized master plan, but we noted a commentary on the same process in great cities such as New York and Paris, and venerable cities such as Venice, and more recently in the format of creative city talk that was and is sweeping North America.

Examples

The UNESCO Declaration of principles and recommendations intended for the safeguarding, study, development and promotion of the intangible cultural heritage (ICH) of nations such as Canada clearly invites study and research related to designating heritage as both a cultural phenomenon and social form in order to preserve and promote the notion under conditions of social change.

The influence of such experiences named by heritage is part of what we mean by culture, the tangible and intangible aspects of the historically shaped spirit of a city that can be affirmed as the identity or "brand" of the city in ways that make that question itself a recurrent index of contentious conflict. Note how recent and yet perennial disputes in cities over what constitutes proper respect or "patriotism" to a place get played out as if a field of choices between affirmations of rites and ritual or other less tangible expressions of loyalty, all sides implicitly ruled by the enigma of the question of what co.

Connected to this is the problem of disseminating the heritage to newcomers or to youth or to those who appear to have been outside of its sphere of influence and need to be oriented to such a force. In the idiom of sociology this makes the fundamental problem of actualizing a heritage one of re-socialization, both re-socializing people to the heritage (newcomers, youth, outsiders of whom we have spoken) and of re-socializing the heritage to make it relevant to the interests of the present. This requires understanding how such knowledge can be disseminated to long term residents as well as to newcomers and each generation of a society. The Conference intends to clarify ways in which this problem of safeguardingheritage takes shape in the re-socialization of participants in civic life to an awareness of the tangible and intangible interrelations of their culture. The primary impact of the UNESCO declaration to safeguard heritage leads to an emphasis on studying and protecting the intangible heritage of cities and other social formations and this proposed event seeks to implement an interdisciplinary conference directed towards realizing such an objective.

The challenge of safeguarding the intangible cultural heritage is due to its very intangibility that makes identification and action in relation to such an "object" more difficult. Unlike the tangible aspect of a heritage such as preservation directed to landmarks, or to the artifacts collected in archives and museums, sociologists have long disclosed the difficulty of mobilizing collective action in projects that seem to lack a tangible and specific objective upon which consensus might be reached. Though in addition to such tangible artifacts archives and structures the ICH Declaration does designate the intangible inheritance by tangible practices such as "oral traditions and expressions, performing arts, rituals and festive events, knowledge and practices concerning nature and the universe, and traditional craftsmanship". These tangible practices exist as part of a history of events and actions that is recognizable. This means that the first step in safeguarding such a heritage lies in recognizing how this tangible history is more than an archive of chance events and activities because it must appear in any present as in part an historical record, but also as an expression of history that is meaningful and significant in shaping the identity of a community. So the first step in safeguarding the heritage is torecognize it as more than a history of external events and milestones ruled by chance but as a field of meaning.

The City in Time

Studies on the city in time treat the city as having to navigate in any present the tension between its past and future, reflected in conceptions of its background recognized in the notion of heritage and in its orientation to change expressed in the notion of innovation. Today, heritage and innovation are conceptions that give us access to the city as a dynamic entity inviting dialectical analysis. The city in the present, in-between past and future, can be seen to work on bringing together conceptions of heritage and innovation that often tend to be separated or kept apart. Here we see that the notion of heritage as a metaphor for the roots of a collective like the city in history and culture, while pointing to a legacy that seems part of the past, requires any active relationship to this past to treat it as a force moving towards the future as a way of transmitting and sustaining the identity of the community. In this way, the past heritage is a resource orienting to the future. Similarly, if work on innovation stresses the future as essential to its aspirations towards change, it is the past that always must be changed, a past sanctified in the present in the conditions that need revision. Thus, the dialectic between past and future is made transparent in conceptions of heritage and innovation, being worked out in any present.

I take the position that one can only approach such an "object" as an urban way of life through the speeches and representations that circulate in society as its system of assumptions and ortho-doxa. Furthermore, since the spirit of a city is grounded historically in more than external milestones but in an oft imperceptible but significant chronology, this notion of spirit points to a deeper conception of what the policy sciences call an intangible heritage, always revealing how the notion of culture as a figure invariably must stand for the background of a city in ways that revitalize heritage as the spiritual inheritance or legacy of an urban way of life. The two-bodied image of heritage must mark it as both a tangible and intangible feature of the urban way of life, disclosed always through tangible effects that can only reveal the intangible influence of its inheritance. I now offer some examples from our research on the gains and losses of the ambiguity of social change.

Gentrification: Progress or Disease?

In her book describing changes in the city, using New York as her model case, the sociologist Sharon Zukin poses the question of whether the tumultuous recent changes New York seems to her to have undergone means that New York has lost its soul. Think of her use of soul here as one way of talking about the spirit of a city, now asking if New York has lost or corrupted its spirit. Of course she cannot answer in one way or another because this either-or question only confirms the disreputable use of such terms in a secular age; yet, soul resonates with identity, quality, and spirit as one of that family of connotations that we connect to what the best philosophy has called the infinitely more that is registered in any finite signifier or characterization. Without being able to create a quantitative solution to such a question, we found that the opinions in such a discourse could still be translated in ways both productive and informative if we could see through its surfaces to various unstated representations of common interests, listening closely to this language as attunbed to its quality.

According to Durkheim, all human societies make reference in their repertoire of ideas and beliefs to some idea of the person as divided, of "the human body as sheltering an interior being as the principle of the life which animates it". Accordingly, this is the function of a conception of the soul as pointing to "what is best and most profound in ourselves, and the pre-eminent part of our being; yet it is also a passing guest which comes from the outside, and which leads in us an existence distinct from that of the body, and which should one day regain its entire independence". This makes the soul a figure of speech for the desire to express our best through the hand we are dealt, through the particular conditions that we inherit.

This begins to politicize the discussion by asking what the spirit of the city means, is it energizing and life-enhancing, or does it tend to turn its citizens into things? This is not simply a question of satisfaction or happiness but of enjoyment: what does thespirit of the city mean for the perpetual human struggle to express its best part through the conditions it inherits? What Zukin means of course is to question how the symptomatic quality of New York, its stigma that marks it as peculiar, is affected by globalization and its consequences? This question has the curious underside of suggesting that the loss of soul, as a loss of peculiarity, might risk making a city such as New York both healthy (free of stigma if that is possible) and indistinct. This is an important question raised by work such as this, suggesting the possible interdependence of soul and symptom, sovereignty and excess. This might be an essential concern animating the lover of a city. Is it possible that the health of a city, as a picture of a city free of excess, can only enforce a view of the good city as tepid and sanitized? Does a city pictured in such a way, whatever its landscapce of amenities and characteristics, appear as true to the nature of a city?

If the city can remain recognizable throughout its changes, as New York can according to Zukin, this raises the question of how change relates to such a loss, or what kind of alteration counts as a real change rather than as an alteration of conditions that are simply incidental. Note again that these are important questions of interpretation that cannot be settled by appeals to brain, genetics, cognition, and the like except through convoluted and circuitous interpretive routes and appeals to evidence; in other words these are questions that must remain irresolute and yet necessary to answer. These are questions raised by what we typically call life or the Real, and if many choose to ignore them, so much the worse for the work they do. Despite theimportance of such concerns, one temptation is always to disregard such questions because they seem to go nowhere. Yet if we desire to engage these concerns by our making explicit the various assumptions they hold in abeyance, we might read Zukin's text for resonances that she leaves unstated.

For example, Zukin's critical voice is meant to impersonate the long-term resident who can remain sensually loyal to the city, seeming to appreciate its stability in the face of change, or in contrast like Zukin herself, might lament the changes as a possible loss of soul. Perhaps Zukin's description of New York's loss is simply resistance to change, or thinly veiled antipathy to youth who must come successively to discount the past as anything other than incidental. Perhaps this is the fate of the city as that everpresent site of change, having to engage this question of the relation of change to loss, of essentials to incidentals, and of the longstanding skepticism of the resident to what each new generation brings to the city, and its melancholia in relation to what seems long gone. The unease that Zukin locates tends to be created by the unsettling character of change that she assumes to disturb that secure sense of regularity and permanence of the village (continuity in work and life, regularity in routines and expectations, in the permanence of buildings and neighbors), bound to destabilize selves in the present who must seek replacements for what is lost. Here, desire for remaking and renovating marks the city in one essential way: it identifies as an urban imaginary this appetite for renovation (authenticity asshe calls it) that leaves both haves and have-nots to pursue such restoration as a condition of the good life. The corporation is seen to exploit the nostalgia market: the resident and tourist consume feverishly to recapture items of authentic value.

Baudrillard described such a system in great detail 40 years ago in the publication of his dissertation on consumption as a symbolic order. The overstimulation created by the anxiety of the death of the referent makes everyone opportune in relation to this object of desire (authenticity) and the struggle over its means of interpretation can only shape the terrain of the city and the everyday life of the resident. Zukin aims to impersonate the voice of the resident and the anxiety expressed for her as indecision over the ambiguity of authenticity itself and the question of whether it is a change for the better or not.

To get some leverage, we can contrast to a city such as New York, Venice as the home of masterpieces, the quintessential beautiful city that attracts all those engaged by the question of good taste. This allows us to begin to work through the notion of gentrification in the spirit of Aristotle who said of being that it has many senses, by following this counsel to examine the many senses of gentrification as part of our work. To this end, we collected interviews with a number of citizens of Venice in order to throw light on the comparative experience in social change. (FNA researcher from the project who was a native resident from Venice, conducted these interviews with ten long-standing older residents of the city, with three exceptions for younger subjects.) What we note is that gentrification is not the only image of change in the city, as the sense of loss is registered in the erosion of a way of life marked by the influx of new people who appear to represent challenges to what is long-standing.

Edification

By and large the interviewees say that the city has not changed and then in the next breath, claim that it has, as reflected in the influx of tourists, foreigners, rising prices and rents, the exodus of youth who leave for employment elsewhere. Thus, it seems that the secret story here is this denial of change or their reluctance to talk about the change they recognize. For example, one subject replies as follows.

What changes have you noticed in the city in the last few years?

The city itself has not changed, it's always the same, but what has changed is the environment of the city because of the migration of many residents to the mainland. The city has more tourists, more foreign workers than in the past. This is the most visible change.

She denies that Venice has changed by distinguishing between the city and the environment as if "migration" belongs to the environment and not the city although its effects are palpable. There is a recurrent need to deny change in the city while affirming what the denial denies.

What do you think about "modern times" and the life style associated with it?

Here in Venice it is difficult to talk about "modern times" or modern life style exactly because of its unique nature. Of course we notice new businesses cropping up to meet the demands of the young or of the tourists but the sense of the "modern" is difficult here. I will tell you that I don't like the way they have "modernized" certain events like the Carnival which instead of being a cultural and artistic expression is turning out to be an excuse for the young to cause havoc and get drunk. This is sad.

Apparently the unique character of Venice, its authenticity, would be compromised by seeing it as modern because modernity as so seen appears to threaten the distinctiveness of the city, being a label that makes all cities comparable. This is the very loss that Zukin fears. Here, new businesseses and a Carnival that meets the demands of youth and tourists are treated as an external alteration and not a real change because she views change from the perspective of the resident. It is interesting that youth and the generational change represented here is not part of the city for this subject. Her sadness shows the melancholia that denies and accepts the loss at the same time. Here, to another question:

What do you think of Venice with respect to other cities? Would you ever want to move away?

We note the reply of a man.

I wouldn't change Venice for any other city because it is a unique city with its own set of advantages as well as disadvantages. Just think that this city is an open air museum: where can one find a place like this?

The unique character of Venice is a function of its status as a work of art, the city as a virtual museum. Yet, that it is a museum has risks: first the tourists that are bound to come and engage it externally as spectators and no more, and then the danger that the museum city neglects its life, e. g., its youth, changing demands of the environment, and the like. The city as a masterpiece has dangers as this subject admits.

Why do you live in Venice?

Because it's fascinating; it's wonderful living here; it's like living within an art masterpiece.

A masterpiece indeed but full of tourists?

To which a subject says:

In the mid-nineteen hundreds there were about a million tourists in the city; by 1998 there were 11 million; today there are 21 million of them. That's 42 million pairs of eyes and many not particularly respectful of the city. I mean that you see many of them with their feet in the canals and eating in Piazza S. Marco bare chested. The Venetians are against the idea of limiting the number of visitors but the city needs to address this problem. Regulations exist and they have to be enforced.

Take for example police in plain clothes who go after the illegal sellers (mostly of purses). They try to catch these people who run away running into people and generally creating havoc to elude the police. The police is more dangerous than the illegal sellers. I've seen horrible scenes like a child's stroller being overturned by one of these people fleeing from the police, and the father catching the child in midair after it was thrown from the stroller. Is the government, I wonder, really trying to eliminate these illegal activities and petty crime or does it allow it seeing it as a necessary social steam valve?

If the masterpiece city attracts spectators, it also attracts life in the shape of misuse, corruption, impurity, and vandalism. It is important for this subject and those like him not to see this corruption as the work of residents but of those who come from elsewhere and use the city for their purposes. It is essential that the work of constructing the city as masterpiece, the time-honored work of Venetians themselves, be disavowed because that would cause them to ask, why did you make a masterpiece if you knew that once you built it, they would come? And if you did not know this, what kind of builder were you, were you similar to Dr. Victor Frankenstein who built his masterpiece and then abandoned it? The residents begin to face the question of whether the masterpiece can be monstrous, giving us an altogether different perspective on the beautiful city. Even more and similar to New York, Venice recognizes that becoming a central city (like Athens at one time) has its consequences insofar as the periphery hates the center and can constantly work not simply to vandalize it but to destroy it and its masterpieces.

How do you see the city socially?

Well, there are still Venetians living in Venice-mostly living in Castello and Cannareggio as well as the Giudecca. But the city is changing. I can see the changes in my own sestiere (area). Half of the businesses are now owned not by Venetians but by, well, Chinese.

Are you pleased by this new international Venice?

Not at all. I prefer to shop at stores owned by the locals with whom I can establish a friendly rapport. With the Chinese it seems rather difficult. They speak their own language and make us feel as outsiders. We are losing our identity because of them. Unfortunately many people shop in their establishments especially because many of them have installed video games...

What do you think is the biggest problem facing the City?

They often talk about the city falling apart. But in my opinion if it's falling apart it's because there are no options for the young people of the city: the city does not have places and open space for the 18-year-old. And the other more significant problem is the number of people leaving the city.

Forty years ago we were a city of over 100, 000 people. Now we number 60, 000. How is it that we can't slow this down? Is there an alternative? For me this is the biggest problem facing the city.

Would you ever leave Venice?

Absolutely not.

Or another:

What has changed in the life of the city?

Well, what has changed is that it's difficult to find Venetians in the historical center. But the common folks are obliged to leave because of the high costs. Consequently, we have lost the real life of the city. Gone is the shoe store where the owner made the shoes himself. Gone are the artisanal shops now replaced by mass produced goods. By encouraging mass tourism and by selling off properties to foreigners we have brought upon the death of the city which is steadily declining.

This mass tourism does not even know how to appreciate the city. Once someone came in the (book) store all worried and asked me how long he had before he needed to leave. Thinking that he was referring to our business hours I told him the time we closed-but he wanted to know at what time the CITY closed down, thinking that like an amusement park the city shut down at a certain time.

The push-pull hypothesis sees the change as a result of foreign influences of immigrants and tourists and the departure of youth for these very reasons. This is because the foreign influences are assumed to contribute to the higher prices and rents and the unemployment that sends youth away. Another subject gives a remarkable avowal of such reasoning.

What changes have you noticed in the city in the last few years?

The city has not changed, it's not like other cities where one can tear down a building and put up a 13, 14-story tower. The changes that are noticeable are in the number of businesses that close down or are owned by foreigners. Then there's the problem of people leaving the city and going to the mainland. Many would return to the city if it weren't for the high prices of homes or for the fact that high waters have "eaten" away many apartments at the lower levels.

So Venice has not changed except for its changes! This contradiction can be avoided by thinking of such changes as inconveniences and not change, alterations that do not have to be decisive.

Has the quality of life changed over the years? Is it better or worse?

We are not badly off now except life is not as quiet as it used to be. In the past we had tourists but not like today which are the masses; once we got a different quality of tourists, who spent more and who were respectful.

Now she distinguishes between inconveniences and "quality of life" and real change, accepting the former as similar to the problem of maintaining a city and of its "working" or not. We also begin to see a distinction between types of tourists, breaking down the homogeneity of the category.

We now get tourists of lower levels; even stores have become ugly, selling ugly things at low prices that are not made in Italy. Once they used to sell beautiful glass items which were really made in Murano. But perhaps this happens in all art cities. I went to Florence a month ago and it appeared ugly to me. Tourism is the same everywhere it seems. Carnival was different than today. We used to get dressed up in costumes to go to house parties. Now it's just for tourists.

Are many people leaving the city?

Yes, because of the high cost of houses. If you are not lucky enough to own a house you can't afford one. The municipality seems to listen only to the needs of the wealthy. The ordinary people don't have a voice. I'm not crazy about the quality of people living in Venice.

There are now many gondoliers especially because now they don't just work in the summer but also through the winter as well. They work when it's raining and at night. They do good business.

I'd have to say that the population of Venice (see graph from the Venice site I sent you) is getting older and there are a few young people. Only the ones that love Venice stay, and those who are lucky enough to have parents who've bought homes for them. A house in Venice now averages 5,000 Euros per square meter and you don't get luxury for that.

These are things that don't work well in Venice but I don't have any plans to leave.

Now it becomes clearer for this person, everything changes but she will not change, she will not imitate the fluctuations of the city that she both denies and then accepts, a fluctuation that includes the decline in the quality of the people.

It's not an easy city to live in maybe because it has lost the characteristics that made it a livable city once?

Absolutely. You are always crowded by people who have no respect for you as a resident or for the city itself. It makes you resentful of the city itself and the people who run the city who are making it unlivable.

It's confusing. On the one hand everyone wants tourists because they bring wealth but on the other hand residents are seeing their government turn Venice into a Disneyland and an attraction destination but with few moments of real life. Many Venetians are abandoning the city and are renting out their homes. On one side you have the vision of the city intended for the tourists but on the other the reality of life for the resident who is not part of the consideration from those who administer the city. The only thing you can do is think that it's a special city, accept it and get on with it.

So, in Venice there are only two possibilities: one stays because you love the city or one can't put up with any more and moves away?

That's right. Most people can't cope anymore especially because of costs but also because it's not a livable city; because it's a city that's becoming more difficult to live in. As a young person maybe you don't realize it because you can't see an alternative but as you grow up you do. As an adolescent I was so bored until I found a sport that helped me out a lot [skating-probably roller skating (Marina)]. But if someone does not have an interest Venice offers you nothing except meeting friends at the bar.

Thus, the residents are resisting the idea that they have killed the city because the influx of foreign businesses suggests that the people who are condemned by the Venetians, such as the Chinese, are doing the business that the Venetians could have done for themselves. The success of the immigrants testifies painfully to the failure of the political and economic will of Venetians, their inability to provide what life the Chinese are doing now. In this sense, the talk raises the possibility that it is the Venetian resident who drives youth away through lethargy, and their accounts of change in the face of rising inconveniences might be attributing to externals (conditions, causes) what they have done to themselves. Venice risks appearing to its residents as a dead city that they have killed, a graveyard evacuated by the young and its future and in the hands of others who are unintelligible. The loss of soul becomes more complex now. If both New York and Venice seem to be changing enough to raise the question of whether such change is a difference of form or degree, whether the change means the city is a new city or more of the same in altered form, it is apparent that residents are confused and yet continue to live in these cities. Just as cities change and so do people, it might be asking too much to avoid treating such a material condition as fatal, asking rather how we might relate to such change as something other than loss, as something other than mournful.

Conclusion: The Dialogue on Change

The world is constantly seen as undergoing change and cities, as sites that vividly bring to view scenes of the changes, are recognized as if in some sense cities are exemplary by virtue of their capacity to exhibit the drama and tensions in worldly change. The city makes a scene of change, makes it into a theatrical occasion. The spectacle of change is typically revealed in the city because the city is the place where learning to engage change is conceived to first become an issue, assuming almost theatrical proportions. In part, social change is seen to reflect the mobility of populations and their patterns of distribution and resettlement that occasion collisions in reference to the evaluation of change, whether it shows a difference in degree or kind. Instead of being seen as maintaining itself or adapting, the city is often viewed as doing both, as maintaining itself in adapting. Concerns for such ambiguity haunt the discourse on change and on the city as the exemplary site of change at any time. The city then functions not just theatrically but somewhat as a school that discloses in very ordinary but dramatic ways the means of learning modernity and the curriculum for self-governance under such conditions.

Principles of Planning Future Cities Based on Artificial Intelligence and Internet of Things

胡 郁[*]

【Abstract】 Artificial Intelligence (AI) and Internet of Things (IoT) brought by the 4th Industrial Revolution will overturn existing modes of living and production, creating new economic opportunities and subsequently, new urban spatial needs. AI and IoT will offer technical supports for improving the harmonious co-existence between city and nature, and make urban life more human-centered. Analyzing the potential revolutionary impacts of emerging technologies like AI and IoT on social life and urban spatial transformation, the plan and design of future cities can consider the following six principles: 1) Small-scale: respect and return to individual comfort; 2) Live/work mix: an outcome of high-density smart cities; 3) Permeable public space: to make urban space more open and resilient in order to improve the efficiency of space use; 4) Interwoven nature: city and nature highly integrate, human and nature co-exist in harmony; 5) Attraction-driven: planning around natural and cultural heritages; 6) Dispersion: dispel urban spatial pressure and allocate resources in a more reasonable and fair way. Although there may exist some technological, moral and social obstacles in the field of AI and IoT, and technological revolution also brings challenges to reemployment and social security, urban

---

* 胡郁，剑桥大学建筑学博士在读。

planners and governors still need to keep an open mind, embracing new technologies and making the best out of them. We need to fully explore the social functions that boost the free and all-round development of people, letting new technologies become the strong power pushing the harmonious and sustainable man-nature and city-nature developments.

【Keywords】 Artificial Intelligence, Internet of Things, Future City, Urban Space, City Planning

Research Background and Scope

Humanity is now at the doorstep of the 4th Industrial Revolution marked by the breakthrough of Artificial Intelligence (AI) and Internet of Things (IoT). This progress will significantly change the look and structure of existing cities. Today's city planning still follows the planning ideas of modernism proposed a century ago. It is unable to adapt to the need of sustainable urban development in our new era, and it does not make enough proactive reaction to the arrival of AI and IoT. Currently, many researches focus on how to use Big Data technology to analyze various urban activities, emphasizing understanding social phenomena and optimizing urban management through Big Data and data visualization, so that cities get more finely and comprehensively scrutinized. Yet these researches have one limit: they view the physical urban space as an unchangeable premise, and improve urban efficiency under the restriction of existing urban spatial conditions. Hence, they cannot foresee the trend of future urban transformation from the perspective of constructing new city form and space. In this way, through an analysis of the social changes and the transforming logic of physical urban spaces induced by AI and IoT, this paper discusses new city planning principles based on the revolution of new technologies, hoping to offer new solution to the question: how to plan sustainable future cities that are more human-centered?

1. Introduction

Modern cities are achievements of the first and second Industrial Revolutions. Modern building techniques characterized by reinforced concrete and steel and modern transportation systems by cars and trains determined the basic structure of modern cities. Urban infrastructure and modern economy support each other; the specialization and interdependence of economic activities push the need for the spatial separation of urban functions, while modern architecture and transportation systems reinforce such a separation. Cities got divided into areas of housing, working, production, consumption, and leisure etc. However, this city model turned out not being human-centered, although its inventors like Le Corbusier claimed that it was intended for a better urban life. [1] Its planning is primarily to ensure the functioning of economy and corresponding institutions, rather than the physical and mental development of human beings. Critiques against high modernism like Jane Jacobs' targeted on modern cities' deprivation of street vibrancy and community trust. [2] On the other hand, this model is not sustainable either: the high energy consumption and pollution brought by construction, transportation, and many economic activities under the idea of consumerism make it difficult for modern cities to co-exist in harmony with ecological systems.

Before discussing AI and IoT's impact on planning future cities, let us get clear about the two terms. AI can be understood as various artificial intelligence algorithms, including different kinds of machine learning and neural network algorithms. Although different algorithms have different functions, the general idea is similar, which is: train a model by "learning" the features of existing data, then make predictions on new data. IoT can simply be understood as the Internet of everything: from a small toaster to a big streetlamp, everything will possess the ability to capture and analyze data with its own sensors and chips, so

---

① Corbusier, L., *The City of To-Morrow and Its Planning*, Jrodker, 1929.
② Jacobs, J., *The Death and life of Great American Cities*, Jonathan Cape, 1962.

everything in the physical world can communicate and interact with each other.

2. Social Changes Brought by AI and IoT and Inspirations for City Planning

AI and IoT will bring three kinds to social change that are significant enough to alter urban form and planning paradigm. They are:

1) Comprehensive improvement in the standard of living

2) Job automation

3) New economy and new industry

2.1　Comprehensive improvement in the standard of living

In the future, AI algorithms will become smarter, so that machines become better at dealing with physical and intellectual challenges for us. For example, we would expect AI algorithms to make more accurate predictions, and devices to process and transfer large amount of data faster with more powerful chips. Smart homes will monitor our health more exhaustively, office software will significantly improve our work efficiency and quality.

Big Data and IoT will not only substantially save human's energy and time (hence greatly improve life quality), but also make more reasonable allocation of urban resources. The physical environment in smart cities will become a sophisticated network of highly performative computing machines in diverse types and forms, being able to process different urban activity data and interact instantly with citizens. We will reach a new high level of using urban infrastructure and experiencing urban life.

2.2　Job Automation

Job automation is a direct result of AI revolution. For a job, when machine does it better and cheaper than human, it will be economically logical to assign it to the machine. We have already seen such a wave of automation during previous industrial revolutions, when machines replaced humans to perform most agricultural and some manufacturing work. In the 4th Industrial Revolution, we will see far more advanced machines replacing humans to perform much more physical and intellectual work.

How job automation would transform urban spaces can be elaborated in the case of Autonomous Vehicles (AV). If AV drives better than human, then the automation of driving will be inevitable. Admittedly AV may never be perfect, but it only needs to be better than humans. Moreover, we are not talking about one AV versus one human driver, but fleets of AVs that communicate and coordinate instantly with each other versus a group of drivers who easily get tired, distracted, or irritated and who do not know each other's intentions well. Obviously, the advantage of AV is preponderant. In addition, AV (in the IoT) is able to take care of itself, they can find a cheap place to park and come pick up their users when called upon. Thus, the full adoption of AV will render many parking lots obsolete: one compact autonomous garage may fulfill the parking demand of an entire neighborhood. This creates opportunities to re-purpose the obsolete parking lots for more meaningful and beneficial purposes, such as housing, park, library, community center and so on.

Similar logic can be applied to other professions or industries; when job automation in a certain industry, such as retail, manufacturing, or health care, starts to invalid certain types of space or architecture, it becomes an opportunity to re-purpose these newly-available spaces.

2.3 New economy and new industry

What comes along with job automation is the emergence of new economy and new industries replacing old ones. This is both an opportunity and challenge for governments and companies. On the one hand, new economies and industries will spring out, creating new jobs and professions. But this will not spontaneously happen, it needs proactive actions from the government side, bearing the labor pains of old-new economic transitions. As an example, city of Shunde in Guangdong Province (China) weeded out its industrial park that used to be filled with small hardware processing workshops and built a new one that brought in robotic industries through preferential policies. The arrival of IoT will give birth to a kaleidoscope of new products and services that depend heavily on data, and AI will use the massive amount of data to create new values. For instance, Microsoft is developing AI for Earth (a portfolio of AI-infused "Earth applications"), which will help monitor, model, and ultimately manage Earth's natural systems[1]. This is the power of the integration of AI and Big Data. With the help of AI, startups around the globe are advancing industries of health-care, education, finance, retail, manufacturing, transportation, construction, management and so on, which is revealing huge benefit and great power that transform society and economy.

On the other hand, governments need to be prepared for the social issues incurred by Job automation, taking care of those social members whose jobs get automated. There is not only the need to help theunemployed to reinvent themselves for the new economy, but also that to build a basic social security net. We have seen how this kind of industrial shift worked before when human civilization transitioned from agricultural to industrial economy a century ago: farmers became workers in factories and offices, modern cities got created during such transition. In our time, the key question becomes: will there be enough new jobs created for the potential displaced workers? Or more fundamentally, will human beings still be valuable in future economies and industries? A report completed by Mckinsey holds a rather optimistic view that as new industries emerge, enough new jobs will be created[2]. Conversely, historian Yuval Harari holds a relatively more pessimistic and radical view; he worries that even though computer scientists and engineers may do pretty well in the coming decades, the accelerating self-evolution of AI will quickly replace them. There will be multiple rounds of re-educating and re-inventing oneself during one's career and the pace will be accelerating. [3]

---

[1] Microsoft AI for Earth, Retrieved November 23, 2019, from https://www.microsoft.com/en-us/ai/ai-for-earth.

[2] Mckinsey Global Institute, Jobs lost, jobs gained: Workforce transitions in a time of automation. https://www.mckinsey.com/~/media/mckinsey/featured% 20insights/Future% 20of% 20Organizations/What% 20the% 20future% 20of% 20work% 20will% 20mean% 20for% 20jobs% 20skills%20and%20wages/MGI-Jobs-Lost-Jobs-Gained-Report-December-6-2017.ashx, 2017.

[3] Harari, Y., 21 *Lessons For The 21st Century*, Vintage, 2018.

Human beings used to devote their labor or intelligence in exchange for living materials and wealth. If people in the future cannot sell their effort for monetary reward through jobs, how will their social value be continued in future economy? Perhaps in the new economic era, the value of human being is no longer limited to traditional professions like driving, cleaning, regular diagnosing or professional consulting, but be carried on in undertakings that are truly beneficial to society or nature, such as spending more time knowing oneself better, understanding bio-diversity, educating children, doing creative work, or exploring outer space. The 4th Industrial Revolution requires us to innovate our value realization, further discovering the incomparable value in human beings. Only by doing so can humans continue to lead civilization.

The trend of job automation and new economy in the future objectively demand the right city planning reactions: how to design an environment that promotes self-awareness and self-discovery? Does it simply mean having more natural elements in the built environment or designing public spaces that encourage social interaction? How to translate these reflections into forms and spaces? William Mitchell, a renowned futuristic urban scholar, touched upon how to make use of the freed-up time achieved by Information Technology when he advocated for a new live/work housing type twenty years ago. He believed that the freed-up time achieved by technology should be used on something truly beneficial to humans. It would be a real success if technology allows us to spend more time and energy on our most valued relationships or on community building. ①

3. Six Planning Principles

The planning of future cities must actively respond to the changes of social life brought by AI and IoT, maximize technologies' benefit while avoid the harm through innovation, and, by taking full advantage of them, build sustainable future cities that promote the all-round free development of man. To realize this

---

① Mitchell, W. J., *E-topia: Urban life, Jim—but not as We Know It*, MIT Press, 1999.

end, we can consider the following six principles in planning future cities.

3.1 Small-scale

Small-scale principle means the design of architectural and urban space should prioritize human comfort. Concretely, rooms and streets need not to be too big or wide, and plazas should not be too open. Chinese traditional architecture has historically paid attention to the convergence of energy and auspice; that the bedroom of Emperor Yongzheng (Qing Dynasty) is only more than a dozen square meters fully reflects this spirit. The idea of small-scale is the dimensional specification of being human-centered and a respect for individual's spatial comfort. In this sense, small-scale rules the other five principles.

The principle of small-scale is based on the range of our perceptible space and of influence of our body energy. Specifically, the radius of normal vision, smell, speech, hearing, walking, and touch is limited to a scale proportional to our body size. We are only able to discern something off a certain distance, smell or hear things from certain ranges, transmit voices or move bodies comfortably within limited radius. In this sense, cities of agricultural age are in line with human scale because most urban activities were carried out literally through physical energy of human beings. The extent of these cities was proportional to humans' walking capacity. This is illustrated by the fact that many historic urban cores, like Boston, Cambridge or Venice, are comfortably walkable. Of course, the small-scale of future cities cannot mechanically copy the urban fabric of agricultural era, but demands innovative spatial planning under new technological conditions. Small-scale, by all means, does not mean everything aims for smallness. The "big" urban structure built in the industrial era would still be the foundation of future cities; highways, high-speed trains and large plaza/arena still have their reasons to exist. Yet big space should not be the core of everyday life, it should only be the framework and support of small spaces.

For cities of different sizes or of different significances, the expression of smallness will be different. It is inherently more challenging for large mono-centric cities (like Beijing) to realize small-scale due to the combined effect of concentrated resources and population pressure. IoT and smart transportation may help to achieve this goal. Studies have shown that with AV, much fewer vehicles and much less parking infrastructure will be needed to fulfill the same traffic demand[1], which opens up opportunities to shrink the overall size of city's road network and of itself. Moreover, if the fragmentation of many traditionally centralized economic activities, such as book purchase, movie watching, education, health care, office working, money saving and so on, do render the corresponding monumental architectures obsolete as predicted by Mitchell[2], then the "big" buildings and "big" blocks may gradually disintegrate into small and comfortable spaces.

The principle of small-scale seems untimely for Chines cities which just finished industrialization as the massive planned and on-going skyscrapersin different cities are repeating America's bustling ostentation during its industrial era. The active Chinese government must reinforce its forward-looking regulation on mega architectures before the arrival of the 4th Industrial Revolution.

3.2   Live/work mix

The principle of live/work mix refers to the overlapping of living and working space in many domains, meaning that people do their work at where they live. This is a natural pattern of high-density smart cities. With the perfection of IoT and telecommunication technologies (with corresponding products like AR/VR devices), more and more work can be done at home, workers do not have to gather together in office buildings. When more and more centralized activities or industries (like retail) become outdated or dispersed into families and communities, more urban space can be allocated for live/work housing. Multifunctional dwelling space may be a significant component in future cities.

The integration of living and working space can eliminate the spatial-temporal segmentation of working and resting, so that living and working proceed coordinately and the consumption of space and energy gets reduced. Currently we

---

① Duarte, F., & Ratti, C., "The Impact of Autonomous Vehicles on Cities: A Review," *Journal of Urban Technology* 4 (2018): 3–18.
② Mitchell, W. J., *City Of Bits: Space, Place, and the Infobahn*, MIT Press, 1996.

are seeing the emergence of co-working spaces like those offered by WeWork, such a mixture will start blurring many divisions between urban functions, hence improving the diversity and tolerance of urban spaces.

3.3 Permeable public space

The principle of permeable public space seeks the maximum seepage of human activities into urban fabric. It asks city to open to and connect various spaces, so as to substantially improve space utilization and subsequently, improve the convenience and comfort of urban life. It targets specifically on the spatial segregation resulted by the closed management of urban spaces. Such a segregation not only leads to the degradation of urban space utilization, but also reinforces the repellence and even hostility between people. This principle demands a blurring of the boundaries between public and private realms, augmenting urban spatial management and usage quality by the effective permeation of different spaces. Creating permeable urban space is consistent with the aim of having accessible urban form in Kevin Lynch's discourse[1], it also helps to re-establish qualities like "eyes on the street" and community trust celebrated by Jane Jacobs.

At the moment, there exists a universal degradation of pedestrian environment among many Chinese mega cities. The main cause is the closed management of urban space: sidewalks not only get cramped between motorways and buildings, but also get cut by motorways and different gated communities or units, severely weakening its traffic function. Permeable public space can help resolve this issue. Danish architect and urban planner Jan Gehl has systematically elaborated the idea of using fine-grain urban fabric to improve urban space utilization[2]. We can also look at Hong Kong or Tokyo's successful cases, where footbridges, escalators, interior corridors, streets, subway stations, building lobbies, shopping mall atriums, interior/exterior plazas, parks, and other kinds of public/private spaces connect together, creating multilevel pedestrian systems and punching through the obstruction of

---

① Lynch, K., *A Theory of Good City Form*, MIT, 1981.
② Gehl, J., *Life between Buildings: Using Public Space*, Washington, DC: Island Press, 2011.

gated communities, thus incorporating alleys and internal streets into one coherent pedestrian network. In this way, urban space gets disintegrated into porous structure and urban mobility gets augmented.

Permeable public space often times is associated with insecurity, so it is traditionally treated as a taboo by city administration. However, AI and IoT are showing us great potential to open up closed spaces and build safe permeable public spaces. AI and IoT would have no difficulty conducting full monitoring over urban public spaces, constructing a completely safe public domain; they can also run fine classification management on space. Classified spaces open to certain identities, citizens' behavioral information forms their credits in urban big database so they have to be responsible for their behavior while enjoying the convenience of permeable public space.

3.4 Interwoven Nature

The principle of interwoven nature means the integration of humanistic and natural ecology in urban space making; urban architecture and living spaces should greatly blend into ecological systems. Living spaces become parks; streets, courtyards and even building facades become homes to plants. Permeable urban space should not only open to people, but also to plants. The extensive urban space utilization during industrial era not only caused the spatial tension between citizens, but also led to the monotony of urban ecology in the process of encroaching various natural systems, thus weakening the resilience of urban ecology. The fine urban management of AI and IoT will release a large amount of urban space, laying the foundation for creating an environment in which diverse urban ecological systems co-exist. An interwoven ecological system can accommodate more plants, hence can improve city's ability to cleans the air and retain water. A poetic environment where birds sing, frogs croak, fireflies shine, and butterflies dance would make urban space more livable and spiritual. Physicist and ecologist Fritjof Capra stresses the importance of "Deep Ecology" that the networks of life are fundamentally interconnected and interdependent[1].

---

[1] Capra, Fritjof, The Web of Life: A New Synthesis of Mind and Matter, Flamingo, 1997.

Many studies and practices, such as "Biophilic Design"[①], have proved the efficacy of being close to natural elements in urban life.

The principle of interwoven nature requires that the planning and design of future urban public space should reflect humanistic care for bio-diversity, reserving homes for birds and fish. Of course, the selection of plants and animals should follow a human-centered principle, using professional knowledge to prioritize human's health and safety. Urban infrastructure should be performative landscape, turning the city itself into a big rich landscape work. A complete principle of interwoven nature can even be implemented in the process of city planning itself, meaning that we invite nature to participate in the planning and design of urban landscape, achieving some kind of balance between planned and unplanned, finishing, via the combined hands of nature and humanity, a variegated drawing that reflects local characteristics. Interwoven nature helps citizens to cultivate the mindset of bio-consonance in a daily life close to nature, building a strong foundation for creating harmonious society and harmonious world.

3.5 Attraction Driven

The principle of attraction driven means making the best of natural and cultural heritage when planning and designing cities: when planning new towns or reviving old ones, one can make proposals around cultural attractions or natural heritage that are rich in urban memories. The site selection of Xiong'an New Area is a god example; its overall plan centers around the Baiyang Lake, the largest freshwater lake in the Huabei area. It uses the lake's landscape and ecological resources to accommodate some city functions and distribute the overload on Beijing's ecology, attracting new industries and elites for local economy.

The principle of attraction driven is consistent with the rules of contemporary and future economic development: the dominant economy in future cities will be service sector, large-scale agriculture and industry will occupy special zones in the suburbs or remote area, some of the agriculture and manufacturing will

---

① Biophilic Desig, https://living-future.org/biophilic-design/? gclid = CjwKCAiA3uDwBRBFEiw A1VsajPsmHHUG1uYvCi3GRkerJHF2uq1w_yHyC_bpaxqormA3768qvFk0yBoCeQcQAvD_BwE.

disperse into families and communities as well. The driving factor of locating cities will no longer be proximity to raw materials or factories, but instead be that to areas with comfortable climate and agreeable sceneries or towns rich in cultural or historic heritage, like Venice or Wuzhen.

3. 6 Dispersion

The principle of dispersion means that overcrowded spaces in urban cores in the industrial era will gradually disintegrate, revealing a decentralizing and balancing trend of urban resources and economic activities; the allocation of urban resources becomes more reasonable and fair. Traditional markets demand agglomeration in order to reduce transaction costs due to dispersion. With the emergence of Internet economy, large markets or trading centers started to break down. The key reason is the easy access to commodity information, making physical trading spaces gradually disappear. New technology revolution would make logistics and urban transportation more convenient and traditional urban agglomeration will further weaken. The breakthrough in future transportation characterized by AV and high-speed train will turn distance into a much less annoying thing for commuters, creating conditions to pull resources (such as health care, education, housing, investment, and consequently, employment) out from existing urban centers. The principles of dispersion and attraction-driven are different sides of the new economic logic.

Because the revolution of Information Technology will make new economy more dependent on telecommunication rather than physical locations, dispersion will reveal a shrinkage in city scale; small-scale network of urban spaces will become the basic pattern of future cities. Many small-scale urban clusters will scatter around future metropolitan centers, each cluster possesses functions of production and consumption. Each cluster may be confined to a radius of 15min walking distance and offers sufficient and diverse amenities for health care, recreation, and other services. Clean and efficient autonomous public transport systems connect different clusters, walking and biking become the dominant traffic within each cluster. The predominant architecture in cluster cores is live/work housing, built for the most energetic and innovative group of young professionals and urban elites.

Xiong'an New Area again can be a model of dispersion. Its implementation is both an inevitable choice to resolve the ecological pressure on Beijing's mega urban space, and a conscious action by the government respecting the trend of dispersion. Dispersion would not only optimize Beijing's city functions, making it more livable, but also more reasonably make use of the natural resources at Beijing's periphery. Such a redistribution of the capital's functions and resources also promotes the coordinated development in its surrounding area.

4. Future Challenges

The prospect of new technology revolution is encouraging. However, there is no guarantee that any new technology would ensure its correct humanistic value, not to mention that the revolution itself is still on its way; many technological details still await breakthrough. For instance, AI research right now is approaching some bottle neck: many computer scientists do not understand the fundamentals of some AI algorithms[1] and some deep-learning algorithms are inherently unpredictable[2]. People can only make guess from existing technological trends. The tougher rub is the traditional Egoism and the deep-rooted sense of hierarchy based on private ownership, both of which are hard to resolve with new technology. Take AV as an example, research shows that people would like others to buy AVs that sacrifice their passengers for the greater good, but they themselves would prefer to ride in AVs that protect their passengers at all costs. [3]Moreover, discriminations (e. g. racial discrimination) unintentionally embedded into AI algorithms is another hotly debated issue.

In addition, the utilization of new technology is restrained by social institution and cultural traditions. For instance, mobile payment technology has

---

[1] Hutson, M., "Has Artificial Intelligence Become Alchemy?" *Science* 360 (2018): 478.

[2] Nunes, A., Reimer, B., & Coughlin, J. F., "People Must Retain Control of Autonomous Vehicles," *Nature* 556 (2018): 169-171.

[3] Bonnefon, J. -F., Shariff, A., & Rahwan, I., "The Social Dilemma of Autonomous Vehicles," *Science* 352 (2016): 1573-1576.

already matured in the US, but the restriction of financial interest group slows its development. On the other hand, Chinese political system requires that financial groups must submit to national interest, thus is capable of promoting the healthy development of mobile payment. Reforming political and cultural environment is far from technology's reach, conversely, effective social reform is the humanistic condition for the rational use of new technology. Although there may exist some technological, moral and social obstacles for AI and IoT, and technological revolution also brings challenges to reemployment and social security, urban planners and administrators still need to keep an open mind, embracing new technology and making the best out of it. We need to fully explore the social functions that boost the free and all-round development of people, letting new technology become the strong power pushing the harmonious and sustainable man-nature and city-nature developments.

5. Conclusion

Artificial Intelligence and Internet of Things brought by the 4th Industrial Revolution will overturn existing modes of living and production, creating new economic opportunities and new urban spatial patterns. They show great prospect for achieving sustainable development, city's harmonious co-existence with nature, and pleasant human-centered urban life. AI + IoT will bring three kinds to social change that are significant enough to alter urban form and planning paradigm. They are: Comprehensive improvement in the standard of living, Job automation, and New economy and new industry. Recognizing these trends, the plan and design of future cities can consider the following six new principles: 1) Small-scale: respect and return to individual comfort; 2) Live/work mix: an outcome of high-density smart cities; 3) Permeable public space: to make urban space more open and resilient in order to improve the efficiency of space utilization; 4) Interwoven nature: city and nature highly integrate, human and nature co-exist in harmony; 5) Attraction-driven: planning around natural and cultural heritages; 6) Dispersion: dispel urban spatial pressure and allocate resources more reasonably and fair.

图书在版编目（CIP）数据

城市治理的理论与实践. 2019~2020／陆丹，包雅钧
主编. -- 北京：社会科学文献出版社，2020.11
　ISBN 978-7-5201-7591-3

　Ⅰ.①城…　Ⅱ.①陆…②包…　Ⅲ.①城市管理-中
国-文集　Ⅳ.①F299.23-53

　中国版本图书馆 CIP 数据核字（2020）第 222682 号

城市治理的理论与实践（2019~2020）

主　　编／陆　丹　包雅钧

出 版 人／王利民
责任编辑／岳梦夏

出　　版／社会科学文献出版社（010）59367156
　　　　　地址：北京市北三环中路甲 29 号院华龙大厦　邮编：100029
　　　　　网址：www. ssap. com. cn
发　　行／市场营销中心（010）59367081　59367083
印　　装／三河市龙林印务有限公司

规　　格／开　本：787mm×1092mm　1/16
　　　　　印　张：14　字　数：238 千字
版　　次／2020 年 11 月第 1 版　2020 年 11 月第 1 次印刷
书　　号／ISBN 978-7-5201-7591-3
定　　价／98.00 元

本书如有印装质量问题，请与读者服务中心（010-59367028）联系